THE COMPLETE JOSEPH SMITH TRANSLATION OF THE OLD TESTAMENT

THE COMPLETE JOSEPH SMITH TRANSLATION OF THE OLD TESTAMENT

A Side-by-Side Comparison with the King James Version

EDITED BY
THOMAS A. WAYMENT

SALT LAKE CITY, UTAH

Visit us at DeseretBook.com

Library of Congress Cataloging-in-Publication Data

Bible. O.T. English. Smith. 2009.
The complete Joseph Smith translation of the Old Testament : a side-by-side comparison with the King James Version / Thomas A. Wayment, editor.
p. cm.
Includes bibliographical references.
ISBN 978-1-60641-131-5 (hardbound : alk. paper)
ISBN 978-1-62972-379-2 (paperback)
1. Bible. O.T.—Versions. I. Wayment, Thomas A. II. Bible. O.T. English. Authorized. 2009. III. Title.
BX8630.A2 2009
220.5'2—dc22 2009014041

Printed in the United States of America
Alexander's Print Advantage, Lindon, UT

10 9 8 7 6 5 4 3

CONTENTS

Acknowledgments

The publication of this volume represents the culmination of many years' work on Joseph Smith's New Translation of the scriptures. It has been a wonderful season for me, as I have made new and now close friends and have met so many who share an equal passion for the Prophet's inspired translation of the Bible.

Many people have helped me along the way. I thank Cory Maxwell for sticking with this project, even when it appeared that it would not see the light of day. I also thank all the wonderful people at Deseret Book Company who have so carefully edited, typeset, designed, and otherwise prepared this volume for publication.

To Robert Lewis at the Community of Christ I owe a particular debt of thanks for guiding me through the permissions process and for answering my numerous inquiries.

Several individuals looked over the manuscript and provided valuable feedback and corrections. In particular I thank Dave LeFever and Tom Sherry, along with the people at the Corvallis Oregon Institute of Religion.

Above all, I thank my wife, Brandi, for doing so much during the early stages of the project and for her continued support throughout.

INTRODUCTION

Our understanding of the Joseph Smith Translation of the Bible has waxed and waned over the past century and more, with many exciting historical twists and changes in our impressions about what the Prophet Joseph Smith's translation is and how he carried out the work of translating. Unlike modern translations of the Bible, the Joseph Smith Translation is not a translation from ancient languages by scholars who are familiar with Hebrew and Greek, nor is it a translation created by diligently comparing a number of modern English translations. Instead, it is an inspired translation of the King James Version of the Bible, and it is specifically tied to that translation, particularly the 1828 H. & E. Phinney edition of the Bible published in Cooperstown, New York, which the Prophet used during the translation process.

Beyond the intimate connections of the Joseph Smith Translation to the King James Version are many of the revelations received by the Prophet while he was translating the scriptures. More than half the revelations in the Doctrine and Covenants, for example, were received in answer to questions Joseph Smith asked the Lord during the translation process. Excerpts from the Joseph Smith Translation that relate to specific scripture passages can be found in the appendix to the Latter-day Saint edition of the King James Version, in the footnotes, and in the Pearl of Great Price (Moses and Joseph Smith–Matthew). These revelations have been translated into many languages and continue to have a broad influence on Latter-day Saints throughout the world.

When the Prophet began his translation of the scriptures, which he and his contemporaries knew as the New Translation, the Church was not even six months old, and it lacked much of the structure it has today. There was no First Presidency, no Quorum of the Twelve Apostles, no temple ordinances for the living or for the dead, and no understanding among Church members of such words and concepts as *telestial* and *celestial kingdoms.* Doctrines related to these and other matters were revealed to the Prophet as he sat down to study his scriptures alone and with some of the men who would become members of the first Quorum of the Twelve Apostles.

During the three years the Prophet worked on the New Translation (June 1830 to July 1833), the revelations recorded in Doctrine and Covenants 24 through 96 and parts of sections 107 and 132 were received—making up 60 percent of the entire book of Doctrine and Covenants. It is evident that as the Prophet was translating the Bible, the Lord was teaching him how to read and understand the scriptures as well as opening his mind to see things that might not have been possible for him to see without such careful and contemplative scripture study.

The Manuscripts of the New Translation

In June 1830, Joseph Smith began his work on the translation of the Bible, starting with Genesis 1, copying out the entire text and making changes as he went. His scribe was Oliver Cowdery, who wrote down the biblical text, with changes, as it was read to him. Work on the Old Testament progressed as far as Genesis 24:42. The scribes for this part of the manuscript were, in chronological order, Oliver Cowdery, John Whitmer, Emma Smith, John Whitmer, and Sidney Rigdon. On March 8, 1831, with Sidney Rigdon acting as scribe, the Prophet began translating the New Testament.

While the Prophet worked on the New Testament, John Whitmer began copying the text of the Old Testament that had been completed previously. These two texts of the Old Testament translation are known as OT1 (the first draft) and OT2 (John Whitmer's copy), respectively.

During his work on the Gospel of John, the Prophet realized that the translation would proceed much more quickly if they were to mark the points of insertion directly in the Bible and then include in the manuscripts only the changes to the text. Using this new system of notation, Joseph Smith and his scribes finished the translation of the New Testament in July 1832. He then returned to his work on the Old Testament, continuing to use the marked Bible to indicate changes. As he approached the end of his work on the Old Testament, the Prophet inquired of the Lord concerning the books collectively known as the Apocrypha, which were printed in his edition of the Bible. The Lord directed him not to translate it (D&C 91:1–6), and on July 2, 1833, the Prophet declared the translation finished. Both the manuscripts and marked Bible are now in the possession of the Community of Christ, formerly known as the Reorganized Church of Jesus Christ of Latter Day Saints.[1]

Was the New Translation Complete?

The question has been raised whether Joseph Smith finished his work on the New Translation. As a result of the work done on the New Translation manuscripts in the past decade, it is now possible to address this question with some confidence. Joseph Smith worked on every book of the Bible, declaring some books complete as already printed. Several books of the Old Testament were recorded as being "correct" in their entirety. For example, Obadiah, Micah, Nahum, Habakkuk, Zephaniah, Haggai, and Malachi are listed simply as "correct."[2] The entry for Ruth in the manuscript reads, "The Book of Ruth is all correct," while each chapter of Esther is listed individually as being correct.[3] The Lamentations of Jeremiah is recorded as being correct, but the entry for the Song of Solomon states, "The Songs of Solomon are not Inspired writings."[4]

After the work had been declared finished, the Prophet did not indicate that he intended to make any more major corrections. The difficulty lies in the fact that the manuscript was never fully prepared for publication. Elder Charles W. Penrose, who served as an apostle from 1904 to 1925, explained, "This important work was not fully completed, and it was his [Joseph Smith's] intention to give it [the manuscript] a careful examination, correcting all errors that might have been made by scribes or other inaccuracies that might have occurred, and preparing it in such a shape that it would be a standard for the Church, before it should be published to the world. The work not being thus completed, its publication has not yet been authorized from the proper source."[5]

For this reason, some have viewed the New Translation as incomplete. But perhaps it is wiser to speak of the *manuscripts* as incomplete, with those manuscripts needing to be carefully compared and corrected for consistency prior to publication. For example, spellings in the manuscripts are not uniform, the chapter headings and system of numbering are not regular, many changes are made inconsistently throughout the manuscripts—such as "saith" being changed to "said," or "ye" to "you"—some points of insertion are unclear, and a few others left unmarked. The verse numbering likewise needs considerable attention, especially in the longer insertions of text that do not contain any verse breaks. Typically, the KJV text includes a single sentence as a verse; the New Translation sometimes includes a lengthy addition within a single verse. Also the punctuation employed by the Prophet's scribes is somewhere between modern punctuation and that of the KJV. A printer's copy, with consistent spelling, punctuation, versification, titles, and so forth, would have required considerable painstaking time and effort—and funding.

Efforts to Print the New Translation

The Prophet sought funds to publish the New Translation, but he was unable to make that endeavor a reality. Joseph Smith's earliest statement regarding the publication of the New Translation of the Bible can be dated to February 1833, when he said that the New Translation "was sealed up, no more to be opened until it arrived in Zion."[6] The Prophet planned to take the manuscripts and marked Bible to Jackson County, Missouri, where he intended to publish the New Translation on the Church's printing press there. Those hopes were dashed in July 1833 when the press was destroyed by a mob. The Prophet likely never took the manuscript to Jackson County, but kept it with him when he and his family moved from Kirtland, Ohio, to Far West, Missouri.

Because of severe persecution in the late 1830s, the manuscripts of the New Translation were taken by Emma Smith to Commerce, Illinois, for safekeeping (Commerce eventually became the city of Nauvoo). In 1840 the Prophet again sought to publish the manuscripts and asked that the Church procure funding to make it possible. Samuel Bent and George W. Harris were given the assignment to seek funding, but apparently the Prophet never received enough money to make publication of the New Translation a reality.[7] Then the Prophet was martyred on July 27, 1844. Exactly how much money the Church had raised at that point is unknown, but the Prophet remained frustrated until the end of his life that he had to attend to temporal matters rather than being able to focus on publishing the New Translation, as well as a new hymnal, a new edition of the Doctrine and Covenants, a new edition of the Book of Mormon, and the book of Abraham.

The manuscripts of the New Translation were kept in the Prophet's home, so at his death they passed directly to Emma Smith, who denied subsequent requests by Willard Richards to obtain the manuscripts. After the

Church moved west, the manuscripts remained in Illinois in the hands of Emma Smith and her descendants.

On July 1, 1867, the Reorganized Church of Jesus Christ of Latter Day Saints began work on publishing the New Translation from a new manuscript that had been created over the course of the previous year. The work proceeded in earnest, and in December 1868 an edition of the translation called The Holy Scriptures was finally made available. In 1892 and 1893 the Reorganized Church again published the New Translation in a book called *The Two Records,* which contained the New Testament and the Book of Mormon. A later edition, published in 1936, included an index. This edition was the first to be titled the Inspired Version. In 1944 a corrected and revised version of the text was set in linotype. Thirty years later, in 1974, the text was reset on computer. The Inspired Version available today is based on the 1944 edition and contains no significant differences from that text. In 1970 the Reorganized Church published a parallel-column version of the New Translation.

Latter-day Saints have relied on the Inspired Version for Joseph Smith Translation changes not published in the footnotes or appendix of the LDS edition of the King James Bible. Over the years, concerns have been raised among Latter-day Saints about the accuracy of the Inspired Version. The general sentiment of LDS scholars and others is that where it agrees with other Restoration scripture, the Inspired Version may be considered correct.[8]

In the last decade of the twentieth century, a team of researchers at Brigham Young University, led by Scott H. Faulring, Kent P. Jackson, and Robert J. Matthews, began working on an edition of the Joseph Smith Translation that would include transcriptions of all the manuscripts and photographs of the Bible that the Prophet marked during the translation process. *Joseph Smith's New Translation of the Bible: Original Manuscripts* was published in 2004 under the direction of the Religious Studies Center at Brigham Young University, which holds copyright for the volume with the Community of Christ. That scholarly edition of the manuscripts provides a complete rendering of every change the Prophet Joseph made to the biblical text. That work, in combination with a growing body of scholarship on the manuscripts' history by LDS and Community of Christ scholars, makes the present day the best time since the Prophet was alive to study the Joseph Smith Translation.

This Volume

My work on a project that depended on the absolute accuracy of the written text of the JST soon showed that no existing text was completely faithful to the original manuscripts of the New Translation, without interpolation or bias. This work, containing Joseph Smith's translation of the Old Testament, partially fills the need for such an accurate text by presenting every JST change to the KJV Old Testament in a reader-friendly, side-by-side format. The reader can easily look up any text to determine whether there is an inspired change for that verse. A companion volume, *The Complete Joseph Smith Translation of the New Testament: A Side-by-Side Comparison with the King James Version* (Salt Lake City: Deseret Book, 2005), contains all the JST changes to the New Testament.

This presentation of the text of the JST is one piece of a rich and sacred history. The work of the Prophet Joseph Smith in revising the text of the Bible has never been so readily available to all members of the Church. While it will become evident that the text still needs correction and improvement, for the first time all changes made to the Old Testament are readily available for study. Having the full revision available permits us to see that the Prophet clarified the text of the Bible to make it easier to read, clarified in a number of instances the relationship between the Father and the Son, harmonized certain portions of the Gospels, and presented the mission of the Son in greater clarity and power.

In a few cases, minor differences do exist between the JST text presented here and the text in the JST appendix of the LDS edition of the Bible. These differences, while not doctrinally significant, are a result of our now having the fully transcribed text and marked Bible available for study. This publication should therefore prove useful to those who wish to study the inspired changes made by Joseph Smith, the Prophet of the Restoration.

Editorial Procedure

The texts of the JST and the KJV are presented in parallel columns, with the KJV text in the left-hand column and the JST in the right-hand column.

In the KJV column, words that were removed or changed are indicated by strikethroughs. In the JST column, changes are noted in bold, so they can be quickly and easily recognized. In cases where the spelling of a word has been modernized from its original KJV spelling, the word has been left in normal typeface instead of placing it in bold, which would otherwise indicate that a genuine change to the KJV language was being made. The same procedure has been adopted for other minor spelling and capitalization differences unless the change may be considered an intentional correction of the KJV text that also changes the meaning of the passage under consideration.

Because the manuscripts of the New Translation were not edited for spelling or consistency, the punctuation of the manuscripts is oftentimes difficult to interpret. Recent publications of the New Translation have frequently adopted modern punctuation to facilitate usage of the text, but this is made more difficult when the New Translation text is printed together or alongside the text of the King James Bible, because it uses punctuation and grammar that is now considered out of date and the punctuation of the manuscripts is not always the same as that printed in the Bible. This publication has attempted to maintain the punctuation of the King James Version where possible, but in situations where the changes are significant, it has been necessary to insert punctuation into the text. In the vast majority of instances, the punctuation of the New Translation manuscripts has been maintained. In the printed text in this volume, when the punctuation associated with a change to the biblical text appears in bold typeface, the punctuation derives from the New Translation manuscripts, but when the punctuation associated with a change to the text appears in normal typeface, the punctuation is that of the King James Version of the Bible.

The Prophet's Bible contains numerous verses in which words have been crossed out, sometimes in pencil and sometimes in ink, but for which there is no corresponding change recorded in the manuscripts. It appears that when the text was dictated to the scribe, the Prophet removed the crossed-out words, indicating that those omissions should be considered JST changes. The process of dictating also resulted in another type of change in the manuscript—omission of entire verses—where it is difficult to determine the Prophet's intent. As the text was being dictated, some verses were omitted entirely: whether these verses were intentionally omitted or were left out unintentionally is no longer clear in most cases. These omissions have been noted in the JST column with an indication of the manuscript where the omission occurs.

The Prophet did not always leave clear instructions where a change in wording should be placed in the Bible. Even though we have the text of the change, we are not certain where to place it in the verse. For example, at Isaiah 13:2, the manuscript records the change "my" to be added to the verse which reads in the KJV, "Lift ye up a banner upon the high mountain, exalt the voice unto them, shake the hand, that they may go into the gates of the nobles." The marked Bible crosses out "the" in the phrase "exalt the voice," suggesting that the Prophet intended to replace "the" with "my," but it is not certain if that is where the change should be located.

In some instances, the copy of the Bible that the Prophet used had typographical errors, such as at Jeremiah 17:5, where his Bible reads "them an," which is changed in the JST to "the man," although this is a change that is unnecessary for our Bibles because the present KJV does not preserve that typo. In other cases, verbs are missing or there are otherwise incomplete ideas. This volume attempts to smooth out those difficulties and notes such places in the footnotes so that the reader is aware that that particular JST change is in question.

Some words and names are spelled differently in the JST from the way they are spelled in the KJV. Those differences have not been noted here. Because we have no evidence that the Prophet dictated the spelling of words and names during his work on the New Translation, such changes have been considered misspellings rather than inspired changes. Only when it is obvious that a change in spelling was intended to alter meaning has it been retained here. Otherwise, the spelling of the KJV has been retained.

Another issue is the numbering of verses. In most instances, the numbering in the manuscripts corresponds to that in our LDS edition of the KJV. In a few instances, however, the JST manuscripts depart from the KJV verse numbering and alter how verses were to be divided and which verses were to be included in each chapter. That information, although critical for laying out the text for publication, does not alter the doctrine.

No attempt has been made here either to note all the differences between the manuscripts of the JST or to record changes made after the Prophet's lifetime. This volume represents only the changes made by the Prophet, without any attempt to harmonize inconsistencies and places of ambiguity or even to correct grammar, unless absolutely necessary for understanding. It is apparent from a close examination of the manuscripts that the issue of grammar was beyond their scope; it seems likely that the Prophet may have intended to address that and other issues before publishing his New Translation. In any case, the grammar of the JST in this volume is the grammar of the KJV.

Although the debate will likely continue about whether the Prophet Joseph Smith completed the New Translation of the scriptures, we now know that he considered every book in the Old Testament and made changes or notations for each one. We can learn as the Prophet learned, from the hand of Lord, and we can maintain our perspective that the JST is perhaps the Lord's endorsement to "seek ye out of the best books words of wisdom, seek learning even by study and also by faith" (D&C 109:7).

NOTES

1. For the most comprehensive study of the scribes and dating of the New Translation, see Faulring, Jackson, and Matthews, eds., *Joseph Smith's New Translation of the Bible,* 55–59.

2. Faulring, Jackson, Matthews. *Joseph Smith's New Translation of the Bible,* 849–851.

3. Ibid., 711, 737.

4. Ibid., 841, 785.

5. Charles W. Penrose, "The Revised Scripture," *Deseret Evening News,* 22 April 1881.

6. Joseph Smith, *History of The Church of Jesus Christ of Latter-day Saints,* edited by B. H. Roberts, 2d ed. rev., 7 vols. (Salt Lake City: The Church of Jesus Christ of Latter-day Saints, 1932–51), 1:324.

7. Smith, *History of the Church,* 4:164; 4:187; 5:293.

8. Robert J. Matthews, "Q&A: Why don't we use the Inspired Version of the Bible in the Church? Would it be helpful to me to read it?" *New Era,* Apr. 1977, 46.

Genesis

Genesis 1
(see Moses 1–2)

Joseph Smith Translation

The words of God, which he spake unto Moses at a time when Moses was caught up into an exceeding high mountain,

And he saw God face to face, and he talked with him, and the glory of God was upon him [OT1 Moses]; therefore he [OT1 Moses] could endure his presence.

And God spake unto Moses, saying: Behold, I[1] am the Lord God Almighty, and Endless is my name; for I am without beginning of days or end of years; and is this not endless?

And, behold, thou art my son; wherefore look, and I will shew thee the workmanship of mine hands; but not all, for my works are without end, and also my words, for they never cease.

Wherefore, no man can behold all my work [OT1 works], except he behold all my glory; and no man can behold all my glory, and afterwards remain in the flesh on the earth [OT1 omits "on the earth"].

And I have a work for thee, Moses, my son; and thou art in the [OT1 omits "the"] similitude of [OT1 to] mine Only Begotten; and mine Only Begotten is and shall be the Savior, for he is full of grace and truth; but there is none other God beside me, and all things are present with me, for I know them all.

And now, behold, this one thing I shew unto thee, Moses, my son, for thou art in the world, and now I shew it thee.

And it came to pass that Moses looked, and beheld the world upon which he was created; and as Moses beheld the world and the ends thereof, and all the children of men which are [OT1 was], and which were [OT1 was] created; of the same he greatly marveled and wondered.

1. Old Testament Manuscript 1 (OT1) repeats the pronoun "I," which could be a mistake or the Prophet may have intended the verse to read, "Behold I, I am the Lord God Almighty."

And the presence of God withdrew from Moses, that his glory was not upon him [OT1 Moses]; and Moses was left unto himself. And as he was left unto himself, he fell unto the earth.

And it came to pass that it was for the space of many hours before he [OT1 Moses] did again receive his natural strength like unto man; and he said [OT1 saith] unto himself: Now, for this once I know that man is nothing, which thing I never had supposed.

But now mine eyes have beheld God; but not mine natural eyes, but my spiritual, for mine natural eyes could not have beheld [OT1 But now mine eyes, mine own eyes but not mine eyes, for mine eyes could not have beheld]; for I should have withered and died in his presence; but his glory was upon me; and I beheld his face, for I was transfigured before him.

And now it came to pass that when Moses had said these words, behold, Satan came tempting him saying: Moses, son of man, worship me,

But [OT1 And it came to pass that] Moses lifted up his eyes and [OT 1 omits "lifted up his eyes and"] looked upon Satan and said [OT1 saith]: Who art thou? For behold, I am a son of God, in the similitude of his Only Begotten; and where is thy glory, that I should worship thee?

For behold, I could not look upon God, except his glory should come upon me, and I was [OT1 were] transfigured before him. But I can look upon thee in the natural man.

Surely [OT1 If not so, surely?] blessed be the name of my God, for his Spirit hath not altogether withdrawn from me, I say [OT1 omits "I say" and adds "or else"], where is thy glory, for it is blackness unto me? And I can judge between thee and God; for God said unto me: Worship God, for him only shalt thou serve.

Get thee hence, Satan; deceive me not; for God said unto me: Thou art after the similitude of mine Only Begotten.

And he also gave unto me commandment when he called unto me out of the burning bush, saying: Call upon God in the name of mine Only Begotten, and worship me.

And again Moses said [OT1 saith]: I will not cease to call upon God, I have other things to inquire of him: for his glory has been upon me and it is glory unto me, wherefore I can judge between [OT1 betwixt] him and thee. Depart hence, Satan.

And now, when Moses had said these words, Satan cried with a loud voice, and rent[2] upon the earth, and commanded, saying: I am the Only Begotten, worship me.

And it came to pass that Moses began to fear exceedingly; and as he began to fear, he saw the bitterness of hell. Nevertheless, calling upon God, he received strength, and he commanded, saying: Depart hence, Satan, for this one God only will I worship, which is the God of glory.

And now Satan began to tremble, and the earth shook; and Moses received [OT1 receiving] strength, and [OT1 omits "and"] called upon God in the name of his Son, saying to Satan [OT1 omits "his Son, saying to Satan," adds "Jesus Christ"], Depart hence [OT1 Satan].

And it came to pass that Satan cried with a loud voice, with weeping, and wailing, and gnashing of teeth; and departed hence, yea from the presence of Moses, that he beheld him not.

And now of this thing Moses bore record; but because of wickedness it is not had among the children of men.

And it came to pass that when Satan had departed from the presence of Moses, that Moses [OT1 he] lifted up his eyes unto heaven, being filled with the Holy Ghost, which beareth record of the Father and the Son;

And calling upon the name of God, he beheld again his glory, for it rested [OT1 was] upon him; and he heard a voice, saying: Blessed art thou, Moses, for I, the Almighty, have chosen thee, and thou shalt be made stronger than the many waters; for they shall obey thy command even as my commandments [OT1 omits "my commandments" and adds "if thou wert God"].

And lo, I am with thee [OT1 you], even unto [OT1 to] the end of thy days; for thou shalt deliver my people from bondage, even Israel my chosen.

And it came to pass, as the voice was still speaking, he cast his eyes and beheld the earth, yea, even all the face of it; and there was not a particle of it which he did not behold, discerning it by the spirit of God.

And he beheld also the inhabitants thereof, and there was not a soul which he beheld not; and he discerned them by the Spirit of God; and their numbers were great, even as numberless as the sand upon the sea shore.

And he beheld many lands; and each land was called earth, and there were inhabitants on [OT1 upon] the face thereof.

2. The spelling of this word is uncertain. The manuscripts contain the reading "wrent," which could be a misspelling of *ranted* (as Moses 1:19) or a misspelled past tense of *rend*.

And it came to pass that Moses called upon God, saying: Shew [OT1 tell] me, I pray thee, why these things are so, and by whom [OT1 what] thou madest them?

And behold, the glory of God was upon Moses, so [OT1 omits "so"] that Moses stood in the presence of God, and he talked with him face to face. And the Lord God said unto Moses: For mine own purpose have I made these things. Here is wisdom and it remaineth in me.

And by the word of my power, have I created them, which is mine Only Begotten Son, who is [OT1 omits "who is"] full of grace and truth.

And worlds without number have I created; and I also created them for mine own purpose; and by the same I created them, which is mine Only Begotten.

And the first man of all men have I called Adam, which is many.

But only an account of this earth, and the inhabitants thereof, give I unto you. For behold, there are many worlds which have passed away by the word of my power. And there are many also which now stand, and numberless are they unto man; but all things are numbered unto me, for they are mine and I know them.

And it came to pass that Moses spake unto the Lord, saying: Be merciful unto thy servant, O God, and tell me concerning this earth, and the inhabitants thereof, and also the heavens, and then thy servant will be content.

And the Lord God spake unto Moses, of the heavens [OT1 omits "of the heavens"], saying: These [OT1 the heavens there] are many, and they cannot be numbered unto man; but they are numbered unto me, for they are mine.

And as one earth shall pass away, and the heavens thereof even so shall another come; and there is no end to my works, neither my words.

For behold, this is my work and [OT1 to] my glory—to bring to pass [OT1 omits "bring to pass"] the immortality and [OT1 the] eternal life of man.

And now, Moses, my son, I will speak unto you concerning this earth upon which you stand [OT1 thou standest]; and you shall [OT1 thou shalt] write the things which I shall speak.

And in a day when the children of men shall esteem my words as naught and take many of them from the book which you shall [OT1 thou shalt] write, behold, I will raise up another like unto you [OT1 thee]; and they shall be had again among the children of men—among even as many as shall believe.

(These words were spoken unto Moses in the mount, the name of which shall not be known among the children of men.) [OT1 adds "And now they are also spoken unto you. Shew them not unto any except them that believe. Amen."]

KING JAMES VERSION	JOSEPH SMITH TRANSLATION
Genesis 1:1 IN the beginning ~~God~~ created the heaven and the earth.	**And it came to pass that the Lord spake unto Moses, saying: Behold, I reveal unto you concerning this heaven, and this earth; write the words which I speak. I am the Beginning and the End, the Almighty God; by mine Only Begotten I created these things; yea,** in the beginning **I** created the heaven, and the earth **upon which thou standest.**
Genesis 1:2 And the earth was without form, and void; and darkness ~~*was*~~ upon the face of the deep. And ~~the~~ Spirit ~~of God~~ moved upon the face of the ~~waters~~.	And the earth was without form, and void; and **I caused** darkness **to come up** upon the face of the deep; and **my** Spirit moved upon the face of the **water**; **for I am God.**
Genesis 1:3 And God said, Let there be light: and there was light.	And **I,** God**,** said, Let there be light: and there was light.
Genesis 1:4 And God saw the light, that *it was* good: and God divided the light from the darkness.	And **I,** God**,** saw the light, **and** that **light** was good: and **I,** God**,** divided the light from the darkness.
	OT1 And **I,** God**,** saw the light, **and the light** was good: and **I,** God**,** divided the light from the darkness.
Genesis 1:5 And God called the light Day, and the darkness ~~he~~ called Night. And the evening and the morning were the first day.	And **I,** God, called the light Day; and the darkness, **I** called Night; **and this I did**[3] **by the word of my power, and it was done as I spake;** and the evening and the morning were the first day.
Genesis 1:6 And God said, Let there be a firmament in the midst of the ~~waters~~, and let it divide the waters from the waters.	And **again, I,** God, said: Let there be a firmament in the midst of the **water**, and **it was so, even as I spake; and I said**: Let it divide the waters from the waters; **and it was done;**

3. OT1 reads "done" instead of "did."

Genesis 1:7 And God made the firmament, and divided the waters ~~which *were*~~ under the firmament from the waters which *were* above the firmament: and it was so.	And **I,** God, made the firmament and divided the waters, **yea, the great waters** under the firmament from the waters which were above the firmament, and it was so **even as I spake**.
Genesis 1:8 And God called the firmament Heaven. And the evening and the morning were the second day.	And **I,** God, called the firmament Heaven. And the evening and the morning were the second day.
Genesis 1:9 And God said, Let the waters under the heaven be gathered together unto one place, and let ~~the~~ dry *land* ~~appear~~: and it was so.	And **I,** God, said: Let the waters under the heaven be gathered together unto one place, and **it was so. And I, God, said:** Let **there be** dry land; and it was so.
Genesis 1:10 And God called the dry *land* Earth; and the gathering together of the waters called ~~he~~ Seas: and God saw that ~~*it was*~~ good.	And **I,** God, called the dry land Earth; and the gathering together of the waters, called **I** Seas; and **I,** God, saw that **all things** that **I had made were** good.
	OT1 And **I**, God, called the dry land Earth; and the gathering together of the waters, called **I the** Seas; and **I,** God, saw that **all things which I had made were** good.
Genesis 1:11 And God said, Let the earth bring forth grass, the herb yielding seed, ~~*and*~~ the fruit tree yielding fruit after his kind, whose seed ~~*is*~~ in itself, upon the earth: and it was so.	And **I,** God, said: Let the earth bring forth grass, the herb yielding seed, the fruit tree yielding fruit, after his kind, **and the tree yielding fruit,** whose seed **should be** in itself upon the earth, and it was so **even as I spake.**
Genesis 1:12 And the earth brought forth grass, ~~*and*~~ herb yielding seed after his kind, and the tree yielding fruit, whose seed ~~*was*~~ in itself, after his kind: and God saw ~~that *it was*~~ good.	And the earth brought forth grass, **every** herb yielding seed after his kind, and the tree yielding fruit, whose seed **should be** in itself, after his kind; and **I,** God, saw that **all things which I had made were** good;
	OT1 And the earth brought forth grass, **every** herb yielding seed after his kind, and the tree yielding fruit, whose seed **should be** in itself, after **its** kind; and **I,** God, saw that **all things which I had made were** good;

Genesis 1:14 And God said, Let there be lights in the firmament of the heaven to divide the day from the night; and let them be for signs, and for seasons, and for days, and years:	And **I,** God, said: Let there be lights in the firmament of the heaven, to divide the day from the night, and let them be for signs, and for seasons, and for days, and **for** years;
Genesis 1:16 And God made two great lights; the greater light to rule the day, and the lesser light to rule the night: ~~*he made*~~ the stars also.	And **I,** God, made two great lights; the greater light to rule the day, and the lesser light to rule the night, **and the greater light was the sun, and the lesser light was the moon;** and the stars also **were**[4] **made even according to my word.**
Genesis 1:17 And God set them in the firmament of the heaven to give light upon the earth,	And **I,** God, set them in the firmament of the heaven to give light upon the earth,
Genesis 1:18 And to rule over the day and over the night, and to divide the light from the darkness: and God saw that ~~*it was*~~ good.	And **the sun** to rule over the day, and **the moon to rule** over the night, and to divide the light from the darkness; and **I,** God, saw that **all things which I had made were** good;
	OT1 And **the sun** to rule over the day, and **the moon to rule** over the night, and to divide the **light** from the darkness; and **I,** God, saw that **all things which I made were** good;
Genesis 1:20 And God said, Let the waters bring forth abundantly the moving creature that hath life, and fowl ~~*that*~~ may fly above the earth in the open firmament of heaven.	And **I,** God, said: Let the waters bring forth abundantly the moving creature that hath life, and fowl **which** may fly above the earth in the open firmament of heaven.
Genesis 1:21 And God created great whales, and every living creature that moveth, which the waters brought forth abundantly, after their kind, and every winged fowl after his kind: and God saw that ~~*it was*~~ good.	And **I,** God, created great whales, and every living creature that moveth, which the waters brought forth abundantly, after their kind, and every winged fowl after his kind; and **I,** God, saw that **all things which I had created were** good.

4. OT1 reads "was" instead of "were."

Genesis 1:22 And God blessed them, saying, Be fruitful, and multiply, and fill the waters in the ~~seas~~, and let fowl multiply in the earth.	And **I,** God, blessed them, saying: Be fruitful, and multiply, and fill the waters in the **sea**; and let fowl multiply in the earth;
Genesis 1:24 And God said, Let the earth bring forth the living creature after his kind, cattle, and creeping ~~thing~~, and ~~beast~~ of the earth after ~~his~~ kind: and it was so.	And **I,** God, said: Let the earth bring forth the living creature after his kind, cattle, and creeping **things**, and **beasts** of the earth after **their** kind, and it was so;
Genesis 1:25 And God made the ~~beast~~ of the earth after ~~his~~ kind, and cattle after their kind, and every thing ~~that~~ creepeth upon the earth after his kind: and God saw that ~~*it was*~~ good.	And **I,** God, made the **beasts** of the earth after **their** kind, and cattle after their kind, and everything **which** creepeth upon the earth after his kind; and **I,** God, saw that **all these things were** good.
Genesis 1:26 And God said, Let us make man in our image, after our likeness: and let them have dominion over the ~~fish~~ of the sea, and over the fowl of the air, and over the cattle, and over all the earth, and over every creeping thing that creepeth upon the earth.	And **I,** God, said **unto mine Only Begotten, which was with me from the beginning:** Let us make man in our image, after our likeness; **and it was so.** And **I, God, said:** Let them have dominion over the **fishes** of the sea, and over the fowl of the air, and over the cattle, and over all the earth, and over every creeping thing that creepeth upon the earth.
Genesis 1:27 ~~So~~ God created man in ~~his~~ *own* image, in the image of ~~God~~ created ~~he~~ him; male and female created ~~he~~ them.	**And I,** God, created man in **mine** own image, in the image of **mine Only Begotten** created **I** him; male and female created **I** them.
Genesis 1:28 And God blessed them, and God said unto them, Be fruitful, and multiply, and replenish the earth, and subdue it: and have dominion over the fish of the sea, and over the fowl of the air, and over every living thing that moveth upon the earth.	And **I,** God, blessed them, and **I,** God said unto them: Be fruitful, and multiply, and replenish the earth, and subdue it, and have dominion over the fish of the sea, and over the fowl of the air, and over every living thing that moveth upon the earth.
Genesis 1:29 And God said, Behold, I have given you every herb bearing seed, which *is* upon the face of all the earth,	And **I,** God, said **unto man:** Behold, I have given you every herb bearing seed, which is upon the face of all the earth,

and every tree, in the which *is* the fruit of a tree yielding seed; to you it shall be for meat.	and every tree in the which **shall be** the fruit of a tree yielding seed; to you it shall be for meat.
Genesis 1:30 And to every beast of the earth, and to every fowl of the air, and to every thing that creepeth upon the earth, wherein ~~*there is*~~ life, ~~*I have*~~ *given* every ~~green~~ herb for meat: and it was so.	And to every beast of the earth, and to every fowl of the air, and to every thing that creepeth upon the earth, wherein **I grant** life, **there shall be** given every **clean** herb for meat; and it was so**, even as I spake**.
Genesis 1:31 And God saw every thing that ~~he~~ had made, and, behold, ~~*it was*~~ very good. And the evening and the morning were the sixth day.	And **I,** God, saw everything that **I** had made, and, behold, **all things which I had made were** very good; and the evening and the morning were the sixth day.

Genesis 2
(see Moses 3)

KING JAMES VERSION	JOSEPH SMITH TRANSLATION
Genesis 2:1 THUS the ~~heavens~~ and the earth were finished, and all the host of them.	Thus the **heaven** and the earth were finished, and all the host of them.
Genesis 2:2 And on the seventh day God ended ~~his~~ work which ~~he~~ had made; and ~~he~~ rested on the seventh day from all ~~his~~ work which ~~he~~ had made.	And on the seventh day **I,** God, ended **my** work, **and all things** which **I** had made; and **I** rested on the seventh day from all **my** work, **and all things** which **I** had made **were finished, and I, God, saw that they were good;** **OT1** And on the seventh day **I,** God, ended **my** work, **and all things** which **I** had made; and **I** rested on the seventh day from all **my** work, **and all things** which **I** had made **were finished, and I saw that they were good;**
Genesis 2:3 And God blessed the seventh day, and sanctified it: because that in it ~~he~~ had rested from all ~~his~~ work which God created and made.	And **I,** God, blessed the seventh day, and sanctified it; because that in it **I** had rested from all **my** work which **I,** God, **had** created and made.

Genesis 2:4 These *are* the generations of the ~~heavens~~ and of the earth when they were created, in the day that the LORD God made the ~~earth~~ and the ~~heavens~~,	**And now, behold, I say unto you, that** these are the generations of the **heaven** and of the earth, when they were created, in the day that **I,** the Lord God, made the **heaven** and the **earth,**
Genesis 2:5 And every plant of the field before it was in the earth, and every herb of the field before it grew: for the LORD God had not caused it to rain upon the earth, and ~~*there was*~~ not a man to till the ground.	And every plant of the field before it was in the earth, and every herb of the field before it grew. **For I, the Lord God, created all things, of which I have spoken, spiritually, before they were naturally upon the face of the earth.** For **I,** the Lord God, had not caused it to rain upon **the face of** the earth. **And I, the Lord God, had created all the children of men;** and not **yet** a man to till the ground**; for in heaven created I them; and there was not yet flesh upon the earth, neither in the water, neither in the air;**
Genesis 2:6 But there went up a mist from the earth, and watered the whole face of the ground.	But **I, the Lord God, spake, and** there went up a mist from the earth, and watered the whole face of the ground.
Genesis 2:7 And the LORD God formed man ~~*of*~~ the dust of the ground, and breathed into his nostrils the breath of life; and man became a living soul.	And **I,** the Lord God, formed man **from** the dust of the ground, and breathed into his nostrils the breath of life; and man became a living soul**, the first flesh upon the earth, the first man also; nevertheless, all things were before created; but spiritually were they created and made according to my word**.
Genesis 2:8 And the LORD God planted a garden eastward in Eden; and there ~~he~~ put the man whom ~~he~~ had formed.	And **I,** the Lord God, planted a garden eastward in Eden, and there **I** put the man whom **I** had formed.
Genesis 2:9 And out of the ground made the LORD God to grow every tree that is pleasant to the sight, and good for food; the tree of life also in the midst of the garden, and the tree of knowledge of good and evil.	And out of the ground made **I,** the Lord God, to grow every tree**, naturally,** that is pleasant to the sight **of man; and man could behold it. And it became also a living soul. For it was spiritual in the day that I created it; for it**

remaineth in the sphere in which I, God, created it, yea, even all things which I prepared for the use of man; and **man saw that it was** good for food**. And I, the Lord God, planted** the tree of life also in the midst of the garden, and **also** the tree of knowledge of good and evil.

OT1 And out of the ground made **I,** the Lord God, to grow every tree**, naturally,** that is pleasant to the sight **of man; and man could behold it. And they became also a living soul. For it was spiritual in the day that I created it; for it remaineth in the sphere which I created it, yea, even all things which I prepared for the use of man;** and **man saw that it was** good for food. **And I, the Lord God, placed** the tree of life also in the midst of the garden, and **also** the tree of knowledge of good and evil.

Genesis 2:10 And a river ~~went~~ out of Eden to water the garden; and from thence it was parted, and became into four heads.

And **I, the Lord God, caused** a river **to go** out of Eden to water the garden; and from thence it was parted, and became into four heads.

Genesis 2:11 The name of the first *is* Pison: ~~that *is*~~ it which compasseth the whole land of Havilah, where ~~*there is*~~ gold;

And I, the Lord God, called the name of the first Pison, **and** it compasseth the whole land of Havilah, where **I, the Lord God, created much** gold;

OT1 And I, the Lord God, called the name of the first Pison, **and** it compasseth the whole land of Havilah, where there **were created much** gold;

Genesis 2:12 And the gold of that land *is* good: there *is* bdellium and the onyx stone.

And the gold of that land **was** good, and there **was** bdellium and the onyx stone.

Genesis 2:13 And the name of the second river *is* Gihon: the same ~~*is* it~~ that compasseth the whole land of Ethiopia.

And the name of the second river **was called** Gihon; the same that compasseth the whole land of Ethiopia.

	OT1 And the name of the second river **was called** Gihon; the same **was** it that compasseth the whole land of Ethiopia.
Genesis 2:14 And the name of the third river ~~*is*~~ Hiddekel: that ~~*is* it~~ which goeth ~~toward~~ the east of Assyria. And the fourth river ~~*is*~~ Euphrates.	And the name of the third river **was** Hiddekel; that which goeth **towards** the east of Assyria. And the fourth river **was** Euphrates.
	OT1 And the name of the third river **was** Hiddekel; that **was** it which goeth **towards** the east of Assyria. And the fourth river **was** Euphrates.
Genesis 2:15 And the LORD God took the man, and put him into the garden of Eden to dress it and to keep it.	And **I,** the Lord God, took the man, and put him into the Garden of Eden, to dress it, and to keep it.
Genesis 2:16 And the LORD God commanded the man, saying, Of every tree of the garden thou mayest freely eat:	And **I,** the Lord God, commanded the man, saying: Of every tree of the garden thou mayest freely eat,
Genesis 2:17 But of the tree of the knowledge of good and evil, thou shalt not eat of it: for in the day that thou eatest thereof thou shalt surely die.	But of the tree of the knowledge of good and evil, thou shalt not eat of it, **nevertheless, thou mayest choose for thyself, for it is given unto thee; but, remember that I forbid it,** for in the day that thou eatest thereof thou shalt surely die.
Genesis 2:18 And the LORD God said, *It* ~~*is*~~ not good that the man should be alone; I will make ~~him~~ an help meet for him.	And **I,** the Lord God, said **unto mine Only Begotten, that** it **was** not good that the man should be alone; **wherefore,** I will make an help meet for him.
Genesis 2:19 And out of the ground the LORD God formed every beast of the field, and every fowl of the air; and ~~brought *them*~~ unto Adam to see what he would call them: and whatsoever Adam called every living creature, that ~~*was*~~ the name thereof.	And out of the ground **I,** the Lord God, formed every beast of the field, and every fowl of the air; and **commanded that they should come** unto Adam, to see what he would call them; **and they were also living souls for I, God, breathed into them the breath of life,** and **commanded that** whatsoever Adam called every living creature, that **should be** the name thereof.

	OT1 And out of the ground **I,** the Lord God, formed every beast of the field, and every fowl of the air; and **commanded that they should be** brought unto Adam, to see what he would call them; **and they were also living souls and it was breathed into them the breath of life,** and whatsoever Adam called every living creature, that was the name thereof.
Genesis 2:20 And Adam gave names to all cattle, and to the fowl of the air, and to every beast of the field; but for Adam there was not found an help meet for him.	And Adam gave names to all cattle, and to the fowl of the air, and to every beast of the field; but **as** for Adam there was not found an help meet for him.
Genesis 2:21 And the LORD God caused a deep sleep to fall upon Adam, and he slept: and ~~he~~ took one of his ribs, and closed up the flesh ~~instead~~ thereof;	And **I,** the Lord God, caused a deep sleep to fall upon Adam; and he slept, and **I** took one of his ribs and closed up the flesh **in the stead** thereof;
Genesis 2:22 And the rib, which the LORD God had taken from man, made ~~he~~ a woman, and brought her unto the man.	And the rib which **I,** the Lord God, had taken from man, made **I** a woman, and brought her unto the man.
Genesis 2:23 And Adam said, This ~~*is*~~ now bone of my bones, and flesh of my flesh: she shall be called Woman, because she was taken out of Man.	And Adam said: This **I know** now **is** bone of my bones, and flesh of my flesh; she shall be called Woman, because she was taken out of man.
Genesis 2:24 Therefore shall a man leave his father and ~~his~~ mother, and shall cleave unto his wife: and they shall be one flesh.	Therefore shall a man leave his father and mother, and shall cleave unto his wife: and they shall be one flesh.

Genesis 3
(see Moses 4)

JOSEPH SMITH TRANSLATION

And I, the Lord God, spake unto Moses saying: That Satan, whom thou hast commanded in the name of mine Only Begotten is the same which was from the beginning, and he came before me saying—Behold, I, send me, I will be thy son, and I will redeem all mankind, that one soul shall not be lost, and surely I will do it; wherefore, give me thine honor.

But, behold, my Beloved Son, which was my Beloved and Chosen from the beginning, said [OT1 saith] unto me—Father, thy will be done, and the glory be thine forever.

Wherefore, because that Satan rebelled against me, and sought to destroy the agency of man, which I, the Lord God, had given him, and also, that I should give unto him mine own power; by the power of mine Only Begotten, I caused that he should be cast down;

And he became Satan, yea, even the devil, the father of all lies, to deceive and to blind men, and to lead them captive at his will, even as many as would not hearken unto my voice.

KING JAMES VERSION	JOSEPH SMITH TRANSLATION
Genesis 3:1 Now the serpent was more subtil than any beast of the field which the LORD God had made. And he said unto the woman, Yea, hath God said, Ye shall not eat of every tree of the garden?	**And** now the serpent was more subtle than any beast of the field which **I,** the Lord God, had made. **And Satan put it into the heart of the serpent, (for he had drew away many after him,) and he sought also to beguile Eve, for he knew not the mind of God, wherefore he sought to destroy the world.** And he said unto the woman: Yea, hath God said—Ye shall not eat of every tree of the garden? **(And he spake by the mouth of the serpent.)** **OT1 And** now the serpent was more subtle than any beast of the field which **I,** the Lord God, had made. **And Satan put it into the heart of the serpent, (for he had drew away many after**

	him,) and he sought also to beguile Eve, for he knew not the mind of God, wherefore he thought to destroy the world. Yea, and he said unto the woman: Yea, hath God said—Ye shall not eat of every tree of the garden? **(And he spake by the mouth of the serpent.)**
Genesis 3:2 And the woman said unto the serpent, We may eat of the fruit of the trees of the garden:	**OT1 verse omitted**
Genesis 3:3 But of the fruit of the tree which ~~*is*~~ in the midst of the garden, God hath said, Ye shall not eat of it, neither shall ye touch it, lest ye die.	But of the fruit of the tree which **thou beholdest** in the midst of the garden, God hath said, Ye shall not eat of it, neither shall ye touch it, lest ye die.
Genesis 3:4 And the serpent said unto the woman, Ye shall not surely die.	**OT1 verse omitted**
Genesis 3:6 And when the woman saw that the tree *was* good for food, and that it ~~*was*~~ pleasant to the eyes, and a tree to be desired to make ~~*one*~~ wise, she took of the fruit thereof, and did eat, and gave also unto her husband with her; and he did eat.	And when the woman saw that the tree was good for food, and that it **became** pleasant to the eyes, and a tree to be desired to make **her** wise, she took of the fruit thereof, and did eat, and gave also unto her husband with her, and he did eat.
Genesis 3:7 And the eyes of them both were opened, and they knew that they ~~*were*~~ naked; and they sewed fig leaves together, and made themselves aprons.	And the eyes of them both were opened, and they knew that they **had been** naked. And they sewed fig leaves together and made themselves aprons.
Genesis 3:8 And they heard the voice of the LORD God walking in the garden in the cool of the day: and Adam and his wife ~~hid~~ themselves from the presence of the LORD God amongst the trees of the garden.	And they heard the voice of the Lord God, **as they were** walking in the garden, in the cool of the day; and Adam and his wife **went to hide** themselves from the presence of the Lord God amongst the trees of the garden.
	OT1 And they heard the voice of the Lord God, **as they were** walking in the garden, in the cool of the day; and Adam and his wife hid themselves from the presence of **I,** the Lord God amongst the trees of the garden.

Genesis 3:9 And the LORD God called unto Adam, and said unto him, Where ~~*art*~~ thou?	And **I,** the Lord God, called unto Adam, and said unto him: Where **goest** thou?
Genesis 3:10 And he said, I heard thy voice in the garden, and I was afraid, because I *was* naked; and I hid myself.	And he said: I heard thy voice in the garden, and I was afraid, because **I beheld that** I was naked, and I hid myself.
Genesis 3:11 And ~~he~~ said, Who told thee that thou *wast* naked? Hast thou eaten of the tree, whereof I commanded thee that thou shouldest not eat?	And **I, the Lord God,** said **unto Adam:** Who told thee that thou wast naked? Hast thou eaten of the tree whereof I commanded thee that thou shouldst not eat**, if so thou shouldst surely die**?
Genesis 3:12 And the man said, The woman whom thou gavest ~~*to be* with~~ me, she gave me of the tree, and I did eat.	And the man said: The woman whom thou gavest me, **and saidest unto her remain with thee**, she gave me of the tree and I did eat.
	OT1 And the man said: The woman whom thou gavest me, **and commanded that she should remain** with me, she gave me **of the fruit** of the tree and I did eat.
Genesis 3:13 And the LORD God said unto the woman, What *is* this ~~*that*~~ thou hast done? And the woman said, The serpent beguiled me, and I did eat.	And **I,** the Lord God, said unto the woman: What is this **thing which** thou hast done? And the woman said: The serpent beguiled me, and I did eat.
	OT1 And **I,** the Lord God, said unto the woman: What is this **thing which** thou hast done? The woman said: The serpent beguiled me, and I did eat.
Genesis 3:14 And the LORD God said unto the serpent, Because thou hast done this, thou ~~*art*~~ cursed above all cattle, and above every beast of the field; upon thy belly shalt thou go, and dust shalt thou eat all the days of thy life:	And **I,** the Lord God said unto the serpent, Because thou hast done this, thou **shalt be** cursed above all cattle, and above every beast of the field; upon thy belly shalt thou go, and dust shalt thou eat all the days of thy life:
	OT1 And **the I,** the Lord God, said unto the serpent: Because thou hast done this thou **shalt be** cursed above

	all cattle, and above every beast of the field; upon thy belly shalt thou go, and dust shalt thou eat all the days of thy life;
Genesis 3:15 And I will put enmity between thee and the woman, ~~and~~ between thy seed and her seed; ~~it~~ shall bruise thy head, and thou shalt bruise his heel.	And I will put enmity between thee and the woman, between thy seed and her seed; **and he** shall bruise thy head, and thou shalt bruise his heel. **OT1** And I will put enmity between thee and the woman, between thy seed and her seed; it shall bruise thy head, and thou shalt bruise his heel.
Genesis 3:16 Unto the woman ~~he~~ said, I will greatly multiply thy sorrow and thy conception; in sorrow thou shalt bring forth children; and thy desire *shall be* to thy husband, and he shall rule over thee.	Unto the woman, **I, the Lord God,** said: I will greatly multiply thy sorrow and thy conception. In sorrow thou shalt bring forth children, and thy desire shall be to thy husband, and he shall rule over thee. **OT1** Unto the woman, **I** said: I will greatly multiply thy sorrow and thy conception. In sorrow thou shalt bring forth children, and thy desire shall be to thy husband, and he shall rule over thee.
Genesis 3:17 And unto Adam ~~he~~ said, Because thou hast hearkened unto the voice of thy wife, and hast eaten of the tree, ~~of~~ which I commanded thee, saying, Thou shalt not eat of it: cursed *is* the ground for thy sake; in sorrow shalt thou eat *of* it all the days of thy life;	And unto Adam, **I, the Lord God,** said: Because thou hast hearkened unto the voice of thy wife, and hast eaten of the tree which I commanded thee, saying—Thou shalt not eat of it, cursed **shall be** the ground for thy sake; in sorrow shalt thou eat of it all the days of thy life. **OT1** And unto Adam, **I, the Lord God,** said: Because thou hast hearkened unto the voice of thy wife, and hast eaten **of the fruit** of the tree of which I commanded thee, saying—Thou shalt not eat of it, cursed **shall be** the ground for thy sake; in sorrow shalt thou eat of it all the days of thy life.

Genesis 3:19 In the sweat of thy face shalt thou eat bread, ~~till~~ thou return unto the ground; for out of it wast thou taken: for dust thou ~~*art*~~, and unto dust shalt thou return.	In the sweat of thy face shalt thou eat bread, **until** thou **shalt** return unto the ground**, for thou shalt surely die**; for out of it wast thou taken: for dust thou **wast**, and unto dust shalt thou return.
	OT1 By the sweat of thy face shalt thou eat bread, **until** thou **shalt** return unto the ground—**for thou shalt surely die**—for out of it wast thou taken: for dust thou **wast**, and unto dust shalt thou return.
Genesis 3:20 And Adam called his wife's name Eve; because she was the mother of all living.	And Adam called his wife's name Eve, because she was the mother of all living**; for thus have I, the Lord God, called the first of all women, which are many**.
Genesis 3:21 Unto Adam also and to his wife did the LORD God make coats of ~~skins~~, and clothed them.	Unto Adam also and to his wife did **I,** the Lord God make coats of **skin**, and clothed them.
	OT1 verse omitted
Genesis 3:22 And the LORD God said, Behold, the man is become as one of us, to know good and evil: and now, lest he put forth his hand, and ~~take~~ also of the tree of life, and eat, and live for ever:	And **I,** the Lord God, said **unto mine Only Begotten**: Behold, the man is become as one of us to know good and evil; and now lest he put forth his hand and **partake** also of the tree of life, and eat and live forever,
Genesis 3:23 Therefore the LORD God ~~sent~~ him forth from the garden of Eden, to till the ground from whence he was taken.	Therefore **I,** the Lord God, **will send** him forth from the Garden of Eden, to till the ground from whence he was taken; **For as I, the Lord God, liveth, even so my words cannot return void, for as they go forth out of my mouth they must be fulfilled.**
Genesis 3:24 So ~~he~~ drove out the man; and ~~he~~ placed at the east of the garden of Eden ~~Cherubims~~, and a flaming sword which turned every way, to keep the way of the tree of life.	So **I** drove out the man, and **I** placed at the east of the Garden of Eden, **cherubim** and a flaming sword, which turned every way to keep the way of the tree of life. **(And these are the words which I spake unto my servant Moses, and they are true even as I will; and I**

	have spoken them unto you. See thou shew them unto no man, until I command you, except they that believe. Amen.) **OT1** So **I** drove out the man, and **I** placed at the east of the Garden of Eden, cherubims and a flaming sword, which turned every way to keep the way of the tree of life. **(And those are the words which I spake unto my servant Moses, and they are true even as I will; and I have spoken them unto you. See thou show them unto no man, until I command you, except they that believe. Amen.)**

Genesis 4
(see Moses 5–Moses 6:4)

JOSEPH SMITH TRANSLATION

And it came to pass that after, I the Lord God,[5] had driven them out, that Adam [OT1 omits "And it came to pass that after, I the Lord God, had driven them out, that Adam" and adds, "A Revelation concerning Adam after he had been driven out of the garden of Eden, for after that he had been driven out he"] began to till the earth, and to have dominion over all the beasts of the field, and to eat his bread by the sweat of the brow, as I [OT1 omits I] the Lord had commanded him; and Eve also, his wife did labor with him.

And Adam [OT1 he] knew his wife [OT1 her], and she bare unto him sons and daughters, and they began to multiply and to replenish the earth.

And from that time forth, the sons and daughters of Adam began to divide two and two in the land, and to till the land, and to tend flocks, and they also begat sons and daughters.

And Adam called upon the name of the Lord, and Eve also, his wife, and they heard the voice of the Lord from the way towards the garden of Eden, speaking unto them, and they saw him not; for they were shut out from his presence.

5. Old Testament Manuscript 2 (OT2) contains the pronoun "he" as the subject of the verb "had," likely as a result of copying the text of OT1, which reads differently.

And he gave unto them commandment, that they should worship the Lord their God, and should offer the firstlings of their flocks for an offering unto the Lord. And Adam was obedient unto the commandments of the Lord.

And after many days an angel of the Lord appeared unto Adam, saying: Why dost thou offer sacrifices unto the Lord? And Adam said unto him, I know not, save the Lord commanded me.

And then the angel spake, saying: This thing is a similitude of the sacrifice of the Only Begotten of the Father, which is full of grace and truth.

Wherefore, thou shalt do all that thou doest in the name of the Son, and thou shalt repent and call upon God in the name of the Son forevermore.

And in that day the Holy Ghost fell upon Adam, which beareth [OT1 bore] record of the Father and the Son, saying: I am the Only Begotten of the Father [OT1 omits "the Only Begotten of the Father" and adds "Jesus Christ"] from the beginning, henceforth and forever, that as thou hast fallen thou mayest be redeemed, and all mankind, even as many as will.

And in that day Adam blessed God and was filled, and began to prophesy concerning all the families of the earth, saying: Blessed be the name of God, for because of [OT1 omits "because of"] my transgression mine eyes are opened [OT1 omits "mine eyes are opened"], and [OT1 for] in this life I shall have joy, and again in the [OT1 my] flesh I shall see God.

And Eve, his wife, heard all these things and was glad, saying: Were it not for our transgression we should never had seed, and should never had known good and evil, and the joy of our redemption, and the eternal life which God giveth unto all the obedient.

And Adam and Eve blessed the name of God, and they made all things known unto their sons and their daughters.

And Satan came [OT1 also] among them, saying: I am also a son of God; and he commanded them, saying: Believe [OT1 it] not; and they believed [OT1 it] not, and loved Satan more than God. And men began from that time forth to be carnal, sensual, and devilish.

And the Lord God called upon men by the Holy Ghost everywhere and commanded them that they should repent;

And as many as believed in the Son, and repented of their sins, should be saved; and as many as believed not and repented not, should be damned; and the words went forth out of the mouth of God in a firm decree; wherefore they must be fulfilled.

And Adam ceased not to call upon God, and Eve also his wife.

KING JAMES VERSION	JOSEPH SMITH TRANSLATION
Genesis 4:1 AND Adam knew Eve his wife; and she conceived, and bare Cain, and said, I have gotten a man from the LORD.	And Adam knew Eve his wife, and she conceived and bare Cain, and said: I have gotten a man from the Lord; **wherefore he may not reject his words. But behold, also Cain hearkened not, saying: Who is the Lord that I should know him?**
Genesis 4:2 And she again bare his brother Abel. And Abel was a keeper of sheep, but Cain was a tiller of the ground.	And she again **conceived and** bare his brother Abel. **And Abel hearkened unto the voice of the Lord.** And Abel was a keeper of sheep, but Cain was a tiller of the ground. **And Cain loved Satan more than God. And Satan commanded him, saying: Make an offering unto the Lord.**
	OT1 And she again **conceived and** bare his brother Abel. **And Abel hearkened unto the voice of the Lord.** And Abel was a keeper of sheep, but Cain was a tiller of the ground. **And he loved Satan more than God. And Satan commanded him, saying: Make an offering unto the Lord.**
Genesis 4:5 But unto Cain and to his offering he had not respect. And Cain was very wroth, and his countenance fell.	But unto Cain, and to his offering, he had not respect. **Now Satan knew this, and it pleased him.** And Cain was very wroth, and his countenance fell.
Genesis 4:6 And the LORD said unto Cain, Why art thou wroth? ~~and~~ why is thy countenance fallen?	And the Lord said unto Cain: Why art thou wroth? Why is thy countenance fallen?
Genesis 4:7 If thou doest well, shalt ~~thou not~~ be accepted? and if thou doest not well, sin lieth at the door. And unto thee ~~*shall be*~~ his desire, and thou shalt rule over him.	If thou doest well, **thou** shalt be accepted. And if thou doest not well, sin lieth at the door, **and Satan desireth to have thee; and except thou shalt hearken unto my commandments, I will deliver thee up,** and **it shall be** unto thee **according to** his desire. And thou shalt rule over him;

JOSEPH SMITH TRANSLATION
For from this time forth thou shalt be the father of his lies; thou shalt be called Perdition; for thou wast also before the world.
And it shall be said in time [OT1 times] to come—That these abominations were [OT1 was] had from Cain; for he rejected the greater counsel[6] which was had from God; and this is a cursing which I will put upon thee, except thou repent.
And Cain was wroth, and listened not any more to the voice of the Lord, neither to Abel, his brother, who walked in holiness before the Lord.
And Adam also and his wife mourned before the Lord, because of Cain and his brethren.
And it came to pass that Cain took one of his brothers' daughters to wife, and they loved Satan more than God.
And Satan saith unto Cain: Swear unto me by thy throat, and if thou tell it thou shalt die; and swear thy brethren by their heads, and by the living God, that they tell it not; for if they tell it, they shall surely die; and this that thy father may not know it; and this day I will deliver thy brother Abel into thine hands.
And Satan sware [OT1 swore] unto Cain that he would do according to his commands. And all these things were done in secret.
And Cain saith: Truly I am Mahan [OT1 Mahon], the master of this great secret, that I may murder and get gain. Wherefore Cain was called Master Mahan [OT1 Mahon], and he gloried in his wickedness.

KING JAMES VERSION	JOSEPH SMITH TRANSLATION
Genesis 4:8 And Cain talked with Abel his brother: and it came to pass, ~~when~~ they were in the field, ~~that~~ Cain rose up against Abel his brother, and slew him.	**And Cain went into the field,** and Cain talked with Abel, his brother. And it came to pass **that while** they were in the field, Cain rose up against Abel, his brother, and slew him. **And Cain gloried in that which he had done, saying: I am free; surely the flocks of my brother falleth into my hands.**

6. OT2 reads "council" here.

Genesis 4:10 And he said, What hast thou done? the voice of thy brother's blood ~~crieth~~ unto me from the ground.	And he said, What hast thou done? the voice of thy brother's blood **cries** unto me from the ground.
Genesis 4:11 And now ~~*art*~~ thou cursed from the earth, which hath opened her mouth to receive thy brother's blood from thy hand;	And now thou **shalt be** cursed from the earth which hath opened her mouth to receive thy brother's blood from thy hand.
Genesis 4:13 And Cain said unto the LORD, My punishment *is* greater than I can bear.	And Cain said unto the Lord**: Satan tempted me because of my brother's flocks. And I was wroth also; for his offering thou didst accept and not mine;** my punishment is greater than I can bear. **OT1** And Cain said unto the Lord**: Satan tempted me because of my brother's flock. And I was wroth also; for his offering thou didst accept and not mine;** my punishment is greater than I can bear.
Genesis 4:14 Behold, thou hast driven me out this day from the face of the ~~earth~~; and from thy face shall I be hid; and I shall be a fugitive and a vagabond in the earth; and it shall come to pass, *that* ~~every one~~ that findeth me ~~shall~~ slay me.	Behold thou hast driven me out this day from the face of the **Lord**, and from thy face shall I be hid; and I shall be a fugitive and a vagabond in the earth; and it shall come to pass, that **he** that findeth me **will** slay me**, because of mine iniquities, for these things are not hid from the Lord**. **OT1** Behold thou hast driven me out this day from the face of the earth, and from thy face shall I be hid; and I shall be a fugitive and a vagabond in the earth; and it shall come to pass, everyone that findeth me shall slay me**, because of mine oath, for these things are not hid from the Lord**.
Genesis 4:15 And the LORD said unto him, ~~Therefore~~ whosoever slayeth ~~Cain~~, vengeance shall be taken on him	And **I,** the LORD said unto him, Whosoever slayeth **thee**, vengeance shall be taken on him sevenfold. And **I,**

sevenfold. And the LORD set a mark upon Cain, lest any finding him should kill him.	the Lord set a mark upon Cain, lest any finding him should kill him.
Genesis 4:16 And Cain ~~went~~ out from the presence of the LORD, and dwelt in the land of Nod, on the east of Eden.	And Cain **was shut** out from the presence of the Lord, **and his wife and many of his brethren** and dwelt in the land of Nod, on the east of Eden.
Genesis 4:17 And Cain knew his wife; and she conceived, and bare Enoch: and he builded a city, and called the name of the city, after the name of his son, Enoch.	And Cain knew his wife, and she conceived and bare Enoch, **and he also begat many sons and daughters.** And he builded a city, and **he** called the name of the city after the name of his son, Enoch.
Genesis 4:18 And unto Enoch was born Irad: and Irad begat Mehujael: and Mehujael begat Methusael: and Methusael begat Lamech.	And unto Enoch was born Irad, **and other sons and daughters.** And Irad begat Mahujael, **and other sons and daughters.** And Mahujael begat Methusael, **and other sons and daughters.** And Methusael begat Lamech.
Genesis 4:19 And Lamech took unto ~~him~~ two wives: the name of ~~the~~ one ~~*being*~~ Adah, and the name of the other Zillah.	And Lamech took unto **himself** two wives; the name of one **being** Adah, and the name of the other, Zillah.
Genesis 4:20 And Adah bare Jabal: he was the father of such as dwell in tents, and ~~*of such as have*~~ cattle.	And Adah bare Jabal; he was the father of such as dwell in tents, and **they were keepers** of cattle;
Genesis 4:21 And his brother's name *was* Jubal: ~~he~~ was the father of all such as handle the harp and organ.	And his brother's name was Jubal, **who** was the father of all such as handle the harp and organ.
Genesis 4:22 And Zillah, she also bare Tubal-cain, an instructer of every artificer in brass and iron: and the sister of Tubal-cain *was* Naamah.	And Zillah, she also bare Tubal Cain, an instructor of every artificer in brass and iron. And the sister of Tubal Cain was **called** Naamah.
Genesis 4:24 If Cain shall be avenged sevenfold, truly Lamech seventy and sevenfold.	If Cain shall be avenged sevenfold, truly Lamech **shall be** seventy and seven fold**;**

JOSEPH SMITH TRANSLATION

For Lamech having entered into a covenant with Satan, after the manner of Cain, wherein he became Master Mahan [OT1 Mahon], master of that great secret which was administered unto Cain by Satan; and Irad [OT1 Irah], the son of Enoch, having known their secret, began to reveal it unto the sons of Adam;

Wherefore Lamech, being angry, slew him, not like unto Cain, his brother Abel, for the sake of getting gain, but he slew him for the oath's sake.

For, from the days of Cain, there was a secret combination, and their works were in the dark, and they knew every man his brother.

Wherefore the Lord cursed Lamech, and his house, and all they that had covenanted with Satan; for they kept not the commandments of God, and it displeased God, and he ministered not unto them, and their works were abominations, and began to spread among all the sons of men. And it was among the sons of men.

And among the daughters of men these things were not spoken, because that Lamech had spoken the secret unto his wives, and they rebelled against him, and declared these things abroad, and had not compassion;

Wherefore Lamech was despised, and cast out, and came not among the sons of men, lest he should die.

And thus the works of darkness began to prevail among all the sons of men.

And God cursed the earth with a sore curse, and was angry with the wicked, with all the sons of men whom he had made;

For they would not hearken unto his voice, nor believe on his Only Begotten Son, even him who [OT1 which] he declared should come in the meridian of time, who [OT1 which] was prepared from before the foundation of the world.

And thus the gospel began to be preached, from the beginning, being declared by holy angels sent forth from the presence of God, and by his own voice, and by the gift of the Holy Ghost.

And thus all things were confirmed unto Adam, by an holy ordinance [OT1 omits "unto Adam by an holy ordinance"], and the Gospel preached, and a decree sent forth, that it should be in the world, until the end thereof; and thus it was. Amen.

KING JAMES VERSION	JOSEPH SMITH TRANSLATION
Genesis 4:25 And Adam knew his wife again; and she bare a son, and called his name Seth: For God, ~~*said she,*~~ hath appointed me another seed instead of Abel, whom Cain slew.	**And Adam hearkened unto the voice of God, and called upon his sons to repent.** And Adam knew his wife again, and she bare a son, and **he** called his name Seth. **And Adam glorified the name of God;** for **he said:** God hath appointed me another seed, instead of Abel, whom Cain slew.
Genesis 4:26 And ~~to Seth,~~ to him also ~~there~~ was born a son; and he called his name Enos: then began men to call upon the name of the LORD.	**And God revealed himself unto Seth, and he rebelled not, but offered an acceptable sacrifice, like unto his brother Abel.** And to him also was born a son, and he called his name Enos. **And** then began **these** men to call upon the name of the Lord**, and the Lord blessed them;**

Genesis 5
(See Moses 6:5–8:12)

KING JAMES VERSION	JOSEPH SMITH TRANSLATION
Genesis 5:1 THIS ~~*is*~~ the book of the ~~generations~~ of Adam. In the day that God created man, in the likeness of God ~~made~~ he him;	**And a book of remembrance was kept, in the which was recorded, in the language of Adam, for it was given unto as many as called upon God to write by the spirit of inspiration; And by them their children were taught to read and write, having a language which was pure and undefiled. Now this same priesthood which was in the beginning, shall be in the end of the world also. Now this prophecy Adam spake, as he was moved upon by the Holy Ghost, and a genealogy was kept of the children of God. And** this **was** the book of the **generation** of Adam, **saying:** In the day that God created man, (in the

	likeness of God **created** he him) **in the image of his own body.** **OT1 And a book of remembrance was kept, in the which was recorded, in the language of Adam, for it was given unto as many as called upon God to write with the finger of inspiration; And by them their children were taught to read and write, having a language which was pure and undefiled. Now this was in the beginning, which shall be in the end of the world. Now this prophecy Adam spake, as he was moved upon, and a genealogy was kept of the children of God. And** this **was** the book of the generations of Adam**, saying:** In the day that God created man, in the likeness of God made he him **in the image of his own body**.
Genesis 5:2 Male and female created he them; and blessed them, and called their ~~name~~ Adam, in the day when they were created.	Male and female, created he them, and blessed them, and called their **names** Adam, in the day when they were created **and became living souls in the land upon the footstool of God.**
Genesis 5:3 And Adam lived ~~an~~ hundred and thirty years, and begat *a son* in his own likeness, after his image; and called his name Seth:	And Adam lived **one** hundred and thirty years, and begat a son in his own likeness, after his **own** image; and called his name Seth:
Genesis 5:4 And the days of Adam after he had begotten Seth were eight hundred years: and he begat sons and daughters:	And the days of Adam after he had begotten Seth were eight hundred years: and he begat **many** sons and daughters: **OT1** And the days of Adam, after he had begotten Seth, were eight hundred **seventy** years, and he begat **many** sons and daughters;
Genesis 5:5 And all the days that Adam lived were ~~nine hundred and thirty~~ years: and he died.	**OT1** And all the days that Adam lived were **one thousand** years, and he died.

Genesis 5:6 ~~And~~ Seth lived ~~an~~ hundred and five years, and begat Enos:	Seth lived **one** hundred and five years, and begat Enos**, and prophesied in all his days, and taught his son Enos in the ways of God; wherefore Enos prophesied also.** **OT1** Seth lived **one** hundred and five years, and begat Enos**, and prophesied in all his days, and taught Enos in the ways of God; wherefore Enos prophesied also.**
Genesis 5:7 And Seth lived after he begat Enos eight hundred and seven years, and begat sons and daughters.	And Seth lived, after he begat Enos, eight hundred and seven years, and begat **many** sons and daughters. **And the children of men were numerous upon all the face of the land. And in these days Satan had great dominion among men, and raged in their hearts. And from thenceforth came wars and bloodshed. And a man's hand was against his own brother in administering death, because of secret works, seeking for power.** **OT1** And Seth lived, after he begat Enos, eight hundred and **seventy-six** years, and begat **many** sons and daughters. **And the children of men were numerous upon all the face of the land. And in those days Satan had great dominion among men, and raged in their hearts. And from thenceforth came wars and bloodsheds. And a man's hand was against his own brother in administering death, because of secret works, seeking for power.**
Genesis 5:8 And all the days of Seth were nine hundred and ~~twelve~~ years: and he died.	And all the days of Seth were nine hundred and **eighty-one** years, and he died.
Genesis 5:9 And Enos lived ninety years, and begat Cainan:	And Enos lived ninety years, and begat Cainan: **And Enos and the residue of the people of God came out from the**

	land, which was called Shulon, and dwelt in a land of promise, which he called after his own son, whom he had named Cainan.
	OT1 And Enos and the residue of the people of God came out from the land, which was called Shulon, and dwelt in a land of promise, which he called after his own son, whom he had named Cainan, whom he begat when he was ninety years old.
Genesis 5:10 And Enos lived after he begat Cainan eight hundred and fifteen years, and begat sons and daughters:	And Enos lived after he begat Cainan eight hundred and fifteen years, and begat **many** sons and daughters:
	OT1 And Enos lived, after he begat Cainan, eight hundred and **fifty** years, and begat **many** sons and daughters.
Genesis 5:11 And all the days of Enos were nine hundred and five years: and he died.	And all the days[7] of Enos were nine hundred and **forty** years, and he died **and thus it was. Amen**.
Genesis 5:12 And Cainan lived seventy years, and begat Mahalaleel:	**OT1** And Cainan lived **one hundred and seventeen** years, and begat Mahalaleel;
Genesis 5:14 And all the days of Cainan were nine hundred and ten years: and he died.	**OT1** And all the days of Cainan were nine hundred and **fifty-seven** years, and he died.
Genesis 5:15 And Mahalaleel lived sixty and five years, and begat Jared:	**OT1** And Mahalaleel lived **one hundred fifteen**, and begat Jared;
Genesis 5:17 And all the days of Mahalaleel were eight hundred and ninety ~~and~~ five years: and he died.	And all the days of Mahalaleel were eight hundred and ninety-five years: and he died.
	OT1 And all the days of Mahalaleel were **nine** hundred and **forty**-five, and he died.

7. OT2 reads "day," here.

Genesis 5:18 And Jared lived ~~an~~ hundred sixty ~~and~~ two years, and ~~he~~ begat Enoch:	And Jared lived **one** hundred **and** sixty-two years, and begat Enoch;
Genesis 5:19 And Jared lived after he begat Enoch eight hundred years, and begat sons and daughters:	And Jared lived, after he begat Enoch, eight hundred years, and begat sons and daughters. **And Jared taught Enoch in all the ways of God. And this is the genealogy of the sons of Adam, who was the son of God, with whom God, himself, conversed. And they were preachers of righteousness, and spake and prophesied, and called upon all men, everywhere, to repent; and faith was taught unto the children of men.** **OT1** And Jared lived, after he begat Enoch, eight hundred years, and begat sons and daughters. **And Jared taught Enoch in all the ways of God. And this is the genealogy of the sons of God, which was the sons of Adam, with whom God, himself, conversed. And they were preachers of righteousness, and spake and prophesied, and called upon all men, everywhere, to repent; and faith was taught unto the children of men.**
Genesis 5:20 And all the days of Jared were nine hundred sixty and two years: and he died.	And **it came to pass that** all the days of Jared were nine hundred sixty and two years, and he died.

JOSEPH SMITH TRANSLATION

And it came to pass that Enoch journeyed in the land, among the people; and as he journeyed, the Spirit of God descended out of heaven, and abode upon him.

And he heard a voice from heaven, saying: Enoch, my son, prophesy unto this people, and say unto them—Repent, for thus saith the Lord: I am angry with this people, and my fierce anger is kindled against them; for their hearts have waxed hard, and their ears are dull of hearing, and their eyes cannot see afar off;

And for these many generations, even since the day that I created them, have they gone astray, and have denied me, and have sought their own counsels in the dark; and in their own abominations have they devised murder, and have not kept the commandments, [OT1 commandment] which I gave unto their father, Adam.

Wherefore, they have foresworn themselves, and, by their oaths, they have brought upon [OT1 omits "have brought upon" and adds "eat unto"] themselves death; and an hell I have prepared for them, if they repent not;

And this is a decree, which I have sent forth in the beginning of the world, from mine own mouth, from the foundation thereof, and by the mouths of my servants, thy fathers, have I decreed it, even as it shall be sent forth into [OT1 in] the world, unto the end thereof.

And when Enoch had heard these words, he bowed himself to the earth, before the Lord, and spake before the Lord, saying: Why is it that I have found favor in thy sight, and am but a lad, and all the people hate me; for I am slow of speech; wherefore am I thy servant?

And the Lord said unto Enoch: Go forth and do as I have commanded thee, and no man shall pierce thee. Open thy mouth, and it shall be filled, and [OT1 omits "and"] I will give thee utterance, for all flesh is in my hands, and I will do as seemeth me good.

Say unto this people: Choose ye this day to serve the Lord [OT1 omits "to serve the Lord" adds "a"] God who made you.

Behold my Spirit is upon you, wherefore all thy words will I justify; and the mountains shall flee before you, and the rivers shall turn from their course; and thou shalt abide in me, and I in you; therefore walk with me.

And the Lord spake unto Enoch, and said unto him: Anoint thine eyes with clay, and wash them, and thou shalt see. And he did so.

And he beheld the spirits that God had created; and he beheld also things which were not visible to the natural eye [OT1 omits "to the natural eye"]; and from thenceforth came the saying abroad in the land: A seer hath the Lord raised up unto his people.

And it came to pass that Enoch went forth in the land, among the people, standing upon the hills and the high places, and cried with a loud voice, testifying against their work [OT1 works]; and all men were offended because of him.

And they came forth to hear him, upon the high places, saying unto the tent keepers: Tarry thou[8] here and keep the tents, while we go yonder to behold the seer, for he prophesieth, and there is a strange thing in the land; a wild man hath come among us.

And it came to pass when they heard him, no man laid their hands on him; for fear came on all them that heard him; for he walked with God.

And there came a man unto him, whose name was Mahijah, and said unto him: Tell us plainly who thou art, and from whence thou came?

And he saith unto them: I came out from the land of Canaan [OT1 Cainan], the land of my fathers, a land of righteousness unto this day. And my father taught me in all the ways of God.

And it came to pass, as I journeyed from the land of Canaan [OT1 Cainan], by the sea east, I beheld a vision; and lo, the heavens I saw, and the Lord spake with me, and gave me commandment; wherefore, for this cause, to keep the commandment, I speak forth these words.

And Enoch continued his speech, saying: The Lord which spake with me, the same is the God of heaven, and he is my God, and your God, and ye are my brethren, and why counsel ye yourselves, and deny the God of heaven?

The heavens [OT1 hath] he made; the earth is his footstool; and the foundation thereof is his. Behold, he laid it, and hosts [OT1 and host] of men hath he brought in upon the face thereof.

And death hath come upon our fathers; nevertheless we know them, and cannot deny, and even the first of all we know, even Adam.

For a book of remembrance we have written among us, according to the pattern given by the finger of God; and it is given in our own language.

And as Enoch spake forth the words of God, the people trembled, and could not stand in [OT1 before] his presence.

And he said [OT1 saith] unto them: Because that Adam fell, we are; and by his fall came death; and we are made partakers of misery and woe.

Behold Satan hath come among the children of men, and tempteth them to worship him; and men have become carnal, sensual, and devilish, and are shut out from the presence of God.

8. A post-1866 scribe added "ye" to replace the singular "thou." See Kent P. Jackson, *The Book of Moses and the Joseph Smith Translation Manuscripts* (Provo: Brigham Young University, Religious Studies Center, 2005), 108.

But God hath made known unto our [OT1 my] fathers that all men must repent.

And he called upon our father Adam by his own voice, saying: I am God; I made the world, and men before they were in the flesh [OT1 omits "in the flesh"].

And he also said unto him: If thou wilt turn unto me, and hearken unto my voice, and believe, and repent of all thy [OT1 their] transgressions, and be baptized, even in [OT1 by] water, in the name of mine Only Begotten Son, who [OT1 which] is full of grace and truth, who [OT1 which] is Jesus Christ, the only name which shall be given under heaven, whereby salvation shall come unto the children of men, and ye shall receive the gift of the Holy Ghost asking [OT1 omits "receive the gift of the Holy Ghost asking" and adds "ask"] all things in his name, and whatsoever ye shall ask, it shall be given you [OT1 omits "you"].

And our father Adam spake unto the Lord, and said: Why is it that men must repent and be baptized in [OT1 by] water? And the Lord said unto Adam: Behold I have forgiven thee thy transgression [OT1 transgressions] in the Garden of Eden.

Hence came the saying abroad among the people, that the Son of God [OT1 omits "Son of God" and adds "Christ"] hath atoned for original guilt, wherein the sins of the parents cannot be answered upon the heads of the children, for they are whole from the foundation of the world.

And the Lord spake unto Adam, saying: Inasmuch as thy children are conceived in sin, even so when they begin to grow up, sin conceiveth in their hearts, and they taste the bitter, that they may know to prize the good.

And it is given unto them to know good from evil; wherefore they are agents unto themselves, and I have given unto you another law and commandment.

Wherefore teach it unto your children, that all men, everywhere, must repent, or they can in nowise inherit the kingdom of God, for no unclean thing can dwell there, or dwell in his presence; for, in the language of Adam, Man of Holiness is his name, and the name of his Only Begotten is the Son a [OT1 of] Man, [OT1 even Jesus Christ,] a righteous Judge, who [OT1 which] shall come in the meridian of time [OT1 omits "meridian of time].

Therefore [OT1 omits "therefore"] I give unto you a commandment, to teach these things freely unto your children, saying:

That by reason of transgression cometh the fall, which fall bringeth death, and [OT1 omits "That by reason of transgression cometh the fall, which fall bringeth death. And"] inasmuch as they were born into the world by water

[OT1 omits "by water" and adds, "the fall, which bringeth death by water"], and blood, and the spirit, which I have made, and so became of dust a living soul, even so ye must be born again into the kingdom of heaven [OT1 omits "into the kingdom of heaven"], of water, and of the Spirit, and be cleansed by blood, even the blood of mine Only Begotten [OT1 adds "into the mysteries of the kingdom of Heaven"]; that ye may be sanctified from all sin, and enjoy the words of eternal life in this world, and eternal life in the world to come, even immortal glory;

For by the water ye keep the commandment; by the Spirit ye are justified, and by the blood ye are sanctified;

Therefore it is [OT1 omits "Therefore it is" and adds "That in you is"] given to abide in you [OT1 omits "to abide in you"]; the record of heaven; the Comforter; the keys of the kingdom of heaven [OT1 omits "keys of the kingdom of heaven" and adds "peaceable things of immortal glory"]; the truth of all things; that which quickeneth all things, which maketh alive all things; that which knoweth all things, and hath all power according to wisdom, mercy, truth, justice, and judgment.

And now, behold, I say unto you: This is the plan of salvation unto all men, through [OT1 omits "through"] the blood of mine Only Begotten, which shall come in the meridian of time.

And behold, all things have their [OT1 has its] likeness, and all things[9] are created and made to bear record of me, both things which are temporal, and things which are spiritual; things which are in the heavens above, and things which are on the earth, and things which are in the earth, and things which are under the earth, both above and beneath: all things bear record of me.

And it came to pass, when the Lord had spoken with Adam, our father, that Adam cried unto the Lord, and he was caught away by the Spirit of the Lord, and was carried down into the water, and was laid under the water, and was brought forth out of the water.

And thus he was baptized, and the Spirit of God descended upon him, and thus he was born of the Spirit, and became quickened in the inner man.

And he heard a voice out of heaven, saying: Thou art baptized with fire, and with the Holy Ghost. This is the record of the Father, and the Son, from henceforth and forever;

And thou art after the order of him who was without beginning of days or end of years, from all eternity to all eternity.

9. OT2 reads "thing" here but contains the plural verb "are."

Behold, thou art one in me, a son of God; and thus may all become my sons. Amen.

[10]And it came to pass that Enoch continued his speech, saying: Behold, our father Adam taught these things, and many have believed and became [OT1 become] the sons of God, and many have believed not, and have perished in their sins, and are looking forth with fear, in torment, for the fiery indignation of the wrath of God to be poured out upon them.

And from that time forth Enoch began to prophesy, saying unto the people, that: As I was journeying, and stood in the place Mahujah, and [OT1 I] cried unto the Lord, there came a voice out of heaven, saying—Turn ye, and get ye upon the mount Simeon.

And it came to pass that I turned and went upon the mount; and as I stood upon the mount, I beheld the heavens open, and I was clothed upon with glory;

And I saw the Lord; and [OT1 omits "and"] he stood before my face, and he talked with me, even as a man talketh one with another, face to face; and he saith unto me: Look, and I will shew [OT1 show] unto thee the world for the space of many generations.

And it came to pass that I beheld in the valley of Shum, and lo, a great people which dwelt in tents, which were the people of Shum.

And again the Lord said unto me: Look; and I looked towards the north, and I beheld the people of Canaan, which dwelt in tents.

And the Lord said unto me: Prophesy; and I prophesied, saying: Behold the people of Canaan, which are numerous, shall go forth in battle array against the people of Shum, and shall slay them that they shall be utterly [OT1 utterly be] destroyed; and the people of Canaan shall divide themselves in the land, and the land shall be barren and unfruitful, and none other people shall dwell there but the people of Canaan;

For behold, the Lord shall curse the land with much heat, and the barrenness thereof shall go forth forever; and there was a blackness come upon all the children of Canaan, that they were despised among all people.

And it came to pass that [OT1 omits "that"] the Lord said unto me: Look; and I looked, and I beheld the land of Sharon, and the land of Enoch, and the land of Omner, and the land of Heni, and the land of Shem, and the land of Haner, and the land of Hananiah [OT1 Hanannihah], and all the inhabitants thereof;

10. Moses 7:1 begins here.

And the Lord said unto me: Go forth to this people, and say unto them—Repent, lest I [OT1 shall] come out and smite them with a curse, and they die.

And he gave unto me a commandment that I should baptize in the name of the Father, and of the Son, which is full of grace and truth, and the Holy Ghost, which beareth record of the Father and the Son.

And it came to pass that Enoch continued to call upon all the people, save it were the people of Canaan, to repent;

And so great was the faith of Enoch that he led the people of God, and their enemies came to battle against them; and he spake the word of the Lord, and the earth trembled, and the mountains fled, even according to his command; and the rivers of water were turned out of their course; and the roar of the lions were [OT1 was] heard out of the wilderness; and all nations feared greatly, so powerful was the word of Enoch, and so great was the power of the language which God had given him.

There also came up a land out of the depth [OT1 depths] of the sea, and so great was the fear of the enemies of the people of God, that they fled and stood afar off and went upon the land which came up out of the depth [OT1 depths] of the sea.

And the giants of the land, also, stood afar off; and there went forth a curse upon all the people which fought against God;

And from that time forth there were [OT1 was] wars and bloodshed [OT1 bloodsheds] among them; but the Lord came and dwelt with his people, and they dwelt in righteousness.

And [OT1 omits "and"] the fear of the Lord was upon all nations, so great was the glory of the Lord, which was upon his people. And the Lord blessed the land, and they were blessed upon the mountains, and upon the high places, and did flourish.

And the Lord called his people Zion, because they were of one heart and of one mind, and dwelt in righteousness; and there were [OT1 was] no poor among them.

And Enoch continued his preaching in righteousness unto the people of God. And it came to pass in his days, that he built a city that was called the City of Holiness, even Zion.

And it came to pass that Enoch talked with the Lord; and he said unto the Lord: Surely Zion shall dwell in safety forever. And [OT1 But] the Lord said unto Enoch: Zion have [OT1 hath] I blessed, but the residue of the people have I cursed.

And it came to pass that the Lord showed unto Enoch all the inhabitants of the earth; and he beheld, and lo, Zion, in process of time, was taken up into heaven. And the Lord said unto Enoch: Behold mine abode forever.

And Enoch also beheld the residue of the people which were the sons of Adam; and they were a mixture of all the seed of Adam save it were the seed of Cain, for the seed of Cain were black, and had not place among them.

And after that Zion was taken up into heaven, Enoch beheld, and lo, all the nations of the earth were before him;

And there came generation upon generation; and Enoch was high and lifted up, even in the bosom of the Father, and the Son of Man; and behold, the powers of Satan were [OT1 was] upon all the face of the earth.

And he saw angels descending out of heaven; and he heard a loud voice saying: Woe, woe be unto the inhabitants of the earth.

And he beheld Satan; and he had a great chain in his hand, and he [OT1 it] veiled the whole face of the earth with darkness; and he looked up and laughed, and his angels rejoiced.

And Enoch beheld angels descending out of heaven, bearing testimony of the Father and of the [OT1 omits "of the"] Son; and the Holy Ghost fell on many, and they were caught up by the power [OT1 powers] of heaven into Zion.

And it came to pass that Enoch [OT1 the God of heaven] looked upon the residue of the people, and [OT1 he] wept; and he beheld, and lo the heavens wept also and shed forth their tears as the rain upon the mountains [OT1 omits "and he beheld, and lo the heavens wept also and shed forth their tears as the rain upon the mountains" and adds, "and Enoch bore record of it, saying: How is it the heavens weep and shed forth her tears as the rain upon the mountains?"]

And Enoch said unto the heavens: How is it that thou canst weep, seeing thou art holy, and from all eternity to all eternity?

And were it possible that man could number the particles of [OT1 the] earth, yea, and millions of such [OT1 omits "such"] earths like this, it would not be a beginning to the number of thy creations; and thy curtains are stretched out still; and [OT1 adds "yet"] thou art there, and thy presence [OT1 bosom] is there; and also thou art just; thou art merciful and kind forever;

Thou hast taken Zion to thine own bosom, from all thy creations, from all eternity to all eternity; [OT1 and] naught but peace, justice, and truth is the habitation of thy throne; and mercy shall go before thy face and have no end; how is it that thou canst weep?

The Lord said unto Enoch: Behold these thy brethren; they are the workmanship of mine own hands, and I gave unto them their intelligence [OT1 omits "intelligence" and adds "knowledge, in the day I created them"]; and in the Garden of Eden man had agency [OT1 omits "man had agency" and adds "gave I unto man his agency"];

And unto thy brethren have I said, and also gave commandment, that they should love one another, and that they should serve me their God [OT1 omits "serve me their God" and adds "choose me their Father"]; but behold, they are without affection, and they hate their own blood;

And the fire of mine indignation is kindled against them; and in my hot displeasure will I send in the floods upon them, for my fierce anger is kindled against them.

Behold, I am God and [OT1 omits "and"] Man of Holiness is my name; Man of Council is my name; and Endless and Eternal is my name, also.

Wherefore, I can stretch forth mine hands and hold all the creations which I have made; and mine eye can pierce them also, and among all the workmanship of mine hands [OT1 hand] there has not been so great wickedness as among thy brethren.

But behold, their sins shall be upon the heads of their fathers; Satan shall be their master [OT1 father], and misery shall be their doom; and the whole heavens shall weep over them, even all the workmanship of mine hands; wherefore should not the heavens weep, seeing these shall suffer?

But behold, these which thine eyes are upon shall perish in the floods; and behold, I will shut them up; a prison have I prepared for them.

And he [OT1 that] whom [OT1 which] I have chosen has [OT1 hath] pled before my face. Wherefore, he suffereth for their sins; inasmuch as they will repent in the day that my Chosen shall return unto me, and until that day they shall be in torment;

Wherefore, for this shall the heavens [OT1 heaven] weep, yea, and all the workmanship of mine hands.

And it came to pass that the Lord spake unto Enoch, and told Enoch all the doings of the children of men; wherefore Enoch knew, and looked upon their wickedness, and their misery, and wept and stretched forth his arms, and he beheld [OT1 omits "and he beheld" and adds "his heart swelled wide as"] eternity; and his bowels yearned; and all eternity shook.

And Enoch saw Noah also, and his family; that the posterity of all the sons of Noah should be saved with a temporal salvation;

Wherefore Enoch [OT1 he] saw that Noah built an ark; and the Lord smiled upon it, and held it in his own hand; but upon the residue of the wicked came the floods and swallowed them up.

And as Enoch saw thus, he had bitterness of soul, and wept over his brethren, and said unto the heavens: I will refuse to be comforted; but the Lord said unto Enoch: Lift up your heart, and be glad; and look.

And it came to pass that Enoch looked[11]; and from Noah, he beheld all the families of the earth; and he cried unto the Lord, saying: When shall the day of the Lord come? When shall the blood of the Righteous be shed, that all they that mourn may be sanctified and have eternal life?

And the Lord said: It shall be in the meridian of time, in the days of wickedness and vengeance.

And behold, Enoch saw the day of the coming of the Son of Man, even in the flesh; and his soul[12] rejoiced, saying: The Righteous is lifted up, and the Lamb is slain from the foundation of the world; and through faith I am in the bosom of the Father, and behold, Zion is with me.

And it came to pass that Enoch looked upon [OT1 the] earth; and he heard a voice from the bowels thereof, saying: Woe, woe is me, the mother of men; I am pained, I am weary, because of the wickedness of my children. When shall I rest, and be cleansed from the wickedness[13] [OT1 filthiness] which has gone forth out of me? When will my Creator sanctify me, that I may rest, and righteousness for a season abide upon my face?

And when Enoch heard the earth mourn, he wept, and cried unto the Lord, saying: O Lord, wilt thou not have compassion upon the earth? Wilt thou not bless the children of Noah?

And it came to pass that Enoch continued his cry unto the Lord, saying: I ask thee, O Lord, in the name of thine [OT1 thy] Only Begotten [OT1 adds "even Jesus Christ"], that thou wilt have mercy upon Noah and his seed, that the earth might never more be covered by the floods.

And the Lord could not withhold; and he covenanted with Enoch [OT1 Noah], and sware [OT1 swore] unto him with an oath, that he would stay the floods; that he would call upon the children of Noah;

11. OT2 likely read "beheld" instead of "looked" as in OT1, but a scribe changed it after the Prophet's lifetime. See Jackson, *Book of Moses and the Joseph Smith Translation,* 129.

12. OT1 likely read "and he saw and rejoiced," but a scribe changed the passage to read like OT2 after 1866. See Jackson, Book of Moses and the Joseph Smith Translation, 129.

13. A later scribe inserted the word "filthiness" into OT2 to correct the passage to OT1. See Jackson, *Book of Moses and the Joseph Smith Translation,* 130.

And he sent forth an unalterable decree, that a[14] remnant of his seed should come [OT1 omits "come" and adds "always be found among"] all nations, while the earth should stand;

And the Lord said: Blessed is he [OT1 him] through whose seed the [OT1 omits "the"] Messiah shall [OT1 should] come; for he saith—I am the [OT1 omits "the"] Messiah, the King of Zion, the Rock of Heaven, which is broad as eternity; and whoso cometh in at the gate and climbeth up by me shall never fall; wherefore, blessed are they of whom [OT1 which] I have spoken, for they shall come forth with songs of everlasting joy.

And it came to pass that Enoch cried unto the Lord, saying: When the Son of Man cometh in the flesh, shall the earth rest? I pray thee, show me these things.

And the Lord said unto Enoch: Look, and he looked and beheld the Son of Man lifted up on the cross, after the manner of men;

And he heard a loud voice; and the heavens were veiled; and all the creation of God mourned; and the earth groaned; and the rocks were rent; and the saints arose, and were [OT1 was] crowned at the right hand of the Son of Man, with crowns of glory;

And as many of the spirits as were in prison came forth, and stood on the right hand of God; and the remainder were [OT1 was] reserved in chains of darkness until the judgment of the great day.

And [OT1 again] Enoch wept and cried unto the Lord, again saying: When shall the earth rest?

And Enoch beheld the Son of Man ascend up unto the Father; and he called unto the Lord, saying: Wilt thou not come again upon the earth? For inasmuch as thou art God, and I know thee, and thou hast sworn unto me, and commanded me that I should ask in the name of thine Only Begotten; thou hast made me, and given unto me a right to thy throne, and not of myself, but through thine own grace; wherefore, I ask thee if thou wilt not come again on the earth.

And the Lord said unto Enoch: As I live, even so will I come in the last days, in the days of wickedness and vengeance, to fulfil the oath which I have made unto you concerning the children of Noah;

And the day shall come that the earth shall rest, but before that day the heavens shall be darkened, and a veil of darkness shall cover the earth; and the

14. OT2 inserts "from" here.

heavens shall shake, and also the earth; a [OT1 and] great tribulation [OT1 tribulations] shall be among the children of men, but my people will I preserve;

And righteousness will I send down out of heaven; [OT1 and] truth will I send forth out of [OT1 omits "of"] the earth, to bear testimony of mine Only Begotten; his resurrection from the dead; yea, and also the resurrection of all men; and righteousness and truth will I cause to sweep the earth as with a [OT1 the] flood, to gather out mine own elect from the four quarters of the earth, unto a place which I shall prepare, an Holy City, that my people may gird up their loins, and be looking forth for the time of my coming; for there shall be my tabernacle, and it shall be called Zion, a New Jerusalem.

And the Lord said unto Enoch: Then shalt thou and all thy city meet them there, and we will receive them into our bosom, and they shall see us; and we will fall upon their necks, and they shall fall upon our necks, and we will kiss each other;

And there shall be mine abode, and it shall be Zion, which shall come forth out of all the creations which I have made; and for the space of a thousand years shall the earth rest.

And it came to pass that Enoch saw the day of the coming of the Son of Man, in the last days, to dwell on the earth in righteousness for the space of a thousand years;

But before that day he saw great tribulations [OT1 tribulation] among the wicked; and he also saw the sea, that it was troubled, and men's hearts failing them, looking forth with fear for the judgments of the Almighty God, which should come upon the wicked.

And the Lord showed Enoch all things, even unto the end of the world; and he saw the day of the righteous, the hour of their redemption, and received a fullness of joy;

And all the days of Zion, in the days of Enoch, were three hundred and sixty-five years.

King James Version	Joseph Smith Translation
Genesis 5:21 And Enoch lived sixty and five years, and begat Methuselah:	**verse omitted**
Genesis 5:22 And Enoch walked with God ~~after he begat Methuselah three hundred years, and begat sons and daughters~~:	And Enoch **and all his people** walked with God, **and he dwelt in the midst of Zion; and it came to pass that Zion was not, for God received it**

	up into his own bosom; and from thence went forth the saying, ZION IS FLED.
Genesis 5:23 ~~And all the days of Enoch were three hundred sixty and five years~~:	[15]**And it came to pass that Methuselah, the son of Enoch, was not taken, that the covenants of the Lord might be fulfilled, which he made to Enoch; for he truly covenanted with Enoch that Noah should be of the fruit of his loins. And it came to pass that Methuselah prophesied that from his loins should spring all the kingdoms of the earth (through Noah), and he took glory unto himself. And there came forth a great famine into the land, and the Lord cursed the earth with a sore curse, and many of the inhabitants thereof died.** **OT1** And all the days of Enoch were **four hundred thirty** years. **And it came to pass that Methuselah, the son of Enoch, was not taken, that the covenants of the Lord might be fulfilled, which he made to Enoch; for he truly covenanted with Enoch that Noah come be the fruit of his loins. And it came to pass that Methuselah prophesied that from his loins should spring all the kingdoms of the earth (from Noah), and he took glory unto himself. And there came forth a great famine into the land, and the Lord cursed the earth with a sore curse, and many of the inhabitants thereof died.**
Genesis 5:24 And Enoch walked with God: and he *was* not; for God took him.	**verse omitted**

15. Moses 8 begins here.

Genesis 5:25 And Methuselah lived ~~an~~ hundred eighty and seven years, and begat Lamech:	And **it came to pass that** Methuselah lived **one** hundred eighty and seven years, and begat Lamech: **OT1 And it came to pass that** Methuselah lived **two** hundred and **eighteen** years, and begat Lamech;
Genesis 5:27 And all the days of Methuselah were nine hundred sixty and nine years: and he died.	**OT1** And all the days of Methuselah were **one thousand** years, and he died.
Genesis 5:29 And he called his name Noah, saying, This *same* shall comfort us concerning our work and toil of our hands, because of the ground which the Lord hath cursed.	**OT1** And he called his name Noah, saying: This **son** shall comfort us concerning our work and toil of our hands, because of the ground which the Lord hath cursed.
Genesis 5:30 And Lamech lived after he begat Noah five hundred ninety and five years, and begat sons and daughters:	And Lamech lived after he begat Noah five hundred **and** ninety and five years, and begat sons and daughters:
Genesis 5:32 And Noah was ~~five~~ hundred years old: and ~~Noah~~ begat Shem, Ham, ~~and Japheth~~.	And Noah was **four** hundred **and fifty** years old and begat **Japeth, and forty two years afterward, he begat** Shem **of her who was the mother of Japeth, and when he was five hundred years old, he begat** Ham.

Genesis 6
(Moses 8:13–30)

King James Version	Joseph Smith Translation
Genesis 6:1 And ~~it came to pass~~, when men began to multiply on the face of the earth, and daughters were born unto them,	And **Noah and his sons hearkened unto the Lord, and gave heed, and they were called the sons of God. And** when **these** men began to multiply on the face of the earth, and daughters were born unto them, **OT1** And it came to pass **that Noah and his sons hearkened unto the Lord, and gave heed, and they were called the sons of God. And** when

	these men began to multiply on the face of the earth, and daughters were born unto them,
Genesis 6:2 That the sons of ~~God~~ saw ~~the~~ daughters ~~of men~~ ~~that they~~ *were* fair; ~~and~~ they took them wives ~~of all which~~ they chose.	That the sons of **men** saw **that their** daughters were fair; they took them wives **even as** they chose. **And the Lord said unto Noah: The daughters of thy sons have sold themselves; for behold mine anger is kindled against the sons of men, for they will not hearken to my voice. And it came to pass that Noah prophesied, and taught the things of God, even as it was in the beginning.**
Genesis 6:3 And the LORD said, My spirit shall not always strive with man, for ~~that~~ he ~~also *is*~~ flesh: yet his days shall be an hundred and twenty years.	And the Lord said **unto Noah:** My Spirit shall not always strive with man, for he **shall know that all** flesh **shall die**; yet his days shall be an hundred and twenty years**; and if men do not repent, I will send in the floods upon them**.
Genesis 6:4 There were giants ~~in~~ the earth ~~in those days~~; and also after that, ~~when~~ the sons of God ~~came in~~ unto ~~the~~ daughters of men, and ~~they~~ bare *children* ~~to them~~, the same ~~*became*~~ mighty men which ~~*were*~~ of old, men of renown.	**And in those days** there were giants **on** the earth, **and they sought Noah to take away his life; but the Lord was with Noah, and the power of the Lord was upon him. And the Lord ordained Noah after his own order, and commanded him that he should go forth and declare his Gospel unto the children of men, even as it was given unto Enoch. And it came to pass that Noah called upon the children of men that they should repent; but they hearkened not unto his words;** And also, after that **they had heard him, they came up before him, saying: Behold, we are** the sons of God**; have we not taken unto ourselves** daughters of men**? And are we not eating and drinking, and marrying and given in marriage?** And **our wives** bare **unto us** children, **and** the

	same **are** mighty men, which **are like unto them** of old, men of **great** renown. **And they hearkened not unto the words of Noah.**
	OT1 And in those days there were giants **on** the earth, **and they sought Noah to take away his life; but the Lord was with Noah, and the power of the Lord was upon him. And the Lord ordained Noah after his own order, and commanded him that he should go forth and declare his Gospel unto the children of men, even as it was given unto Enoch. And it came to pass that Noah called upon men that they should repent; but they hearkened not unto his words;** And also, after that **they had heard him, they came up before him, saying: Behold, we are** the sons of God**; have we not taken** unto **ourselves** the daughters of men**? And are we not eating and drinking, and marrying and given in marriage?** And **our wives** bare **unto us** children, **and** the same **are** mighty men, which **are like unto them** of old, men of **great** renown. **And they hearkened not unto the words of Noah.**
Genesis 6:5 And God saw that the wickedness of man *was* great in the earth, and *that* every imagination of the thoughts of his heart *was* only evil continually.	And God saw that the wickedness of man **had become** great in the earth; and every **man was lifted up in the** imagination of the thoughts of his heart, **being** only evil continually. **And it came to pass that Noah continued his preaching unto the people, saying: Hearken, and give heed unto my words; Believe and repent of your sins and be baptized in the name of Jesus Christ, the Son of God, even as our fathers did, and ye shall receive the Holy Ghost, that ye may have all things made manifest; and if ye do**

	not this, the floods will come in upon you; nevertheless they hearkened not. **OT1** And God saw that the wickedness of man **had become** great in the earth; and every **man was lifted up in the** imagination of the thoughts of his heart, **being** only evil continually. **And it came to pass that Noah continued his preaching unto the people, saying: Hearken, and give heed unto my words; Believe and repent of your sins and be baptized in the name of Jesus Christ, the Son of God, even as our fathers did, and ye shall receive the gift of the Holy Ghost, that ye may have all things made manifest; and if ye do not do this, the floods will come in upon you; nevertheless they hearkened not.**
Genesis 6:6 And it repented ~~the LORD~~ that ~~he had~~ made man on the earth, and it grieved him at ~~his~~ heart.	And it repented **Noah, and his heart was pained** that **the Lord** made man on the earth, and it grieved him at **the** heart. **OT1** And it repented **Noah, and his heart was pained** that **the Lord** had made man on the earth, and it grieved him at his heart.
Genesis 6:7 And the LORD said, I will destroy man whom I have created from the face of the earth; both ~~man~~, and ~~beast~~, and the creeping ~~thing~~, and the fowls of the air; for it repenteth ~~me~~ that I have made them.	And the Lord said: I will destroy man whom I have created, from the face of the earth, both **men** and **beasts**, and the creeping **things**, and the fowls of the air; for it repenteth **Noah that I have created them, and** that I have made them**; and he hath called upon me; for they have sought his life**. **OT1** And the Lord said: I will destroy man whom I have created, from the face of the earth, both man and beast, and the creeping **things**, and the fowls of the air; for it repenteth **Noah that I have created them, and** that I have

	made them**; and he hath called upon me; and they have sought his life.**
Genesis 6:8 ~~But~~ Noah found grace in the eyes of the LORD	**And thus** Noah found grace in the eyes of the Lord.
Genesis 6:9 ~~These *are* the generations of Noah~~: Noah was a just man *and* perfect in his ~~generations~~, *and* ~~Noah~~ walked with God.	**For** Noah was a just man, and perfect in his **generation**, and **he** walked with God, **OT1 And** Noah was a just man, and perfect in his generations; and Noah walked with God,
Genesis 6:10 And ~~Noah begat~~ three sons, Shem, Ham, ~~and~~ Japheth.	And **also his** three sons, Shem, Ham, Japheth. **OT1** And **also his** three sons, Shem, Ham, and Japheth.
Genesis 6:11 The earth ~~also~~ was corrupt before God, ~~and the earth~~ was filled with violence.	**But** the earth was corrupt before God, **it** was filled with violence.
Genesis 6:12 And God looked upon ~~the earth~~, and, behold, it was corrupt; for all flesh had corrupted ~~his~~ way upon the earth.	And God looked upon **it**, and, behold, it was corrupt; for all flesh had corrupted **its** way upon the earth.
Genesis 6:13 And God said unto Noah, The end of all flesh is come before me; for the earth is filled with violence ~~through them~~; and, behold, I will destroy ~~them with~~ the earth.	And God said unto Noah, The end of all flesh is come before me; for the earth is filled with violence; and, behold, I will destroy **all flesh from off** the earth.
Genesis 6:14 Make thee an ark of gopher wood; rooms shalt thou make in the ark, and shalt pitch it within and without with pitch.	Make thee **therefore** an ark of gopher wood; rooms shalt thou make in the ark, and **thou** shalt pitch it within and without with pitch. **OT1** Make thee an ark of gopher wood; rooms **shalt** thou make in the ark, and **shall** pitch it within and without with pitch.
Genesis 6:15 And ~~this *is the fashion* which thou shalt make it *of*~~*:* The length	And the length of the ark **thou shalt make** three hundred cubits, the breadth

of the ark ~~*shall be*~~ three hundred cubits, the breadth of it fifty cubits, and the height of it thirty cubits.	of it fifty cubits, and the height of it thirty cubits.
Genesis 6:16 ~~A window~~ shalt thou make to the ark, and in a cubit shalt thou finish it above; and the door of the ark shalt thou set in the side thereof; ~~*with*~~ lower, second, and third ~~*stories*~~ shalt thou make it.	**And windows** shalt thou make to the ark, and in a cubit shalt thou finish it above; and the door of the ark shalt thou set in the side thereof; lower, second, and third **chambers** shalt thou make **in** it.
Genesis 6:17 And, behold, I, even I, ~~do~~ bring a flood of ~~waters~~ upon the earth, to destroy all flesh, wherein *is* the breath of life, from under heaven; ~~*and*~~ every thing that ~~*is* in~~ the earth shall die.	And, behold, I, even I, **will** bring **in** a flood of **water** upon the earth, to destroy all flesh, wherein is the breath of life, from under heaven; every thing that **liveth on** the earth shall die. **OT1** And, behold, I, even I, will bring **in** a flood of waters upon the earth, to destroy all flesh, wherein **shall be** the breath of life, from under heaven every thing that **liveth on** the earth shall die.
Genesis 6:18 But with thee will I establish my covenant; and thou shalt come into the ark, thou, and thy sons, and thy wife, and thy sons' wives with thee.	But with thee will I establish my covenant; **even as I have sworn unto thy father Enoch, that a remnant**[16] **of thy posterity should come all nations.** And thou shalt come into the ark, thou, and thy sons, and thy wife, and thy sons' wives with thee. **OT1** But with thee will I establish my covenant; **even as I have sworn unto thy father Enoch that a remnant of thy posterity should be preserved among all nations which shall come** and thou shalt come into the ark, thou, and thy sons, and thy wife, and thy sons' wives with thee.
Genesis 6:19 And of every living thing of all flesh, two of every ~~*sort*~~ shalt thou	And of every living thing of all flesh, two of every **kind** shalt thou bring into

16. OT2 reads, "~~remnant~~ <of> of thy posterity."

bring into the ark, to keep ~~*them*~~ alive with thee; they shall be male and female.	the ark, to keep alive with thee; they shall be male and female.
Genesis 6:20 Of fowls after their kind, and of cattle after their kind, of every creeping thing of the earth after his kind, two of every ~~*sort* shall come unto thee~~, to keep ~~*them*~~ alive.	Of fowls after their kind, and of cattle after their kind, of every creeping thing of the earth after his kind, two of every **kind shalt thou take into the ark** to keep alive.
Genesis 6:21 And take thou unto thee of all food that is eaten, and thou shalt gather ~~*it* to~~ thee; and it shall be for food for thee, and for them.	And take thou unto thee of all food that is eaten, and thou shalt gather **fruit of every kind unto** thee **in the ark**; and it shall be for food for thee, and for them.
Genesis 6:22 Thus did Noah; according to all that God commanded him, ~~so did he~~.	Thus did Noah; according to all that God commanded him. **OT1** Thus did Noah; according to all that God commanded him, **even** so. **Amen.**

Genesis 7

KING JAMES VERSION	JOSEPH SMITH TRANSLATION
Genesis 7:1 AND the LORD said unto Noah, Come thou and all thy house into the ark; for thee have I seen righteous before me in this generation.	And the Lord said unto Noah, Come thou and all thy house into the ark; for thee **only** have I seen righteous before me in this generation.
Genesis 7:3 Of fowls also of the air by sevens, the male and the female; to keep seed alive upon the face of ~~all~~ the earth.	Of fowls also of the air by sevens, the male and the female; to keep seed alive upon the face of the earth.
Genesis 7:5 And Noah did according ~~unto~~ all that the LORD commanded him.	And Noah did according **to** all that the Lord commanded him.
Genesis 7:8 Of clean beasts, and of beasts that ~~*are*~~ not clean, and of fowls, and of every thing that creepeth upon the earth,	Of clean beasts, and of beasts that **were** not clean, and of fowls, and of every thing that creepeth upon the earth,

Genesis 7:11 In the six hundredth year of Noah's life, in the second month, the seventeenth day of the month, the same day were all the fountains of the great deep broken up, and the windows of heaven were opened.	In the six hundredth year of Noah's life, in the second month, **and** the seventeenth day of the month, the same day were all the fountains of the great deep broken up, and the windows of heaven were opened.
Genesis 7:13 In the selfsame day entered Noah, and Shem, and Ham, and Japheth, the sons of Noah, and Noah's wife, and the three wives of his sons with them, into the ark;	**OT1** In the selfsame day entered Noah, and Shem, Ham, and[17] Japheth, the sons of Noah, and Noah's wife, and the three wives of his sons with them, into the ark;
Genesis 7:14 They, and every beast after his kind, and all the cattle after their kind, and every creeping thing that creepeth ~~upon~~ the earth after his kind, and every fowl after his kind, every bird of every sort.	They, and every beast after his kind, and all the cattle after their kind, and every creeping thing that creepeth **on** the earth after his kind, and every fowl after his kind, **and** every bird of every sort.
	OT1 verse omitted
Genesis 7:15 And they went ~~in~~ unto Noah into the ark, two and two of all flesh, wherein *is* the breath of life.	And they went unto Noah into the ark, two and two of all flesh, wherein is the breath of life.
	OT1 verse omitted
Genesis 7:17 And the flood was forty days upon the earth; and the waters increased, and bare up the ark, and it was ~~lift~~ up above the earth.	And the flood was forty days upon the earth; and the waters increased, and bare up the ark, and it was **lifted** up above the earth.
Genesis 7:18 And the waters prevailed, and ~~were~~ increased greatly upon the earth; and the ark went upon the face of the waters.	And the waters prevailed, and increased greatly upon the earth; and the ark went upon the face of the waters.
Genesis 7:19 And the waters prevailed exceedingly upon the earth; and all the high hills, that ~~*were*~~ under the whole heaven, were covered.	And the waters prevailed exceedingly upon **the face of** the earth; and all the high hills, that **are** under the whole heaven, were covered.

17. This "and" is omitted in OT1, most likely through an error in copying or dictation.

Genesis 7:20 Fifteen cubits upward did the waters prevail; and the mountains were covered.	Fifteen cubits **and** upward did the waters prevail; and the mountains were covered.
Genesis 7:21 And all flesh died that moved upon the earth, both of fowl, and of cattle, and of ~~beast~~, and of every creeping thing that creepeth upon the earth, and every man:	And all flesh died that moved upon **the face of** the earth, both of fowl, and of cattle, and of **beasts**, and of every creeping thing that creepeth upon the earth, and every man:
Genesis 7:22 All in whose nostrils ~~*was*~~ the breath of life, of all that ~~*was* in~~ the dry *land,* died.	All in whose nostrils **the Lord had breathed** the breath of life, of all that **were on** the dry land, died.
Genesis 7:23 And every living substance was destroyed which was upon the face of the ground, both ~~man~~, and cattle, and the creeping things, and the ~~fowl~~ of the heaven; and they were destroyed from the earth: and Noah only remained ~~*alive,*~~ and they that *were* with him in the ark.	And every living substance was destroyed which was upon the face of the ground, both **men**, and cattle, and the creeping things, and the **fowls** of the heaven; and they were destroyed from the earth: and Noah only remained, and they that were with him in the ark.
Genesis 7:24 And the waters prevailed ~~upon~~ the earth ~~an~~ hundred and fifty days.	And the waters prevailed **on** the earth **one** hundred and fifty days.

Genesis 8

KING JAMES VERSION	JOSEPH SMITH TRANSLATION
Genesis 8:1 AND God remembered Noah, ~~and~~ every living thing, and all the cattle that ~~*was*~~ with him in the ark: and God made a wind to pass over the earth, and the waters assuaged;	And God remembered Noah, every living thing, and all the cattle that **were** with him in the ark: and God made a wind to pass over the earth, and the waters assuaged;
Genesis 8:3 And the waters returned from off the earth continually: and after the end of the hundred and fifty days the waters were abated.	**OT1** And the waters returned from off the earth: and after the end of the hundred and fifty days the waters were abated.

Genesis 8:4 And the ark rested in the seventh month, on the seventeenth day of the month, upon the ~~mountains~~ of Ararat.	And the ark rested in the seventh month, on the seventeenth day of the month, upon the **mountain** of Ararat.
Genesis 8:5 And the waters decreased continually until the tenth month: in the tenth *month,* on the first *day* of the month, were the tops of the mountains seen.	And the waters decreased continually until the tenth month: **and** in the tenth [month], on the first [day] of the month[18] were the tops of the mountains seen.
Genesis 8:8 ~~Also~~ he sent forth a dove from him, to see if the waters were abated from off the face of the ground;	He **also** sent forth a dove from him, to see if the waters were abated from off the face of the ground;
Genesis 8:9 But the dove found no rest for the sole of her foot, and she returned unto him into the ark, for the waters ~~*were* on~~ the face of the whole earth: then he put forth his hand, and took her, and pulled her in unto him into the ark.	But the dove found no rest for the sole of her foot, and she returned unto him into the ark, for the waters **had not receded from off** the face of the whole earth: then he put forth his hand, and took her, and pulled her in unto him into the ark.
Genesis 8:10 And he stayed yet other seven days; and again he sent ~~forth~~ the dove out of the ark;	And he stayed yet other seven days; and again he sent the dove out of the ark;
Genesis 8:11 And the dove came in to him in the evening; and, lo, in her mouth ~~*was*~~ an olive leaf pluckt off: so Noah knew that the waters were abated from off the earth.	And the dove came in to him in the evening; and, lo, in her mouth an olive leaf plucked off: so Noah knew that the waters were abated from off the earth.
Genesis 8:12 And he stayed yet other seven days; and sent forth ~~the~~ dove; which returned not again unto him any more.	And he stayed yet other seven days; and sent forth **a** dove; which returned not again unto him any more.
Genesis 8:16 Go forth of the ark, thou, and thy wife, and thy sons, and thy sons' wives with thee.	Go forth **out** of the ark, thou, and thy wife, and thy sons, and thy sons' wives with thee.

18. OT2 reads, "until the tenth month ~~& [i]~~<o>n <& in> the tenth ~~day of~~ <on> the <first of the> month were the tops of the mountains seen."

Genesis 8:19 Every beast, every creeping thing, and every fowl, *and* whatsoever creepeth upon the earth, after their kinds, went forth out of the ark.	**And** every beast, **and** every creeping thing, and every fowl, and whatsoever creepeth upon the earth, after their kinds, went forth out of the ark. **OT1** Every beast, every creeping thing, and every fowl upon the earth, after their kinds, went forth out of the ark.
Genesis 8:20 And Noah builded an altar unto the LORD; and took of every clean beast, and of every clean fowl, and offered burnt offerings on the altar.	And Noah builded an altar unto the Lord; and took of every clean beast, and of every clean fowl, and offered burnt offerings on the altar**, and gave thanks unto the Lord, and rejoiced in his heart. And the Lord spake unto Noah and he blessed him.**
Genesis 8:21 And ~~the LORD~~ smelled a sweet savour; and ~~the LORD~~ said in his heart, I will not again curse the ground any more for man's sake; for the imagination of man's heart *is* evil from his youth; ~~neither~~ will ~~I~~ again smite any more every thing living, as ~~I have~~ done.	And **Noah** smelled a sweet savour; and **he** said in his heart, I **will call on the name of the Lord that he** will not again curse the ground any more for man's sake; for the imagination of man's heart is evil from his youth; **and that he** will **not** again smite any more every thing living, as **he hath**[19] done.
Genesis 8:22 While the earth remaineth, seedtime and harvest, and cold and heat, and summer and winter, and day and night ~~shall~~ not cease.	While the earth remaineth, **and that** seedtime and harvest, and cold and heat, and summer and winter, and day and night **may** not cease **with man**.

Genesis 9

King James Version	Joseph Smith Translation
Genesis 9:2 And the fear of you and the dread of you shall be upon every beast of the earth, and upon every fowl of the air, upon all that moveth *upon* the earth, and upon all the fishes of the sea; ~~into~~ your hand are they delivered.	And the fear of you and the dread of you shall be upon every beast of the earth, and upon every fowl of the air, upon all that moveth upon the earth, and upon all the fishes of the sea; **unto** your hand are they delivered.

19. OT1 modernizes the verb "hath" to "has."

	OT1 And the fear of you and the dread of you shall be upon every beast of the earth, and upon every fowl of the air, upon all that moveth **on** the earth, and upon all the fishes of the sea; into your hand are they delivered.
Genesis 9:4 But ~~flesh with~~ the life thereof, ~~*which is*~~ the blood ~~thereof~~, shall ~~ye~~ not eat.	But **the blood of all which I have given you for meat shall be shed upon** the **ground which taketh** life thereof, **and** the blood **ye** shall not eat.
	OT1 But **the blood of all** flesh **which I have given you for meat shall be shed upon** the **ground which taketh** life thereof, **and** the blood, **ye** shall not eat.
Genesis 9:5 And surely ~~your~~ blood ~~of~~ your lives ~~will I require; at~~ the ~~hand~~ of every beast will I require ~~it, and~~ at ~~the hand of man; at the hand of every man's brother will I require the life of man~~.	And surely blood **shall not be shed only for meat to save** your lives **and** the **blood** of every beast will I require at **your hands.**
Genesis 9:6 Whoso sheddeth man's blood, by man shall his blood be shed: for in ~~the~~ image ~~of God~~ made ~~he~~ man.	**And** whoso sheddeth man's blood, by man shall his blood be shed: **for man shall not shed the blood of man. For a commandment I give that every man's brother shall preserve the life of man** for in **mine own** image **have I** made man.
Genesis 9:7 And you, be ye fruitful, and multiply; bring forth abundantly ~~in~~ the earth, and multiply therein.	And **a commandment I give unto** you, be ye fruitful, and multiply; bring forth abundantly **on** the earth, and multiply therein.
Genesis 9:9 And I, behold, ~~I~~ establish my covenant with you, ~~and with~~ your seed after you;	And I, behold, **will** establish my covenant with you, **which I made unto your father Enoch concerning** your seed after you;
	OT1 And I, behold, **I will** establish my covenant with you **which I made unto your father Enoch concerning** your seed after you;

Genesis 9:10 And ~~with~~ every living creature that *is* with you, of the fowl, of the cattle, and of ~~every~~ beast of the earth with you; ~~from all that~~ go out of the ark, ~~to every beast of the earth~~.	And **it shall come to pass that** every living creature that is with you, of the fowl, **and** of the cattle, and of **the** beast of the earth **that is** with you, **which shall** go out of the ark, **shall not altogether perish**.
Genesis 9:11 ~~And I will establish my covenant with you~~; neither shall all flesh be cut off any more by the waters of a flood; neither shall there any more be a flood to destroy the earth.	Neither shall all flesh be cut off any more by the waters of a flood; neither shall there any more be a flood to destroy the earth. **And I will establish my covenant with you which I made unto Enoch concerning the remnants of your posterity.**
Genesis 9:12 And God said, This *is* the token of the covenant ~~which~~ I make between me and you and every living creature ~~that *is*~~ with you, for perpetual generations:	And God **made a covenant with Noah and** said, This **shall be** the token of the covenant I make between me and you and **for** every living creature with you, for perpetual generations:[20]
Genesis 9:13 I ~~do~~ set my bow in the cloud, and it shall be for a token of a covenant between me and the earth.	**And** I **will** set my bow in the cloud, and it shall be for a token of a covenant between me and the earth.
Genesis 9:15 And I will remember my covenant, which *is* between me and you ~~and~~ every living creature of all flesh; and the waters shall no more become a flood to destroy all flesh.	And I will remember my covenant, which **I have made** between me and you **for** every living creature of all flesh; and the waters shall no more become a flood to destroy all flesh.
Genesis 9:16 And the bow shall be in the cloud; and I will look upon it, that I may remember the everlasting covenant between ~~God~~ and every living creature of all flesh that *is* upon the earth.	And the bow shall be in the cloud; and I will look upon it, that I may remember the everlasting covenant **which I made unto thy father Enoch that, when men should keep all my commandments Zion should again come on the earth, the city of Enoch which I have caught up unto myself. And this is mine everlasting covenant that I establish with you that [OT1 omits "I establish with you that"] when thy**

20. OT2 has a singular "generation," which appears to be a copying error for "generations."

	posterity shall embrace the truth and look upward; then shall Zion look downward. And all the heavens shall shake with gladness and the earth shall tremble with joy and the general assembly of the church of the firstborn shall come down out of heaven and possess the earth and shall have place until the end come. And this is mine everlasting covenant which I made with thy father Enoch and the bow shall be in the cloud and I will establish my covenant unto thee which I have made between **me** and **thee for** every living creature of all flesh that **shall be** upon the earth.
Genesis 9:17 And God said unto Noah, This *is* the token of the covenant, which I have established between me and all flesh that ~~*is*~~ upon the earth.	And God said unto Noah, This is the token of the covenant, which I have established between me and **thee for** all flesh that **shall be** upon the earth.
Genesis 9:18 And the sons of Noah, that went forth of the ark, were Shem, and Ham, and Japheth: and Ham ~~*is*~~ the father of Canaan.	And the sons of Noah, that went forth of the ark, were Shem, and Ham, and Japheth: and Ham **was** the father of[21] Canaan.
Genesis 9:19 These ~~*are*~~ the three sons of Noah: and of them was the whole earth overspread.	These **were** the three sons of Noah: and of them was the whole earth overspread.
Genesis 9:20 And Noah began *to* ~~*be*~~ an husbandman, and he planted a vineyard:	And Noah began to **till the earth, and he was** an husbandman, and he planted a vineyard:
Genesis 9:22 And Ham, the father of Canaan, saw the nakedness of his father, and told his ~~two~~ brethren without.	**OT1** And Ham, the father of Canaan, saw the nakedness of his father, and told his two brethren without.
Genesis 9:23 And Shem and Japheth took a garment, and laid ~~*it*~~ upon both their shoulders, and went backward,	And Shem and Japheth took a garment, and laid upon both their shoulders, and went backward, and covered the

21. OT1 omits "of" through scribal or dictation error.

and covered the nakedness of their father; and their faces *were* backward, and they saw not their father's nakedness.	nakedness of their father; and their faces were backward, and they saw not their father's nakedness. **OT1** And Shem and Japheth took a garment, and laid upon both their shoulders, and went backward, and they saw not their father's nakedness.
Genesis 9:24 And Noah awoke from his wine, and knew what his ~~younger~~ son had done unto him.	And Noah awoke from his wine, and knew what his **youngest** son had done unto him.
Genesis 9:26 And he said, Blessed *be* the Lord God of Shem; and Canaan shall be his servant.	And he said, Blessed be the Lord God of Shem; and Canaan shall be his servant **and a veil of darkness shall cover him that he shall be known among all men**.
Genesis 9:27 God shall enlarge Japheth, and he shall dwell in the tents of Shem; and Canaan shall be his ~~servant~~.	God shall enlarge Japheth, and he shall dwell in the tents of Shem; and Canaan shall be his **servants**.

Genesis 10

King James Version	Joseph Smith Translation
Genesis 10:1 Now these ~~*are*~~ the generations of the sons of Noah, Shem, Ham, and Japheth: and unto them were sons born after the flood.	Now these **were** the generations of the sons of Noah, Shem, Ham, and Japheth: and unto them were sons born after the flood.
Genesis 10:2 The sons of Japheth; Gomer, and Magog, ~~and~~ Madai, and Javan, and Tubal, and Meshech, and Tiras.	The sons of Japheth; Gomer, and Magog, Madai, and Javan, and Tubal, and Meshech, and Tiras.
Genesis 10:3 And the sons of Gomer; Ashkenaz, and Riphath, and Togarmah.	And **these are** the sons of Gomer; Ashkenaz, and Riphath, and Togarmah.
Genesis 10:4 And the sons of Javan; Elishah, and Tarshish, Kittim, ~~and~~ Dodanim.	**OT1** And the sons of Javan; Elishah, and Tarshish, Kittim, Dodanim.

Genesis 10:5 By these were the isles of the Gentiles divided in their lands; every one after ~~his tongue~~, after their families, in their nations.	By these were the isles of the Gentiles divided in their lands; every one after **the same tongues**, after their families, in their nations. **OT1** By these were the isles of the Gentiles divided in their lands; every one after **the same** tongue, after their families, in their nations.
Genesis 10:7 And the sons of Cush; Seba, and Havilah, and Sabtah, and Raamah, and Sabtecha: and ~~the~~ sons of Raamah; Sheba, ~~and~~ Dedan.	And the sons of Cush; Seba, and Havilah, and Sabtah, and Raamah, and Sabtecha: and sons of Raamah; Sheba, Dedan. **OT1** And the sons of Cush; Seba, and Havilah, and Sabtah, and Raamah, and Sabtecha: and the sons of Raamah; Sheba, Dedan.
Genesis 10:9 He was a mighty hunter ~~before~~ the ~~LORD~~: wherefore it is said, Even as Nimrod the mighty hunter ~~before~~ the ~~LORD~~.	He was a mighty hunter **in** the **land**: wherefore it is said, Even as Nimrod the mighty hunter **in** the **land**.[22]
Genesis 10:10 And the beginning of his kingdom was Babel, and Erech, and Accad, and Calneh, in the land of Shinar.	**And he began a kingdom,** and the beginning of his kingdom was Babel, and Erech, and Accad, and Calneh, in the land of Shinar.
Genesis 10:12 And Resen between Nineveh and Calah: the same ~~*is*~~ a great city.	And Resen between Nineveh and Calah: the same **was** a great city.
Genesis 10:16 And the Jebusite, and the Amorite, and ~~the~~ Girgasite,	And the Jebusite, and the Amorite, and Girgasite,
Genesis 10:17 And the Hivite, and the Arkite, and the Sinite,	**OT1** And Hivite, and the Arkite, and the Sinite,
Genesis 10:18 And the Arvadite, and the Zemarite, and the Hamathite: and afterward were the families of the Canaanites spread abroad.	**OT1** And the Arvadite, and Zemarite, and the Hamathite: and afterward were the families of the Canaanites spread abroad.

22. A copying error from OT1 to OT2 occurs here. The text reads "even & Nimrod as mighty hunter in the land."

Genesis 10:19 And the ~~border~~ of the Canaanites ~~was~~ from Sidon, as thou comest to Gerar, unto Gaza; as thou goest, ~~unto~~ Sodom, and Gomorrah, and Admah, and Zeboim, even unto Lasha.	And the **borders** of the Canaanites **were** from Sidon, as thou comest to Gerar, unto Gaza; as thou goest, **to** Sodom, and Gomorrah, and Admah, and Zeboim, even unto Lasha.
Genesis 10:20 These ~~*are*~~ the sons of Ham, after their families, after ~~their tongues~~, in their countries, *and* in their nations.	These **were** the sons of Ham, after their families, after **the same tongue**, in their countries, and in their nations.
Genesis 10:21 Unto Shem also, the father ~~of all the children~~ of Eber, ~~the brother of Japheth the elder~~, even to him were *children* born.	Unto Shem also, **which was the elder, children were born; And he was** the father of Eber, **and** even to him were children born.
Genesis 10:22 The children of Shem; Elam, and Asshur, and Arphaxad, and Lud, and Aram.	**And these are** the children of Shem; **Eber, and** Elam, and Asshur, and Arphaxad, and Lud, and Aram. **OT1 And these are** the children of Shem; **Eber,** Elam, and Asshur, and Arphaxad, and Lud, and Aram.
Genesis 10:23 And the children of Aram; Uz, and Hul, and Gether, and Mash.	And **these are** the children of Aram; Uz, and Hul, and Gether, and Mash **and Arphaxad**. **OT1** And **these were** the children of Aram; Uz, and Hul, and Gether, and Mash **and Arphaxad**.
Genesis 10:25 And unto Eber were born two sons: the name of one *was* Peleg; for in his days was the earth divided; ~~and his brother's name *was* Joktan~~.	And unto Eber were born two sons: the name of **the** one was Peleg; **the other Joktan. And Peleg was a mighty man,** for in his days was the earth divided. **OT1** And unto Eber were born two sons: the name of one Peleg; **the other Joktan**. **And Peleg was a mighty man** for in his days was the earth divided.
Genesis 10:29 And Ophir, and Havilah, ~~and~~ Jobab: all these *were* the sons of Joktan.	And Ophir, and Havilah, Jobab: all these were the sons of Joktan.

Genesis 10:30 And their dwelling ~~was~~ from Mesha, as thou goest unto Sephar a mount of the east.	**OT1** And their dwelling from Mesha, as thou goest unto Sephar a mount of the east.
Genesis 10:31 These ~~*are*~~ the sons of Shem, after their families, after their tongues, in their lands, after their nations.	These **were** the sons of Shem, after their families, after their tongues, in their lands, after their nations.
Genesis 10:32 These ~~*are*~~ the families of the sons of Noah, after their generations, in their nations: and by these were the nations divided ~~in~~ the earth after the flood.	These **were** the families of the sons of Noah, after their generations, in their nations: and by these were the nations divided **on** the earth after the flood.

Genesis 11

KING JAMES VERSION	JOSEPH SMITH TRANSLATION
Genesis 11:1 AND the whole earth was of ~~one~~ language, and of ~~one~~ speech.	And the whole earth was of **the same** language, and of **the same** speech.
Genesis 11:2 And it came to pass, ~~as they~~ journeyed from the east, ~~that~~ they found a plain in the land of Shinar; and ~~they~~ dwelt there.	And it came to pass, **that many** journeyed from the east, **and as they journeyed from the east,** they found a plain in the land of Shinar; and dwelt there **in the plain of Shinar**.
Genesis 11:3 And they said one to another, Go to, let us make brick, and burn them throughly. And they had brick for stone, and slime ~~had they~~ for morter.	And they said one to another, **Come,** go to, let us make brick, and burn them throughly. And they had brick for stone, and **they had** slime for morter.
Genesis 11:4 And they said, Go to, let us build us a city and a tower, whose top ~~*may reach*~~ unto heaven; and let us make us a name, lest we be scattered abroad upon the face of the whole earth.	And they said, **Come,** go to, let us build us a city and a tower, whose top **will be high, nigh** unto heaven; and let us make us a name, lest we be scattered abroad upon the face of the whole earth.
Genesis 11:5 And the LORD came down ~~to see~~ the city and the tower, which the children of men ~~builded~~.	And the Lord came down **beholding** the city and the tower, which the children of men **were building**.

Genesis 11:6 And the LORD said, Behold, the people ~~*is* one~~, and they have ~~all one~~ language; and this they begin to ~~do~~: and now nothing will be restrained from them, which they have imagined ~~to do~~.	And the Lord said, Behold, the people **are the same**, and they **all** have **the same** language; and this **tower** they begin to **build**: and now nothing will be restrained from them, which they have imagined.
Genesis 11:7 ~~Go to, let us go down, and there~~ confound their language, that they may not understand one another's speech.	**Except I, the Lord,** confound their language, that they may not understand one another's speech.
Genesis 11:8 So the LORD ~~scattered~~ them abroad from thence upon the face of ~~all~~ the earth: and they left off to build the city.	So **I,** the Lord**, will scatter** them abroad from thence upon **all** the face of the **land and unto every quarter of the** earth: and they **were confounded and** left off to build the city **and they hearkened not unto the Lord**. **OT1** So **I,** the Lord**, will scatter** them abroad from thence upon **all** the face of the **land and into every quarter of the** earth: and they **were confounded and** left off to build the city **and they hearkened not unto the Lord**.
Genesis 11:9 Therefore is the name of it called Babel; because the LORD did there confound the language of all the earth: and from thence did the LORD scatter them abroad upon the face ~~of all the earth~~.	Therefore is the name of it called Babel; because the Lord **was displeased with their works and** did there confound the language of all the earth: and from thence did the Lord scatter them abroad upon the face **thereof**.
Genesis 11:10 These ~~*are*~~ the generations of Shem: Shem ~~*was*~~ an hundred years ~~old~~, ~~and~~ begat Arphaxad two years after the flood:	**And** these **were** the generations of Shem: **And** Shem **being** an hundred **and ten** years, begat Arphaxad two years after the flood: **OT1 And** these **were** the generations of Shem: Shem **being** an hundred years old, begat Arphaxad two years after the flood:
Genesis 11:25 And Nahor lived after he begat Terah an hundred and nineteen years, and begat sons and daughters.	**OT1** And Nahor lived after he begat Terah a hundred nineteen years, and begat sons and daughters.

Genesis 11:27 Now these ~~*are*~~ the generations of Terah: Terah begat Abram, Nahor, and Haran; and Haran begat Lot.	Now these **were** the generations of Terah: Terah begat Abram, Nahor, and Haran; and Haran begat Lot.
Genesis 11:28 And Haran died before his ~~father~~ Terah in the land of his nativity, in Ur of the Chaldees.	And Haran died before his **fathers** Terah in the land of his nativity, in Ur of the Chaldees.
Genesis 11:29 And Abram and Nahor took them wives: the name of Abram's wife *was* Sarai; and the name of Nahor's wife, Milcah, the daughter of Haran, the father of Milcah, and the father of Iscah.	And Abram and Nahor took them wives: **and** the name of Abram's wife was Sarai; and the name of Nahor's wife, Milcah, the daughter of Haran, the father of Milcah, and the father of[23] Iscah.
Genesis 11:30 But Sarai was barren; she ~~*had*~~ no child.	But Sarai was barren; **and** she **bare** no child.
Genesis 11:32 And the days of Terah were two hundred and five years: and Terah died in Haran.	**OT1** And the days of Terah **was** two hundred and five years: and Terah died in Haran.

Genesis 12

KING JAMES VERSION	JOSEPH SMITH TRANSLATION
Genesis 12:3 And I will bless them that bless thee, and curse ~~him~~ that ~~curseth~~ thee: and in thee shall ~~all~~ families of the earth be blessed.	And I will bless them that bless thee, and curse **them** that **curse** thee: and in thee shall **the** families of the earth be blessed.
Genesis 12:6 And Abram passed through the land unto the place of Sichem, unto the plain of Moreh. And the ~~Canaanite *was*~~ then in the land.	And Abram passed through the land unto the place of Sichem, unto the plain of Moreh. And the **Canaanites were** then in the land.
Genesis 12:8 And he removed from thence unto a mountain on the east of Beth-el, and pitched his tent, ~~*having*~~	And he removed from thence unto a mountain on the east of Beth-el, and pitched his tent, **leaving** Beth-el on

23. The Prophet's scribe omitted the word "of" apparently in error in OT2.

Beth-el on the west, and Hai on the east: and there he builded an altar unto the LORD, and called upon the name of the LORD.	the west, and Hai **was** on the east: and there he builded an altar unto the Lord, and called upon the name of the Lord.
Genesis 12:10 And there was a famine in the land: and Abram went down into Egypt to sojourn there; for the famine ~~*was*~~ grievous in the land.	And there was a famine in the land: and Abram went down into Egypt to sojourn there; for the famine **became** grievous in the land.
Genesis 12:11 And it came to pass, when he was come near to enter into Egypt, that he said unto Sarai his wife, Behold now, I know ~~that thou *art*~~ a fair woman to look upon:	And it came to pass, when he was come near to enter into Egypt, that he said unto Sarai his wife, Behold now, I know **thee to be** a fair woman to look upon:
Genesis 12:13 Say, I pray thee, ~~thou *art* my~~ sister: that it may be well with me for thy sake; and my soul shall live because of thee.	Say, I pray thee **unto them, I am his** sister: that it may be well with me for thy sake; and my soul shall live because of thee.
Genesis 12:15 The princes also of Pharaoh saw her, and ~~commended~~ her before Pharaoh: and the woman was taken into Pharaoh's house.	The princes also of Pharaoh saw her, and **commanded** her **to be brought** before Pharaoh: and the woman was taken into Pharaoh's house.
Genesis 12:16 And he entreated Abram well for her sake: and he had sheep, and oxen, and he asses, and menservants, ~~and maidservants, and she asses~~, and camels.	And he entreated Abram well for her sake: and he had sheep, and oxen, and he asses, and menservants, and camels.
Genesis 12:18 And Pharaoh called Abram, and said, What ~~*is* this *that*~~ thou ~~hast~~ done unto me? why didst thou not tell me that she *was* thy wife?	And Pharaoh called Abram, and said, What **hast** thou done unto me **in this thing**? why didst thou not tell me that she was thy wife?
Genesis 12:19 Why saidst thou, She *is* my sister? so I might have taken her to me to wife: now therefore behold thy wife, ~~take *her*~~, and go thy way.	Why saidst thou, She is my sister? so I might have taken her to me to wife: now therefore behold **I say unto thee take** thy wife, and go thy way.
Genesis 12:20 And Pharaoh commanded ~~*his*~~ men concerning him: and they sent him away, and his wife, and all that he had.	And Pharaoh commanded men concerning him: and they sent him away, and his wife, and all that he had.

Genesis 13

KING JAMES VERSION	JOSEPH SMITH TRANSLATION
Genesis 13:3 And he went on his ~~journeys~~ from the south even to Beth-el, unto the place where his tent had been at the beginning, between Beth-el and Hai;	And he went on his **journey** from the south even to Beth-el, unto the place where his tent had been at the beginning, between Beth-el and Hai;
Genesis 13:6 And the land was not able to bear them, that they might dwell together: for their substance was great, ~~so~~ that they could not dwell together.	**OT1** And the land was not able to bear them, that they might dwell together: for their substance was great, that they could not dwell together.
Genesis 13:7 And there was a strife between the herdmen of Abram's cattle and the herdmen of Lot's cattle: and the Canaanite and the Perizzite dwelled then in the land.	And there was a strife between the herdmen of Abram's cattle and the herdmen of Lot's cattle**, that they could not dwell together**: and the Canaanite and the Perizzite dwelled then in the land.
Genesis 13:8 And Abram said unto Lot, Let there be no strife, I pray thee, between me and thee, and between my herdmen and thy herdmen; for we ~~*be*~~ brethren.	And Abram said unto Lot, Let there be no strife, I pray thee, between me and thee, and between my herdmen and thy herdmen; for we **are** brethren.
Genesis 13:9 *Is* not the whole land before thee? separate thyself, I pray thee, from me: if *thou* ~~*wilt take*~~ the left hand, then I will go to the right; ~~or~~ if *thou* ~~*depart*~~ to the right hand, then I will go to the left.	Is not the whole land before thee? separate thyself, I pray thee, from me: if thou **go to** the left hand, then I will go to the right; if thou **go** to the right hand, then I will go to the left.
Genesis 13:10 And Lot lifted up his eyes, and beheld all the plain of Jordan, that it *was* well watered every where, before the LORD destroyed Sodom and Gomorrah, ~~*even*~~ as the garden of the LORD, like the land of Egypt, ~~as thou comest unto Zoar~~.	And Lot lifted up his eyes, and beheld all the plain of Jordan, that it was well watered every where, before the Lord destroyed Sodom and Gomorrah, **like** as the garden of the Lord, like the land of Egypt.

Genesis 13:11 Then Lot chose him all the plain of Jordan; and Lot journeyed ~~east~~: and they separated themselves the one from the other.	Then Lot chose him all the plain of Jordan; and Lot journeyed **out**: and they separated themselves the one from the other.
Genesis 13:13 But the men of Sodom ~~*were* wicked and~~ sinners before the LORD ~~exceedingly~~.	But the men of Sodom[24] **becoming** sinners **and exceedingly wicked** before the Lord. **The Lord was angry with them.**
Genesis 13:14 And the LORD said unto Abram, after that Lot was separated from him, Lift up now thine eyes, and look from the place where thou art northward, and southward, and eastward, and westward:	And the Lord said unto Abram, after that Lot was separated from him, Lift up now thine eyes, and look from the place where thou art northward, and southward, and eastward, and westward: **And remember the covenant which I make with thee, for it shall be an everlasting covenant, and thou shalt remember the days of Enoch thy father.**
Genesis 13:15 For all the land which thou seest, ~~to thee~~ will I give ~~it~~, and to thy seed for ever.	For all the land which thou seest, will I give **thee**, and to thy seed for ever.
Genesis 13:16 And I will make thy seed as the dust of the earth: so that if a man can number the dust of the earth, ~~*then* shall~~ thy seed also be numbered.	And I will make thy seed as the dust of the earth: so that if a man can number the dust of the earth, thy seed **shall** also be numbered.
Genesis 13:18 Then ~~Abram~~ removed *his* tent, and came and ~~dwelt~~ in the plain of Mamre, which ~~*is*~~ in Hebron, and built there an altar unto the LORD.	Then **Abraham** removed his tent, and came and **dwelled** in the plain of Mamre, which **was** in Hebron, and built there an altar unto the Lord.

24. Likely the word "were" is omitted following "Sodom"; otherwise, the sentence lacks a finite verb.

Genesis 14

KING JAMES VERSION	JOSEPH SMITH TRANSLATION
Genesis 14:1 AND it came to pass in the days of Amraphel king of Shinar, Arioch king of Ellasar, Chedorlaomer king of Elam, and Tidal king of nations;	And it came to pass in the days of Amraphel king of Shinar, **and** Arioch king of Ellasar, Chedorlaomer king of Elam, and Tidal king of nations;
Genesis 14:2 *That these* made war with Bera king of Sodom, and with Birsha king of Gomorrah, Shinab king of Admah, and Shemeber king of Zeboiim, and the king of Bela, which is Zoar.	That these **kings** made war with Bera king of Sodom, and with Birsha king of Gomorrah, Shinab king of Admah, and Shemeber king of Zeboiim, and the king of Bela, which is Zoar.
Genesis 14:6 And the Horites in their mount Seir, unto El-paran, which ~~*is*~~ by the wilderness.	And the Horites in their mount Seir, unto El-paran, which **was** by the wilderness.
Genesis 14:7 And they returned, and came to En-mishpat, which *is* Kadesh, and smote all the country of the Amalekites, and also the Amorites, ~~that dwelt in~~ Hazezon-tamar.	And they returned, and came to En-mishpat, which is Kadesh, and smote all the country of the Amalekites,[25] and also the Amorites, Hazezon-tamar.
Genesis 14:8 And there went out the king of Sodom, and the king of Gomorrah, and the king of Admah, and the king of Zeboiim, and the king of Bela (~~the same~~ *is* Zoar;) and they joined battle with them in the vale of Siddim;	And there went out the king of Sodom, and the king of Gomorrah, and the king of Admah, and the king of Zeboiim, and the king of Bela (**which** is Zoar;) and they joined battle with them in the vale of Siddim;
Genesis 14:9 With Chedorlaomer ~~the~~ king of Elam, and with Tidal king of nations, and Amraphel king of Shinar, ~~and~~ Arioch king of Ellasar; four kings with five.	With Chedorlaomer king of Elam, and with Tidal[26] king of nations, and Amraphel king of Shinar, Arioch king of Ellasar; four kings with five.

25. OT2 reads "Amebakites."

26. OT2 reads "Sidal."

Genesis 14:10 And the vale of Siddim *was* ~~*full of*~~ slimepits; and the kings of Sodom and Gomorrah fled, and fell there; and they that remained fled to the mountain.	And the vale of Siddim was **filled with** slimepits; and the kings of Sodom and Gomorrah fled, and fell there; and they that remained fled to the mountain**, which is called Hanabal**. **OT1** And the vale of Siddim was **filled with** slimepits; and the kings of Sodom and Gomorrah fled, and fell there; and they that remained fled to the mountain**, which was called Hanabal**.
Genesis 14:13 And there came one that had escaped, and told Abram the Hebrew; for he dwelt in the plain of Mamre the Amorite, brother of Eshcol, and brother of Aner: and these *were* confederate with Abram.	And there came one that had escaped, and told Abram the Hebrew; **the man of God,** for he dwelt in the plain of Mamre the Amorite,[27] brother of Eshcol, and brother of Aner: and these were confederate with Abram.
Genesis 14:14 And when Abram heard that his ~~brother~~ was taken captive, he armed his trained ~~*servants*~~, born in his own house, three hundred and eighteen, and pursued ~~*them*~~ unto Dan.	And when Abram heard that **Lot,** his **brother's son,** was taken captive, he armed his trained **men**, **and they which were** born in his own house, three hundred and eighteen, and pursued unto Dan.
Genesis 14:15 And he divided himself against them, he and his ~~servants~~, by night, and smote them, and pursued them unto Hobah, which ~~*is*~~ on the left hand of Damascus.	And he divided himself against them, he and his **men**, by night, and smote them, and pursued them unto Hobah, which **was** on the left hand of Damascus.
Genesis 14:16 And he brought back all ~~the goods, and also brought again his brother Lot, and~~ his goods, and the women also, and the people.	And he brought back **Lot, his brother's son, and** all his goods, and the women also, and the people.
Genesis 14:17 And the king of Sodom went out to meet him after his return from the slaughter of Chedorlaomer, and of the kings that *were* with him, at the valley of Shaveh, which ~~*is*~~ the king's dale.	And the king of Sodom **also** went out to meet him after his return from the slaughter of Chedorlaomer, and of the kings that were with him, at the valley of Shaveh, which **was** the king's dale.

27. OT2 reads "Amonite."

Genesis 14:18 And Melchizedek king of Salem brought forth bread and wine: and he ~~*was*~~ the priest of the most high God.	And Melchizedek king of Salem brought forth bread and wine: and he **break bread and blessed it and he blessed the wine, he being** the priest of the most high God**, and he gave to Abram**.
Genesis 14:19 And he blessed him, and said, Blessed ~~*be*~~ Abram of the most high God, possessor of heaven and earth:	And he blessed him, and said, Blessed Abram**, thou art a man** of the most high God, possessor of heaven and **of** earth:
Genesis 14:20 And blessed ~~be~~ the most high God, which hath delivered thine enemies into ~~thy~~ hand. And ~~he~~ gave him tithes of all.	And blessed **is the name of** the most high God, which hath delivered thine enemies into **thine** hand. And **Abram** gave him tithes of all **he had taken**.
Genesis 14:22 And Abram said to the king of Sodom, I have ~~lift~~ up ~~mine~~ hand unto the LORD, the most high God, the possessor of heaven and earth,	And Abram said to the king of Sodom, I have **lifted** up **my** hand unto the Lord, the most high God, the possessor of heaven and **of** earth,
Genesis 14:23 That I will not *take* from a thread even to a shoelatchet, and that I will not take any thing that *is* thine, lest thou shouldest say, I have made Abram rich:	**And have sworn** that I will not take **of thee** from a thread even to a shoe-latchet, and that I will not take any thing that is thine, lest thou shouldest say, I have made Abram rich:

JOSEPH SMITH TRANSLATION

And Melchizedek lifted up his voice and blessed Abram.

Now Melchizedek was a man of faith, who wrought righteousness; and when a child he feared God, and stopped the mouths of lions, and quenched the violence of fire.

And thus, having been approved of God, he was ordained a high priest after the order of the covenant which God made with Enoch,

It being after the order of the Son of God; which order came, not by man, nor the will of man [OT1 "men"]; neither by father nor mother; neither by beginning of days nor end of years; but of God;

And it [OT1 omits "it"] was delivered unto men by the calling of his own voice, according to his own will, unto as many as believed on his name.

For God having sworn unto Enoch and unto his seed with an oath by himself; that every one being ordained after this order and calling should have power, by faith, to break mountains, to divide the seas, to dry up waters, to turn them out of their course;

To put at defiance the armies of nations, to divide the earth, to break every band, to stand in the presence of God; to do all things according to his will, according to his command, subdue principalities and powers; and this by the will of the Son of God which was from before the foundation of the world.

And men having this faith, coming up unto this order of God, were translated and taken up into heaven.

And now, Melchizedek was a priest of this order; therefore he obtained peace in Salem, and was called the Prince of peace.

And his people wrought righteousness, and obtained heaven, and sought for the city of Enoch which God had before taken, separating it from the earth, having reserved it unto the latter days, or the end of the world;

And hath said, and sworn with an oath, that the heavens and the earth should come together; and the sons of God should be tried so as by fire.

And this Melchizedek, having thus established righteousness, was called the king of heaven by his people, or, in other words, the King of peace.

And he lifted up his voice, and he blessed Abram, being the high priest, and the keeper of the storehouse of God;

Him whom God had appointed to receive tithes for the poor.

Wherefore, Abram paid unto him tithes of all that he had, of all the riches which he possessed, which God had given him more than that which he had need.

And it came to pass, that God blessed Abram, and gave unto him riches, and honor, and lands for an everlasting possession; according to the covenant which he had made, and according to the blessing wherewith Melchizedek had blessed him.

Genesis 15

KING JAMES VERSION	JOSEPH SMITH TRANSLATION
Genesis 15:1 AFTER these things the word of the LORD came unto Abram in a vision, saying, Fear not, Abram: I ~~*am*~~ thy shield, ~~*and*~~ thy exceeding great reward.	**And it came to pass that** after these things the word of the Lord came unto Abram in a vision, saying, Fear not, Abram: I **will be** thy shield, **I will be** thy exceeding great reward **and according to the blessings of my servant I will give unto thee**.
Genesis 15:2 And Abram said, Lord GOD, what wilt thou give me, seeing I go childless, and the steward of my house ~~*is* this Eliezer of Damascus?~~	And Abram said, Lord God, what wilt thou give me, seeing I go childless, and **Eliezer of Damascus was made** the steward of my house? **OT1** And Abram said, Lord God, what wilt thou give me, seeing I go childless, and **Eliezer of Damascus is made** the steward of my house?
Genesis 15:3 And Abram said, Behold, to me thou hast given no seed: and, lo, one born in ~~my~~ house is mine heir.	And Abram said, Behold, to me thou hast given no seed: and, lo, one born in **mine** house is mine heir.
Genesis 15:4 And, behold, the word of the LORD *came* unto him, saying, This shall not be thine heir; but he that shall come forth out of thine own bowels shall be thine heir.	And, behold, the word of the Lord came unto him **again**, saying, This shall not be thine heir; but he that shall come forth out of thine own bowels shall be thine heir.
Genesis 15:5 And he brought him forth abroad, and said, Look now ~~toward~~ heaven, and tell the stars, if thou be able to number them: and he said unto him, So shall thy seed be.	And he brought him forth abroad, and **he** said, Look now **towards** heaven, and tell the stars, if thou be able to number them: and he said unto him, So shall thy seed be. **And Abram said, Lord God, how wilt thou give me this land for an everlasting inheritance? And the Lord said, Though thou was dead, yet am I not able to give it thee? And if thou shalt die, yet thou shalt possess it, for the day cometh, that the Son of Man shall live; but**

	how can he live if he be not dead? he must first be quickened. And it came to pass, that Abram looked forth and saw the days of the Son of Man, and was glad, and his soul found rest,
	OT1 And he brought him forth abroad, and **he** said, Look now toward heaven, and tell the stars, if thou be able to number them: and he said unto him, So shall thy seed be. **And Abram said, Lord God, how wilt thou give me this land for an everlasting inheritance? And the Lord said, Though thou was dead, yet am I not able to give it thee? And if thou shall die, yet thou shalt possess it, for the day cometh, that the Son of Man shall live; but how can he live if he be not dead? he must first be quickened. And it came to pass, that Abram looked forth and saw the days of the Son of Man, and was glad, and his soul found rest,**
Genesis 15:6 And he believed in the LORD; and ~~he~~ counted it ~~to~~ him for righteousness.	And he believed in the Lord; and **the Lord** counted it **unto** him for righteousness.
Genesis 15:7 And ~~he~~ said unto him, I ~~*am*~~ the LORD ~~that~~ brought thee out of Ur of the Chaldees, to give thee this land to inherit it.	And **the Lord** said unto him, I the Lord brought thee out of Ur of the Chaldees, to give thee this land to inherit it.
Genesis 15:8 And ~~he~~ said, Lord ~~GOD~~, whereby shall I know that I shall inherit it?	And **Abram** said, Lord, whereby shall I know that I shall inherit it? **Yet he believed God.**
Genesis 15:9 And ~~he~~ said unto him, Take me an heifer of three years old, and a she goat of three years old, and a ram of three years old, and a turtledove, and a young pigeon.	And **the Lord** said unto him, Take me a heifer of three years old, and a she goat of three years old, and a ram of three years old, and a turtledove, and a young pigeon.
Genesis 15:10 And he took unto him all these, and divided them in the	And he took unto him all these, and **he** divided them in the midst, and **he** laid

midst, and laid each piece one against ~~another~~: but the birds divided he not.	each piece one against **the other**: but the birds divided he not.
Genesis 15:12 And when the sun was going down, a deep sleep fell upon Abram; and, lo, an horror of ~~great~~ darkness fell upon him.	And when the sun was going down, a deep sleep fell upon Abram; and, lo, a **great** horror of darkness fell upon him. **OT1** And when the sun was going down, a deep sleep fell upon Abram; and, lo, **a great** horror of great darkness fell upon him.
Genesis 15:13 And he said unto Abram, Know of a surety that thy seed shall be a stranger in a land ~~*that is*~~ not theirs, and shall serve ~~them~~; and they shall ~~afflict~~ them four hundred years;	**And the Lord spake,** and he said unto Abram, Know of a surety that thy seed shall be a stranger in a land **which shall** not **be** theirs, and shall serve **strangers**; and they shall **be afflicted and serve** them four hundred years;
Genesis 15:14 And also that nation, whom they shall serve, will I judge: and ~~afterward~~ shall they come out with great ~~substance~~.	And also that nation, whom they shall serve, will I judge: and **afterwards** shall they come out with great **sustenance**.
Genesis 15:15 And thou shalt go to thy fathers in peace; thou shalt be buried in a good old age.	And thou shalt **die and** go to thy fathers in peace; thou shalt be buried in a good old age. **OT1** And thou shalt **die and** go to thy fathers in peace; thou **shall** be buried in a good old age.
Genesis 15:17 And it came to pass, that, when the sun went down, and it was dark, behold a smoking furnace, and a burning lamp ~~that~~ passed between those pieces.	And it came to pass, that, when the sun went down, and it was dark, behold a smoking furnace, and a burning lamp **which** passed between those pieces **which Abram had divided**.
Genesis 15:18 In ~~the~~ same day the LORD made a covenant with Abram, saying, Unto thy seed have I given this land, from the river of Egypt unto the great river, the river Euphrates:	**And** in **that** same day the Lord made a covenant with Abram, saying, Unto thy seed have I given this land, from the river of Egypt unto the **great** river Euphrates: **OT1 And** in **that** same day the Lord made a covenant with **Abraham**, saying, Unto thy seed have I given this

	land, from the river of Egypt unto the great river, the river Euphrates:

Genesis 16

KING JAMES VERSION	JOSEPH SMITH TRANSLATION
Genesis 16:2 And Sarai said unto Abram, Behold now, the LORD hath restrained me from bearing: I pray thee, go in unto my maid; it may be that I may obtain children by her. And Abram hearkened ~~to~~ the voice of Sarai.	And Sarai said unto Abram, Behold now, the Lord hath restrained me from bearing: I pray thee, go in unto my maid; it may be that I may obtain children by her. And Abram hearkened **unto** the voice of Sarai.
Genesis 16:5 And Sarai said unto Abram, My wrong ~~*be*~~ upon thee: I have given my maid into thy bosom; and when she saw that she had conceived, I was despised in her eyes: the LORD judge between me and thee.	And Sarai said unto Abram, My wrong **is** upon thee: I have given my maid into thy bosom; and when she saw that she had conceived, I was despised in her eyes: the Lord judge between me and thee.
Genesis 16:6 But Abram said unto Sarai, Behold, thy maid *is* in thy hand; do to her as ~~it~~ pleaseth thee. And when Sarai dealt hardly with her, she fled from her face.	But Abram said unto Sarai, Behold, thy maid is in thy hand; do to her as pleaseth thee. And when Sarai dealt hardly with her, she fled from her face.
Genesis 16:7 And ~~the~~ angel of the LORD found her by a fountain of water in the wilderness, by the fountain in the way to Shur.	And **an** angel of the LORD found her by a fountain of water in the wilderness, by the fountain in the way to Shur.
Genesis 16:8 And he said, Hagar, Sarai's maid, whence ~~camest~~ thou? and whither wilt thou go? And she said, I flee from the face of my mistress Sarai.	**OT1** And he said, Hagar, Sarai's maid, whence **comest** thou? and whither wilt thou go? And she said, I flee from the face of my mistress Sarai.
Genesis 16:10 And the angel of the LORD said unto her, ~~I~~ will multiply thy seed exceedingly, that it shall not be numbered for multitude.	And the angel of the Lord said unto her, **the Lord** will multiply thy seed exceedingly, **so** that it shall not be numbered for multitude.
Genesis 16:11 And the angel of the LORD said unto her, Behold, thou *art* with child, and shalt bear a son, and	And the angel of the LORD said unto her, Behold, thou art with child, and shalt bear a son, and shalt call his name

shalt call his name Ishmael; because the Lord ~~hath~~ heard thy affliction.	Ishmael; because the Lord **has** heard thy affliction.
Genesis 16:12 And he will be a wild man; his hand *will be* against every man, and every man's hand against him; and he shall dwell in the presence of all his brethren.	And he will be a wild man; **and** his hand will be against every man, and every man's hand against him; and he shall dwell in the presence of all his brethren.
Genesis 16:13 And she called the name of the Lord ~~that~~ spake unto her, Thou God ~~seest me: for~~ she said, Have ~~I~~ also here looked after him ~~that seeth me~~?	And she called the name **of the Angel** of the Lord **and he** spake unto her **saying**, **Knowest** thou **that** God **seeth thee**: **and** she said, **I know that God seeth me for I** have also here looked after him**,**
Genesis 16:14 Wherefore the well was called Beer-lahai-roi; behold, *it is* between Kadesh and Bered.	**And there was a well between Kadesh and Bered, near where Hagar saw the Angel and the name of the Angel was Beer-lahai-roi.** Wherefore the well was called Beer-lahai-roi; **for a memorial.**

Genesis 17

King James Version	Joseph Smith Translation
Genesis 17:1 And when Abram was ninety years old ~~and nine~~, the Lord appeared to Abram, and said unto him, I ~~*am*~~ the Almighty God; walk before me, and be ~~thou~~ perfect.	And when Abram was ninety **and nine** years old, the Lord appeared to Abram, and said unto him, I, the Almighty God, **give unto thee a commandment that thou shalt** walk **uprightly** before me, and be perfect. **OT1** And when Abram was ninety **and nine** years old, the Lord appeared **unto** Abram, and said unto him, I, the Almighty God, **give unto thee a commandment that thou shalt** walk **uprightly** before, and be perfect.
Genesis 17:3 And Abram fell on his face: and God talked with him, saying,	And **it came to pass that** Abram fell on his face: **and called upon the name of the Lord,** and God talked with him, saying, **My people have gone astray from my precepts and have not kept**

	mine ordinances which I gave unto their fathers and they have not observed mine anointing and the burial or baptism wherewith I commanded them, but have turned from the commandment and taken unto themselves the washing of children and the blood of sprinkling and have said that the blood of the righteous Abel was shed for sins and have not known wherein they are accountable before me.
Genesis 17:4 As for ~~me~~, behold, my covenant ~~*is*~~ with thee, and thou shalt be a father of many nations.	**But** as for **thee**, behold, **I will make** my covenant with thee, and thou shalt be a father of many nations.
Genesis 17:5 Neither shall thy name any more be called Abram, but thy name shall be Abraham; for a father of many nations have I made thee.	**And this covenant I make that thy children may be known among all nations.** Neither shall thy name any more be called Abram, but thy name shall be **called** Abraham; for a father of many nations have I made thee.
Genesis 17:6 And I will make thee ~~exceeding~~ fruitful, and I will make nations of thee, and kings shall come ~~out~~ of thee.	And I will make thee **exceedingly** fruitful, and I will make nations of thee, and kings shall come **up** of thee **and of thy seed**.
Genesis 17:7 And I will establish ~~my~~ covenant between me and thee and thy seed after thee in their generations ~~for an everlasting covenant, to~~ be a God unto thee, and ~~to~~ thy seed after thee.	And I will establish **a** covenant **of circumcision with thee and it shall be my covenant** between me and thee and thy seed after thee in their generations **that thou mayest know forever that children are not accountable before me until they are eight years old and thou shalt observe to keep all my covenants wherein I covenanted with thy fathers and thou shalt keep the commandments which I have given thee with mine own mouth and I will** be a God unto thee, and thy seed after thee.
Genesis 17:8 And I will give unto thee, and ~~to~~ thy seed after thee, ~~the~~	And I will give unto thee, and thy seed after thee, **a** land wherein thou art a

land wherein thou art a stranger, all the land of Canaan, for an everlasting possession; and I will be their God.	stranger, all the land of Canaan, for an everlasting possession; and I will be their God.
Genesis 17:9 And God said unto Abraham, Thou shalt keep my covenant ~~therefore~~, thou, and thy seed after thee in their generations.	And God said unto Abraham, **Therefore** thou shalt keep my covenant, thou, and thy seed after thee in their generations.
Genesis 17:10 This ~~*is*~~ my covenant, which ye shall keep, between me and ~~you~~ and thy seed after thee; Every man child among you shall be circumcised.	**And** this **shall be** my covenant, which ye shall keep, between me and **thee** and thy seed after thee; Every man child among you shall be circumcised.
Genesis 17:15 And God said unto Abraham, As for Sarai thy wife, thou shalt not call her name Sarai, but Sarah ~~*shall*~~ her name ~~*be*~~.	And God said unto Abraham, As for Sarai thy wife, thou shalt not call her name Sarai, but Sarah **thou shalt call** her name.
Genesis 17:16 And I will bless her, and give thee a son ~~also~~ of her: yea, I will bless her, and she shall be ~~*a*~~ *mother* of nations; kings ~~of~~ people shall be of her.	And I will bless her, and **I will** give thee a son of her: yea, I will bless her, and she shall be **blessed, the** mother of nations; kings **and** people shall be of her.
Genesis 17:17 Then Abraham fell ~~upon~~ his face~~, and laughed~~, and said in his heart, Shall *a child* be born unto him that is an hundred years old? and ~~shall~~ Sarah, that is ninety years ~~old,~~ bear?	Then Abraham fell **on** his face, and **rejoiced**, and said in his heart, **there** shall a child be born unto him that is an hundred years old and Sarah, that is ninety years, **shall** bear**.**
Genesis 17:18 And Abraham said unto God, O that Ishmael might live before thee!	And Abraham said unto God, O that Ishmael might live **uprightly** before thee!
Genesis 17:19 And God said, Sarah thy wife shall bear thee a son ~~indeed~~; and thou shalt call his name Isaac: and I will establish my covenant with him for an everlasting covenant, ~~*and*~~ with his seed after him.	And God said, Sarah thy wife shall bear thee a son; and thou shalt call his name Isaac: and I will establish my covenant with him **also** for an everlasting covenant with his seed after him.
Genesis 17:21 But my covenant will I establish with Isaac, ~~which~~ Sarah shall bear unto thee at this set time in the next year.	But my covenant will I establish with Isaac, **whom** Sarah shall bear unto thee at this set time in the next year.

Genesis 17:24 And Abraham *was* ninety years old ~~and nine~~, when he was circumcised in the flesh of his foreskin.	And Abraham was ninety **and nine** years old, when he was circumcised in the flesh of his foreskin.
Genesis 17:25 And Ishmael ~~his son~~ *was* thirteen years old, when he was circumcised in the flesh of his foreskin.	And Ishmael was thirteen years old, when he was circumcised in the flesh of his foreskin.
Genesis 17:26 In the selfsame day ~~was~~ Abraham circumcised, and Ishmael his son.	In the selfsame day Abraham **was** circumcised, and Ishmael his son.
Genesis 17:27 And all the men of his house, born in ~~the~~ house, and bought with money of ~~the stranger~~, were circumcised with him.	And all the men of his house, **which were** born in **his** house, and bought with money of **strangers**, **they** were **also** circumcised with him. **OT1** And all the men of his house, **which were** born in the house, and bought with money of **a**[28] stranger, were circumcised with him.

Genesis 18

KING JAMES VERSION	JOSEPH SMITH TRANSLATION
Genesis 18:1 AND the LORD appeared unto ~~him~~ in the ~~plains~~ of Mamre: and he sat in ~~the~~ tent door in the heat of the day;	And the Lord appeared unto **Abraham** in the **plain** of Mamre: and he sat in **his** tent door in the heat of the day;
Genesis 18:2 And he ~~lift~~ up his eyes and looked, and, lo, three men stood by him: and when he saw ~~*them*~~, he ran to meet them from ~~the~~ tent door, and bowed himself toward the ground,	And he **lifted** up his eyes and looked, and, lo, three men stood by him: and when he saw, he ran to meet them from **his** tent door, and bowed himself toward the ground,
Genesis 18:3 And said, My ~~Lord~~, if now I have found favour in ~~thy~~ sight, pass not away, I pray ~~thee~~, from thy servant:	And said, My **brethren**, if now I have found favour in **your** sight, pass not away, I pray **you**, from thy servant:

28. OT1 includes "the" after "a." Most likely the Prophet's scribes intended to cross out the word as unnecessary.

Genesis 18:5 And I will fetch a morsel of bread, and comfort ye your hearts; after that ~~ye~~ shall pass on: for therefore are ye come to your servant. And they said, So do, as thou hast said.	And I will fetch a morsel of bread, and comfort ye your hearts; after that **you** shall pass on: for therefore are ye come to your servant. And they said, So do, as thou hast said. **OT1** And I will fetch a morsel of bread, and comfort ye your hearts; after that **you** shall pass on: for therefore are ye come to your servant. And they said, So do, as thou **has** said.
Genesis 18:6 And Abraham hastened into the tent unto Sarah, and said, Make ready quickly three measures of fine meal, knead ~~*it*~~, and make cakes upon the hearth.	And Abraham hastened into the tent unto Sarah, and said, Make ready quickly three measures of fine meal, knead, and make cakes upon the hearth.
Genesis 18:8 And he took butter, and milk, and the calf which he had dressed, and set ~~*it*~~ before them; and he stood by them under the tree, and they did eat.	And he took butter, and milk, and the calf which he had dressed, and set before them; and he stood by them under the tree, and they did eat.
Genesis 18:9 And they said unto him, Where *is* Sarah thy wife? And he said, Behold, in the tent.	And they said unto him, Where is Sarah thy wife? And he said, Behold, in the tent. **And one of them blessed Abraham.**
Genesis 18:10 And he said, I will certainly return unto thee ~~according to the time of life~~; and, lo, Sarah thy wife shall have a son. And Sarah heard ~~*it*~~ in the tent door, ~~which *was* behind him~~.	And he said, I will certainly return unto thee **from my journey**; and, lo, **according to the time of life,** Sarah thy wife shall have a son. And Sarah heard **him** in the tent door.
Genesis 18:11 Now Abraham and Sarah ~~*were*~~ old *and* ~~well~~ stricken in age; ~~*and*~~ it ceased to be with Sarah after the manner of women.	**And** now Abraham and Sarah **being** old and stricken in age; **therefore** it **had** ceased to be with Sarah after the manner of women.
Genesis 18:12 Therefore Sarah laughed within herself, saying, After I ~~am~~ waxed old shall I have pleasure, my lord being old also?	Therefore Sarah laughed within herself, saying, After I **have** waxed old shall I have pleasure, **in** my lord being old also?
Genesis 18:13 And the LORD said unto Abraham, Wherefore did Sarah	And the **angel of the** Lord said unto Abraham, Wherefore did Sarah laugh,

laugh, saying, Shall I of ~~a~~ surety bear a child, which am old?	saying, Shall I of surety bear a child, which am old?
Genesis 18:14 Is any thing too hard for the LORD? At the time appointed I will return unto thee, according to the time of life, ~~and~~ Sarah shall have a son.	Is any thing too hard for the Lord? At the time appointed **behold** I will return unto thee **from my journey which the Lord hath sent me and** according to the time of life, **thou mayest know that** Sarah shall have a son.
Genesis 18:16 And the ~~men~~ rose up from thence, and looked ~~toward~~ Sodom: and Abraham went with them to bring them on the way.	And the **angels** rose up from thence, and looked **towards** Sodom: and Abraham went with them to bring them on the way.
Genesis 18:17 And the LORD said, Shall I hide from Abraham that thing which ~~I~~ do;	And the **angel of the** Lord said, Shall I hide from Abraham that thing which **the Lord will** do **for him;**
Genesis 18:19 For I know him, that he will command his children and his household after him, and they shall keep the way of the LORD, to do justice and judgment; that the LORD may bring upon Abraham that which he ~~hath~~ spoken of him.	For I know him, that he will command his children and his household after him, and they shall keep the way of the Lord, to do justice and judgment; that the Lord may bring upon Abraham that which he **has** spoken of him.
Genesis 18:20 And the LORD said, Because the cry of Sodom and Gomorrah is great, and because their sin is very grievous;	And the **angel of the** Lord said **unto Abraham, The Lord said unto us,** Because the cry of Sodom and Gomorrah is great, and because their sin is very grievous; **I will destroy them,**
Genesis 18:21 I will go down now, and see ~~whether they~~ have done altogether according to the cry of it, which is come unto me; and if not, I will ~~know~~.	**And** I will **send you and ye shall** go down now, and see **that their iniquities are rewarded unto them and ye shall** have **all things** done altogether according to the cry of it, which is come **up** unto me; and if **ye do it** not **it shalt be upon your heads, for I will destroy them and you shall know that** I will **do it for it shall be before your eyes**.
	OT1 And I will **send you and ye shall** go down now, and **that their iniquities**

	are rewarded unto them and ye shall have **all things** done altogether according to the cry of it, which is come **up** unto me; and if **ye do it** not **it shalt be upon your heads, for I will destroy them and you shall know that** I will **do it for it shall be before your eyes**.
Genesis 18:22 And the men turned their faces from thence, and went toward Sodom: but Abraham stood yet before the LORD.	And the **angels which were holy** men **and were sent forth after the order of God,** turned their faces from thence, and went toward Sodom: but Abraham stood yet before the Lord **remembering the things which had been told him**.
Genesis 18:23 And Abraham drew near, and said, Wilt thou ~~also~~ destroy the righteous with the wicked?	And Abraham drew near **to Sodom**, and said **unto the Lord calling upon his name saying**, Wilt thou destroy the righteous with the wicked?
Genesis 18:24 Peradventure there be fifty righteous within the city: wilt thou also destroy and not spare the place for the fifty righteous that ~~*are*~~ therein?	**Wilt thou not spare them** peradventure there **may** be fifty righteous within the city: wilt thou also destroy and not spare the place for the fifty righteous that **may be** therein?
Genesis 18:25 That be far from thee to do after this manner, to slay the righteous with the wicked: and that the righteous should be as the wicked, that be far from thee: Shall not the Judge of all the earth do right?	**Oh! May** that be far from thee to do after this manner, to slay the righteous with the wicked: and that the righteous should be as the wicked, **Oh! God may** that be far from thee: **For** shall not the Judge of all the earth do right?
Genesis 18:26 And the LORD said, If ~~I find~~ in Sodom fifty righteous within the city, then I will spare all ~~the~~ place for their sakes.	And the Lord said **unto Abraham**, If **thou findest** in Sodom fifty righteous within the city, then I will spare all **this** place for their sakes.
Genesis 18:27 And Abraham answered and said, Behold now, I have taken upon me to speak unto the Lord, which ~~*am but*~~ dust and ashes:	And Abraham answered and said, Behold now, I have taken upon me to speak unto the Lord, which **is able to destroy the city and lay all the people in** dust and ashes:
Genesis 18:28 Peradventure there ~~shall~~ lack five of the fifty righteous: wilt thou destroy all the city for ~~*lack of*~~ five?	**Will the Lord spare them** peradventure there lack five of the fifty righteous: wilt thou destroy all the city for

And he said, ~~If I find there forty and five~~, I will not destroy *it*.	**their wickedness if I find there forty and** five **righteous**? And he said, I will not destroy **but spare them**.
Genesis 18:29 And he spake unto him ~~yet~~ again, and said, Peradventure there ~~shall~~ be forty found there. And he said, I will not ~~do~~ *it* for forty's sake.	And he spake unto him again, and said, Peradventure there **should** be forty found there. And he said, I will not **destroy** it for forty's sake.
Genesis 18:30 And he said *unto ~~him~~*, Oh let not the Lord be angry, and I will speak: Peradventure there shall thirty be found there. And he said, I will not ~~do *it*~~, if ~~I~~ find thirty there.	And he said **again** unto **the Lord**, Oh let not the Lord be angry, and I will speak: Peradventure there shall thirty be found there. And he said, I will not **destroy them**, if **thou shalt** find thirty there.
Genesis 18:31 And he said, Behold now, I have taken upon me to speak unto the Lord: Peradventure there shall be twenty found there. And he said, I will not destroy *it* for twenty's sake.	And he said, Behold now, I have taken upon me to speak unto the Lord: **Wilt thou destroy** peradventure there shall be twenty found there. And he said, I will not destroy **them** for twenty's sake.
	OT1 And he said, Behold now, I have taken upon me to speak unto the Lord: **Wilt thou destroy them if** peradventure there shall be twenty found there. And he said, I will not destroy **them** for twenty's sake.
Genesis 18:32 And ~~he~~ said, Oh let not the Lord be angry, and I will speak ~~yet~~ but this once: Peradventure ten shall be found there. And ~~he~~ said, I will not destroy *it* for ten's sake.	And **Abraham** said **unto the Lord**, Oh let not the Lord be angry, and I will **yet** speak but this once: Peradventure ten shall be found there. And **the Lord** said, I will not destroy **them** for ten's sake.
Genesis 18:33 And the LORD ~~went his way~~, as soon as he had left communing with Abraham: and Abraham returned unto his ~~place~~.	And the Lord **ceased speaking with Abraham and** as soon as he had left communing with **the Lord,** Abraham **went his way**: and **it came to pass that** Abraham returned unto his **tent**.

Genesis 19

KING JAMES VERSION	JOSEPH SMITH TRANSLATION
Genesis 19:1 AND there came ~~two~~ angels to Sodom ~~at even~~; and Lot sat in the ~~gate~~ of Sodom: and Lot seeing ~~*them*~~ rose up to meet them; and he bowed himself ~~with his face~~ toward the ground;	And **it came to pass that** there came **three** angels to Sodom **in the evening**; and Lot sat in the **door of his house in the city** of Sodom: and Lot seeing **the angels** rose up to meet them; and he bowed himself toward the ground;
Genesis 19:2 And he said, Behold now, my lords, turn in, I pray you, into your servant's house, and tarry all night, and wash your feet, and ye shall rise up early, and go on your ways. And they said, Nay; but we will abide in the ~~street~~ all night.	And he said, Behold now, my lords, turn in **now**, I pray you, into your servant's house, and tarry all night, and wash your feet, and ye shall rise up early, and go on your ways. And they said, Nay; but we will abide in the **streets** all night.
Genesis 19:4 But before they lay down, the men of the city, ~~*even* the men~~ of Sodom, compassed the house round, both old and young, ~~all~~ the people from every quarter:	But before they lay down **to rest**, the men of the city of Sodom, compassed the house round, **even men which were** both old and young, **even** the people from every quarter:
Genesis 19:5 And they called unto Lot, and said unto him, Where *are* the men which came in ~~to~~ thee this night? bring them out unto us, that we may know them.	And they called unto Lot, and said unto him, Where are the men which came in **unto** thee this night? bring them out unto us, that we may know them.
Genesis 19:6 And Lot went out ~~at~~ the door unto them, and shut the door after him,	And Lot went out **of** the door unto them, and shut the door after him,
Genesis 19:8 ~~Behold now, I have two daughters which have not known man; let me~~, I pray you, ~~bring them out unto you, and do ye to them as *is* good in your eyes: only unto these men do nothing; for therefore came they under the shadow of my roof.~~	**And said,** I pray you **brethren, do not so wickedly.**
Genesis 19:9 And they said, Stand back. And they said ~~*again*~~, This one ~~*fellow*~~ came in to sojourn, and he will	And they said **unto him**, Stand back. **And they were angry with him.** And they said **among themselves**, This one

needs be a judge: now ~~will~~ we deal worse with ~~thee~~, than with them. And they ~~pressed sore upon the man, *even*~~ Lot, and came near to break the door.	**man** came in to sojourn **among us**, and he will needs **now make himself to** be a judge: now we **will** deal worse with **him**, than with them. **Wherefore they said unto the man, We will have the men and thy daughters also and we will do unto [OT1 with] them as seemeth [OT1 us] good. Now this was after the wickedness of Sodom. And Lot said, Behold now I have two daughters which have not known man, let me I pray you plead with my brethren that I may not bring them out unto you and ye shall not do unto them as seemeth good in your eyes. For God will not justify his servant in this thing, wherefore let me plead with my brethren this once only that unto these men ye do nothing that they may have peace in my house for therefore came they under the shadow of my roof** and they **were angry with** Lot, and came near to break the door.
Genesis 19:10 But the ~~men~~ put forth their hand, and pulled Lot into the house ~~to~~ them, and shut to the door.	But the **angels of God, which were holy men,** put forth their hand, and pulled Lot into the house **unto** them, and shut to the door.
Genesis 19:11 And they smote the men ~~that *were* at the door of the house~~ with blindness, both small and great: ~~so~~ that they wearied themselves to find the door.	And they smote the men with blindness, both small and great: that they **could not come at the door and they were angry so that they** wearied themselves to find the door **and could not find it**.
Genesis 19:12 And ~~the~~ men said unto Lot, Hast thou here ~~any~~ besides? ~~son~~ in law, and thy sons, and thy daughters, and whatsoever thou hast in the city, bring ~~*them*~~ out of this place:	And **these holy** men said unto Lot, Hast thou **any** here besides **thy sons** in law, and thy sons,[29] and thy daughters, and **they commanded Lot saying,** whatsoever thou hast in the city, **thou shalt** bring out of this place:

29. OT2 reads "thy sons sons."

Genesis 19:13 For we will destroy this place, because the cry of them is waxen great before the face of the LORD; and the LORD hath sent us to destroy it.	For we will destroy this place, because the cry of them is waxen great **and their abominations have come up** before the face of the Lord; and the Lord hath sent us to destroy it.
Genesis 19:14 And Lot went out, and spake unto his sons in law, which married his daughters, and said, Up, get ~~you~~ out of this place; for the LORD will destroy this city. But he seemed as one that mocked unto his sons in law.	And Lot went out, and spake unto his sons in law, which married his daughters, and said, Up, get **ye** out of this place; for the Lord will destroy this city. But he seemed as one that mocked unto his sons in law.
Genesis 19:15 And when the morning ~~arose, then~~ the angels hastened Lot, saying, Arise, take thy wife, and thy two daughters, which are here; lest thou be consumed in the iniquity of the city.	And when the morning **was come**, the angels **arose and** hastened Lot, saying, Arise, take thy wife, and thy two daughters, which are here; lest thou be consumed in the iniquity of the city.
Genesis 19:16 And while he lingered, the ~~men~~ laid hold upon his hand, and upon the hand of his wife, and upon the hand of his two daughters; the LORD being merciful unto ~~him~~: and they brought ~~him~~ forth, and set ~~him~~ without the city.	And while he lingered, the **angels** laid hold upon his hand, and upon the hand of his wife, and upon the hand of his two daughters; the Lord being merciful unto **them**: and they brought **them** forth, and set **them down** without the city.
Genesis 19:17 And it came to pass, when they had brought them forth abroad, that ~~he~~ said, Escape for ~~thy life~~; look not behind ~~thee~~, neither stay ~~thou~~ in all the plain; escape to the mountain, lest ~~thou~~ be consumed.	And it came to pass, when they had brought them forth abroad, that **they** said **unto them**, Escape for **your lives**; look not behind **you**, neither stay **you** in all the plain; escape to the mountain, lest **you** be consumed.
Genesis 19:18 And Lot said unto them, Oh, not so, my Lord:	And Lot said unto **one of** them, Oh, not so, my Lord:
Genesis 19:19 Behold now, thy servant ~~hath~~ found grace in thy sight, and thou hast magnified thy mercy, which thou hast shewed unto me in saving my life; and I cannot escape to the mountain, lest some evil ~~take~~ me, and I die:	Behold now, thy servant **has** found grace in thy sight, and thou hast magnified thy mercy, which thou hast shewed unto me in saving my life; and I cannot escape to the mountain, lest some evil **overtake** me, and I die:
Genesis 19:20 Behold now, ~~this~~ city *is* near to flee unto, and it *is* a little one:	Behold now, **here is another** city**, and this** is near to flee unto, and it is a little

Oh, let me escape thither, ~~(*is it not a little one?*)~~ and my soul shall live.	one: Oh, let me escape thither, **and may not the Lord destroy it** and my soul shall live.
Genesis 19:21 And ~~he~~ said unto him, See, I have accepted thee concerning this thing also, that I will not overthrow this city, for the which thou hast spoken.	And **the angel** said unto him, See, I have accepted thee concerning this thing also, that I will not overthrow this city, for the which thou hast spoken.
Genesis 19:22 Haste thee, escape thither; for I cannot do any thing ~~till~~ thou be come thither. ~~Therefore~~ the name of the city was called Zoar.	Haste thee, escape thither; for I cannot do any thing **until** thou be come thither. **And** the name of the city was called Zoar.
Genesis 19:23 The sun was risen upon the earth when Lot entered into Zoar.	**Therefore** the sun was risen upon the earth when Lot entered into Zoar. **And the Lord did not destroy Sodom until Lot had entered into Zoar.**
Genesis 19:24 Then the LORD rained upon Sodom and upon Gomorrah brimstone and fire from the LORD out of heaven;	**And** then **when Lot had entered into Zoar,** the Lord rained upon Sodom and upon Gomorrah**, for the angels called upon the name of the Lord for** brimstone and fire from the Lord out of heaven;
Genesis 19:25 And ~~he~~ overthrew those cities, and all the plain, and all the inhabitants of the cities, and that which grew upon the ground.	And **thus they** overthrew those cities, and all the plain, and all the inhabitants of the cities, and that which grew upon the ground.
Genesis 19:26 But his wife looked back from behind him, and ~~she~~ became a pillar of salt.	But **it came to pass that when Lot fled,** his wife looked back from behind him, and became a pillar of salt.
Genesis 19:27 And Abraham ~~gat~~ up early in the morning to the place where he stood before the LORD:	And Abraham **got** up early in the morning to the place where he stood before the Lord:
Genesis 19:28 And he looked toward Sodom and Gomorrah, and toward all the land of the plain, and ~~beheld, and~~, lo, the smoke of the country went up as the smoke of a furnace.	And he looked toward Sodom and Gomorrah, and toward all the land of the plain, and **behold**, lo, the smoke of the country went up as the smoke of a furnace.

Genesis 19:29 And it came to pass, when God destroyed the cities of the plain, that God ~~remembered~~ Abraham, and sent ~~Lot~~ out of the midst of the overthrow, when ~~he~~ overthrew the ~~cit-ies~~ in the which Lot dwelt.	And it came to pass, when God **had** destroyed the cities of the plain, that God **spake unto** Abraham **saying, I have remembered Lot** and sent **him** out of the midst of the overthrow **that thy brother might not be destroyed** when **I** overthrew the **city** in the which **thy brother** Lot dwelt. **And Abraham was comforted.**
Genesis 19:31 And the firstborn said unto the younger, Our father ~~*is*~~ old, and ~~*there is*~~ not a man ~~in~~ the earth to come in unto us after the manner of all the earth:	And the firstborn **dealt wickedly and** said unto the younger, Our father **has become** old, and **we have** not a man **on** the earth to come in unto us **to live with us** after the manner of all **that live on** the earth:
	OT1 And the firstborn **dealt wickedly and** said unto the younger, Our father **has become** old, and **we have** not a man **on** the earth to come in unto us **to live with us** after the manner of all **they that live on** the earth:
Genesis 19:32 Come, let us make our father drink wine, and we will lie with him, that we may preserve seed of our father.	**Therefore** come, let us make our father drink wine, and we will lie with him, that we may preserve seed of our father.
Genesis 19:33 And they made their father drink wine that night: and the firstborn went in, and lay with her fa-ther; and he perceived not when she lay down, nor when she arose.	And they **done wickedly and** made their father drink wine that night: and the firstborn went in, and lay with her father; and he perceived not when she lay down, nor when she arose.
Genesis 19:34 And it came to pass on the morrow, that the firstborn said unto the younger, Behold, I lay yester-night with my father: let us make him drink wine this night also; and go thou in, *and* ~~lie~~ with him, that we may pre-serve seed of our father.	And it came to pass on the morrow, that the firstborn said unto the younger, Behold, I lay yesternight with my fa-ther: let us make him drink wine this night also; and go thou in, and **lay** with him, that we may preserve seed of our father.
	OT1 And it came to pass on the mor-row, that the firstborn said unto the younger, Behold, I lay **yesterday** night

	with my father: let us make him drink wine this night also; and go thou in, and lie with him, that we may preserve seed of our father.
Genesis 19:37 And the firstborn bare a son, and called his name Moab: ~~the same *is*~~ the father of the Moabites unto this day.	And the firstborn bare a son, and called his name Moab: the father of the Moabites **the same which is** unto this day.
Genesis 19:38 And the younger, she also bare a son, and called his name Benammi: ~~the same *is*~~ the father of the children of ~~Ammon~~ unto this day.	And the younger, she also bare a son, and called his name Benammi: the father of the children of **which are Ammonites the same which are** unto this day.

Genesis 20

KING JAMES VERSION	JOSEPH SMITH TRANSLATION
Genesis 20:1 AND Abraham journeyed from thence toward the south country, and ~~dwelled~~ between Kadesh and Shur, and sojourned in Gerar.	And Abraham journeyed from thence toward the south country, and **dwelt** between Kadesh and Shur, and sojourned in Gerar. **OT1** And Abraham journeyed from thence **towards** the south country, and **dwelt** between Kadesh and Shur, and sojourned in Gerar.
Genesis 20:2 And Abraham said of Sarah his wife, She *is* my sister: and Abimelech king of Gerar sent, and took Sarah.	And Abraham said **again** of Sarah his wife, She is my sister: and Abimelech king of Gerar sent, and took Sarah.
Genesis 20:3 But God came to Abimelech in a dream by night, and said ~~to~~ him, Behold, thou ~~*art but a* dead man, for the woman which thou~~ hast taken; for she *is* ~~a man's~~ wife.	But God came to Abimelech in a dream by night, and said **unto** him, Behold, thou hast taken **a woman which is not thine own** for she is **Abraham's** wife. **And the Lord said unto him, Thou shalt return her unto Abraham for if thou do it not, thou shalt die.**

Genesis 20:4 ~~But~~ Abimelech had not come near her: and he said, Lord, wilt thou slay also a righteous nation?	**And** Abimelech had not come near her**, for the Lord had not suffered him**: and he said, Lord, wilt thou slay **me and** also a righteous nation?
Genesis 20:5 Said he not unto me, She *is* my sister? and she, even she herself said, He *is* my brother: in the integrity of my heart and innocency of my hands have I done this.	**Behold** said he not unto me, She is my sister? and she, even she herself said, He is my brother: **and** in the integrity of my heart and innocency of my hands have I done this.
Genesis 20:6 And God said unto him in a dream, Yea, I know that thou didst this in the integrity of thy heart; for I also withheld thee from sinning against me: therefore suffered I thee ~~not~~ to touch her.	And God said unto him in a dream, Yea, I know that thou didst **do** this in the integrity of thy heart; for I also withheld thee from sinning against me: therefore suffered I **not** thee to touch her.
Genesis 20:7 Now therefore restore the ~~man *his*~~ wife; for he *is* a prophet, and he shall pray for thee, and thou shalt live: and if thou ~~restore~~ *her* not, know thou that thou shalt surely die, thou, and all that *are* thine.	Now therefore restore the **man's** wife **to him**; for he is a prophet, and he shall pray for thee, and thou shalt live: and if thou **return** her not **to him**, know thou that thou shalt surely die, thou, and all that are thine.
Genesis 20:8 Therefore Abimelech rose early in the morning, and called ~~all~~ his servants, and told all these things in their ears: and the men were sore afraid.	Therefore Abimelech arose early in the morning, and called his servants, and told all these things in their ears: and the men were sore afraid.
Genesis 20:9 Then Abimelech called Abraham, and said unto him, What hast thou done unto us? and what have I offended thee, that thou hast brought on me and on my kingdom a great sin? thou hast done ~~deeds~~ unto me that ought not to be done.	Then Abimelech called Abraham, and said unto him, What hast thou done unto us? and **in** what have I offended thee, that thou hast brought on me and on my kingdom a great sin? thou hast done **things** unto me that ought not to be done.
Genesis 20:11 And Abraham said, Because I thought, ~~Surely~~ the fear of God ~~*is*~~ not in this place; and they ~~will~~ slay me for my wife's sake.	And Abraham said, Because I thought, **Assuredly** the fear of God **was** not in this place; and they **would** slay me for my wife's sake.
Genesis 20:12 And yet indeed *she* ~~*is*~~ my sister; she ~~*is*~~ the daughter of my	And yet indeed she **was** my sister; she **was** the daughter of my father, but not

father, but not the daughter of my mother; and she became my wife.	the daughter of my mother; and she became my wife.
Genesis 20:13 And it came to pass, when God caused me to wander from my father's house, that I said unto her, This ~~*is*~~ thy kindness which thou shalt shew unto me; at every place whither we shall come, say of me, He *is* my brother.	And it came to pass, when God caused me to wander from my father's house, that I said unto her, This **shall be** thy kindness which thou shalt shew unto me; at every place whither we shall come, say of me, He is my brother.
Genesis 20:14 And Abimelech took sheep, and oxen, and menservants, and womenservants, and gave ~~*them*~~ unto Abraham, and restored him Sarah his wife.	And Abimelech took sheep, and oxen, and menservants, and womenservants, and gave unto Abraham, and restored **unto** him Sarah his wife.
Genesis 20:15 And Abimelech said, Behold, my land ~~*is*~~ before thee: dwell where it pleaseth thee.	And Abimelech said, Behold, my land **layeth** before thee: dwell where it pleaseth thee.
Genesis 20:16 And unto Sarah he said, Behold, I have given thy brother a thousand *pieces* of silver: behold, he ~~*is* to~~ thee a covering of the eyes, unto all that ~~*are* with thee~~, and ~~with all *other*:~~ thus she was reproved.	And unto Sarah he said, Behold, I have given thy brother a thousand pieces of silver: behold, he **shall give unto** thee a covering of the eyes, **and it shall be a token** unto all that **thou mayest not be taken again from Abraham thy husband**, and thus she was reproved.
Genesis 20:17 So Abraham prayed unto God: and God healed Abimelech, and his wife, and his maidservants; and they bare *children*.	So Abraham prayed unto God: and God healed Abimelech, and his wife, and his maidservants; and they bare **unto him** children.
Genesis 20:18 For the Lord had fast closed up all the wombs of the house of Abimelech, ~~because of Sarah Abraham's wife~~.	For **because of Sarah, Abraham's wife,** the Lord had fast closed up all the wombs of the house of Abimelech.

Genesis 21

King James Version	Joseph Smith Translation
Genesis 21:1 AND the LORD visited Sarah as he had said, and the LORD did unto Sarah as he had spoken.	And the Lord visited Sarah as he had said, and the Lord did unto Sarah as he had spoken **by the mouth of his angels**.
Genesis 21:2 For Sarah conceived, and bare Abraham a son in his old age, at the set time of which God had spoken to him.	For Sarah conceived, and bare Abraham a son in his old age, at the set time of which **the angels of** God had spoken to him.
Genesis 21:3 And Abraham called the name of his son that was born unto him, ~~whom~~ Sarah bare ~~to~~ him, Isaac.	And Abraham called the name of his son that was born unto him, **which** Sarah bare **unto** him, Isaac.
Genesis 21:6 And Sarah said, God ~~hath~~ made me to ~~laugh~~, ~~*so that*~~ all that ~~hear~~ will ~~laugh~~ with me.	And Sarah said, God **has** made me to **rejoice**, **and also** all that **know me** will **rejoice** with me.
Genesis 21:7 And she said, Who would have said ~~unto Abraham~~, that Sarah should have given children suck? for I have born ~~*him*~~ a son in his old age.	And she said **unto Abraham**, Who would have said that Sarah should have given children suck? for **I was barren, but the Lord promised and** I have born **unto Abraham** a son in his old age.
Genesis 21:8 And the child grew, and was weaned: and Abraham made a great feast ~~the *same* day that Isaac was weaned~~.	And the child grew, and was weaned: and **the day that Issac was weaned,** Abraham made a great feast.
Genesis 21:9 And Sarah saw the son of Hagar the Egyptian, which ~~she~~ had born unto Abraham, mocking.	And Sarah saw the son of Hagar the Egyptian, which **Hagar** had born unto Abraham, mocking.
Genesis 21:10 Wherefore she said unto Abraham, Cast out this bondwoman and her son: for the son of this bondwoman shall not be heir with my son, ~~*even* with~~ Isaac.	**And she was troubled,** wherefore she said unto Abraham, Cast out this bondwoman and her son: for the son of this bondwoman shall not be heir with my son, Isaac.

Genesis 21:11 And ~~the~~ thing was very grievous ~~in Abraham's sight~~ because of his son.	And **this** thing was very grievous **unto** Abraham because of his son.
Genesis 21:12 And God said unto Abraham, Let it not be grievous in thy sight because of the lad, and because of thy bondwoman; in all that Sarah ~~hath~~ said unto thee, hearken unto her voice; for in Isaac shall thy seed be called.	And God said unto Abraham, Let it not be grievous in thy sight because of the lad, and because of thy bondwoman; in all that Sarah **has** said unto thee, hearken unto her voice; for in Isaac shall thy seed be called.
Genesis 21:14 And Abraham rose up early in the morning, and took bread, and a bottle of water, and gave ~~*it*~~ unto Hagar, ~~putting *it* on her shoulder~~, and the child, and sent her away: and she departed, and wandered in the wilderness of Beer-sheba.	And Abraham rose up early in the morning, and took bread, and a bottle of water, and gave unto Hagar, and **she took** the child, and **he** sent her away: and she departed, and wandered in the wilderness of Beer-sheba.
Genesis 21:15 And the water was spent in the bottle, and she cast the child under one of the shrubs.	And **it came to pass that** the water was spent in the bottle, and she cast the child under one of the shrubs.
Genesis 21:16 And she went, and sat her down over against ~~*him*~~ a good way off, as it were a bowshot: for she said, Let me not see the death of the child. And she sat over against ~~*him*~~, and ~~lift~~ up her voice, and wept.	And she went, and sat her down over against **the child** a good way off, as it were a bowshot: for she said, Let me not see the death of the child. And she sat over against **the child**, and **lifted** up her voice, and wept.
Genesis 21:17 And God heard the voice of the lad; and the angel of ~~God~~ called to Hagar out of heaven, and said unto her, What aileth thee, Hagar? fear not; for God hath heard the voice of the lad where he ~~*is*~~.	And God heard the voice of the lad; and the angel of **the Lord** called to Hagar out of heaven, and said unto her, What aileth thee, Hagar? fear not; for God hath heard the voice of the lad where he **layeth**.
	OT1 And God heard the voice of the lad; and the angel of God called to Hagar out of heaven, and said unto her, What aileth thee, Hagar? fear not; for God hath heard the voice of the lad where he **lies**.
Genesis 21:18 Arise, lift up the lad, and hold him in thine hand; for I will make him a great nation.	Arise, lift up the lad, and hold him in thine hand; for I will make **of** him a great nation.

Genesis 21:21 And he dwelt in the wilderness of Paran: and his mother took him a wife out of the land of Egypt.	And he dwelt in the wilderness of Paran: **he** and his mother**, and he** took him a wife out of the land of Egypt.
Genesis 21:22 And it came to pass at ~~that~~ time, that Abimelech and Phichol the chief captain of his host spake unto Abraham, saying, God *is* with thee in all that thou doest:	And it came to pass at **the** time, that Abimelech and Phichol the chief captain of his host spake unto Abraham, saying, God is with thee in all that thou doest:
Genesis 21:23 Now therefore swear unto me here by God ~~that~~ thou wilt not deal falsely with me, nor with my son, nor with my son's son: *but* according to the kindness that I have ~~done~~ unto thee, thou shalt do unto me, and to the land wherein thou hast sojourned.	Now therefore swear unto me here **that** by **the help of** God thou wilt not deal falsely with me, nor with my son, nor with my son's son: but **that** according to the kindness that I have **shewn** unto thee, thou shalt do unto me, and to the land wherein thou hast sojourned.
Genesis 21:25 And Abraham reproved Abimelech because of a well of water, which Abimelech's servants had ~~violently~~ taken away.	And Abraham reproved Abimelech because of a well of water, which Abimelech's servants had **recently** taken away.
Genesis 21:26 And Abimelech said, I ~~wot~~ not who ~~hath~~ done this thing: neither ~~didst thou tell me, neither~~ yet heard ~~I *of it,*~~ ~~but to~~ day.	And Abimelech said, **Thou didst not tell me and** I **knew** not who **has** done this thing: neither yet **have I** heard **that** it **was done until this** day. **OT1** And Abimelech said, **Thou didst not tell me and** I **know** not who hath done this thing: neither yet **have I** heard **that** it **was done until this** day.
Genesis 21:29 And Abimelech said unto Abraham, What ~~*mean*~~ these seven ewe lambs which thou hast set by themselves?	And Abimelech said unto Abraham, What **wilt thou do with** these seven ewe lambs which thou hast set by themselves?
Genesis 21:30 And he said, ~~For *these*~~ seven ewe lambs shalt thou take ~~of~~ my hand, that they may be a witness unto me, that I have digged this well.	And he said, Seven ewe lambs shalt thou take **at** my hand, that they may be a witness unto me, that I have digged this well.

Genesis 21:31 Wherefore he called that place Beer-sheba; ~~because there they sware both of them~~.	**And because they swear both of them,** wherefore he called that place Beer-sheba.
Genesis 21:32 Thus they made a covenant at Beer-sheba: then Abimelech ~~rose up~~, and Phichol the chief captain of his host, ~~and they returned into the land of the Philistines~~.	**And** thus they made a covenant at Beer-sheba: then Abimelech and Phichol the chief captain of his host **rose up,**
Genesis 21:33 And ~~*Abraham*~~ planted a grove in Beer-sheba, and called there on the name of the Lord, ~~the everlasting God~~.	And **they** planted a grove in Beer-sheba, and called there on the name of the Lord, **and they returned unto the land of the Philistines**. **OT1** And **they** planted a grove in Beer-sheba, and called there on the name of the Lord, **and they returned into the land of the Philistines**.
Genesis 21:34 And Abraham sojourned in the ~~Philistines~~' land many days.	And Abraham **worshipped the everlasting God and** sojourned in the land **of the Philistines** many days.

Genesis 22

King James Version	Joseph Smith Translation
Genesis 22:1 And it came to pass after these things, that God did ~~tempt~~ Abraham, and said unto him, Abraham: and ~~he~~ said, Behold, *here* I ~~*am*~~.	And it came to pass after these things, that God did **try** Abraham, and said unto him, Abraham: and **Abraham** said, Behold, here **am** I.
Genesis 22:2 And ~~he~~ said, Take now thy son, thine only ~~*son*~~ Isaac, whom thou lovest, and get thee into the land of Moriah; and offer him there for a burnt offering upon one of the mountains which I will tell thee ~~of~~.	And **the Lord** said,[30] Take now thy son, thine only Isaac, whom thou lovest, and get thee into the land of Moriah; and offer him there for a burnt offering upon one of the mountains **of** which I will tell thee.

30. OT2 omits "said."

Genesis 22:5 And Abraham said unto his young men, Abide ~~ye~~ here with the ass; and I and the lad will go yonder and worship, and come ~~again~~ to you.	And Abraham said unto his young men, Abide **you** here with the ass; and I and the lad will go yonder and worship, and come to you **again**.
Genesis 22:6 And Abraham took the wood of the burnt offering, and laid *it* upon ~~Isaac~~ his ~~son~~; and he took the fire in his hand, and a knife; and they went both of them together.	And Abraham took the wood of the burnt offering, and laid it upon his **back**; and he took the fire in his hand, and a knife **and Isaac his son**; and they went both of them together.
Genesis 22:9 And they came to the place which God had told him ~~of~~; and Abraham built an altar there, and laid the wood in order, and bound Isaac his son, and laid him on the altar upon the wood.	And they came to the place **of** which God had told him; and Abraham built an altar there, and laid the wood in order, and bound Isaac his son, and laid him on the altar upon the wood.
Genesis 22:11 And the angel of the LORD called unto him out of heaven, and said, Abraham, Abraham: and ~~he~~ said, Here *am* I.	And the angel of the Lord called unto him out of heaven, and said, Abraham, Abraham: and **Abraham** said, Here am I.
Genesis 22:12 And ~~he~~ said, Lay not thine hand upon the lad, neither do thou any thing unto him: for now I know that thou fearest God, seeing thou hast not withheld thy son, thine only ~~*son*~~ from me.	And **the angel** said, Lay not thine hand upon the lad, neither do thou any thing unto him: for now I know that thou fearest God, seeing thou hast not withheld thy son, thine only **Isaac** from me.
Genesis 22:13 And Abraham lifted up his eyes, and looked, and behold behind ~~*him*~~ a ram caught in ~~a thicket~~ by his horns: and Abraham went and took the ram, and offered him up for a burnt offering in the stead of his son.	And Abraham lifted up his eyes, and looked, and behold behind **a thicket there was** a ram caught in **it** by his horns: and Abraham went and took the ram, and offered him up for a burnt offering in the stead of his son.
	OT1 And Abraham lifted up his eyes, and looked, and behold behind **a thicket there was** a ram caught in **it** by his **horn**: and Abraham went and took the ram, and offered him up for a burnt offering in the stead of his son.
Genesis 22:14 And Abraham called the name of that place Jehovah-jireh:	And Abraham called the name of that place Jehovah-jireh: as it is said **unto**

as it is said ~~*to*~~ this day, In the mount of the LORD it shall be seen.	this day, **and** in the mount of the Lord it shall be seen.
Genesis 22:16 And said, ~~By myself have~~ I sworn, ~~saith the LORD, for~~ because thou hast done this thing, and hast not withheld thy son, thine only ~~son~~:	And said, **Thus saith the Lord,** I **have** sworn **by myself that** because thou hast done this thing, and hast not withheld thy son, thine only **Isaac from me**:
Genesis 22:17 That in ~~blessing~~ I will bless thee, and in multiplying I will multiply thy seed as the stars of ~~the~~ heaven, and as the sand which *is* upon the sea shore; and thy seed shall possess the gate of his enemies;	That in **blessings** I will bless thee, and in multiplying I will multiply thy seed as the stars of heaven, and as the sand which is upon the sea shore; and thy seed shall possess the gate of his enemies;
Genesis 22:19 So Abraham returned unto his young men, and they rose up and went ~~together~~ to Beer-sheba; and Abraham dwelt at Beer-sheba.	So Abraham returned unto his young men, and they rose up and went to Beer-sheba; and Abraham dwelt at Beer-sheba.
Genesis 22:20 And it came to pass after these things, that it was told Abraham, saying, Behold, Milcah, she ~~hath~~ also born children unto thy brother Nahor;	And it came to pass after these things, that it was told Abraham, saying, Behold, Milcah, she **has** also born children unto thy brother Nahor;
Genesis 22:21 Huz his firstborn, and Buz his brother, and Kemuel the father of Aram,	Huz **is** his firstborn, and Buz **is** his brother, and Kemuel **is** the father of Aram,
Genesis 22:22 And Chesed, ~~and~~ Hazo, and Pildash, and Jidlaph, and Bethuel.	And Chesed, Hazo, and Pildash,[31] and Jidlaph, and Bethuel.

31. OT2 reads "Bildash, & Sidlaph."

Genesis 23

KING JAMES VERSION	JOSEPH SMITH TRANSLATION
Genesis 23:1 AND Sarah was an hundred and seven and twenty years old: ~~*these were*~~ the years of the life of Sarah.	And Sarah was an hundred and seven and twenty years old **and she died. And thus ended** the years of the life of Sarah.
Genesis 23:2 And Sarah died in Kirjath-arba; the same is Hebron in the land of Canaan: and Abraham came to mourn for Sarah, and to weep for her.	And Sarah died in Kirjath-arba; the same is **now called** Hebron in the land of Canaan: and Abraham came to mourn for Sarah, and to weep for her**, his wife which was dead**.
Genesis 23:6 Hear us, my lord: thou *art* a mighty prince among us: in the ~~choice~~ of our sepulchres bury thy dead; none of us shall withhold from thee his sepulchre, but that thou mayest bury thy dead.	Hear us, my lord: thou art a mighty prince among us: in the **choicest** of our sepulchres bury thy dead; none of us shall withhold from thee his sepulchre, but that thou mayest bury thy dead.
Genesis 23:7 And Abraham stood ~~up~~, and bowed himself to the people of the land, ~~*even*~~ to the children of Heth.	And Abraham stood, and bowed himself to the people of the land, **and** to the children of Heth.
Genesis 23:8 And he communed with them, saying, If it be your ~~mind~~ that I should bury my dead out of my sight; hear me, and intreat ~~for me to~~ Ephron the son of Zohar,	And he communed with them, saying, If it be your **minds** that I should bury my dead out of my sight; hear me, and intreat Ephron the son of Zohar **for me**,
Genesis 23:9 That he may give me the cave of Machpelah, which he hath, ~~which *is*~~ in the end of his field; for as much money as it is worth he shall give it me for a possession of a buryingplace ~~amongst~~ you.	That he may give me the cave of Machpelah, which he hath in the end of his field; for as much money as it is worth he shall **have if he will** give it me for a possession of a buryingplace **among** you.
Genesis 23:10 And Ephron dwelt among the children of Heth: and Ephron the Hittite answered Abraham in the audience of the children of Heth, ~~*even* of~~ all that went in at the ~~gate~~ of his city, saying,	And Ephron dwelt among the children of Heth: and Ephron the Hittite answered Abraham in the audience of the children of Heth, **among** all **of them** that went in at the **gates** of his city, saying,

Genesis 23:11 ~~Nay~~, my lord, hear me: the field ~~give~~ I thee, and the cave that *is* therein, I give it thee; in the presence of the sons of my people give ~~I~~ it thee: bury thy dead.	**Hearken**, my lord, **and** hear me: the field I **give** thee, and the cave that is therein, I give it thee; in the presence of the sons of my people **and** I **give** it thee: **therefore,** bury thy dead.
Genesis 23:13 And he spake unto Ephron in the audience of the people of the land, saying, ~~But if thou *wilt give it*,~~ I pray thee, hear me: I will give thee money for the field; ~~take *it* of me~~, and I will bury my dead there.	And he spake unto Ephron in the audience of the people of the land, saying, I pray thee, hear me: **If thou wilt take it of me,** I will give thee money for the field; and I will bury my dead there**; but I will give thee money for it**.
Genesis 23:15 My lord, hearken unto me: the land ~~*is worth*~~ four hundred shekels of silver; what ~~*is*~~ that betwixt me and thee? bury therefore thy dead.	My lord, hearken unto me: the land **thou shalt have for** four hundred shekels of silver; what **shall** that **be** betwixt me and thee? bury therefore thy dead.
Genesis 23:16 And Abraham hearkened unto Ephron; and Abraham weighed to Ephron the silver, which he had named in the audience of the sons of Heth, four hundred shekels of silver, current ~~money~~ with the merchant.	And Abraham hearkened unto Ephron; and Abraham weighed to Ephron the silver, which he had named in the audience of the sons of Heth, four hundred shekels of silver, **which was** current with the merchant.
Genesis 23:17 And the field of Ephron, which *was* in Machpelah, which *was* before Mamre, the field, and the cave which *was* therein, and all the trees that *were* in the field, that *were* in all the borders round about, were made sure.	**OT1** And the field of Ephron, which was in Machpelah, which was before Mamre, the field, and the cave which was therein, and all the trees that were in the field, **and** that were in all the borders round about, were made sure.
Genesis 23:18 Unto Abraham for a possession in the presence of the children of Heth, before all that went in at the gate of ~~his~~ city.	Unto Abraham for a possession in the presence of the children of Heth, before all that went in at the gate of **the** city. **OT1** Unto Abraham for a possession in the presence of the children of Heth, before all that went in at the **gates** of his city.
Genesis 23:19 And after this, Abraham buried Sarah his wife in the cave of the field of Machpelah before Mamre: the same *is* Hebron in the land of Canaan.	And after this, Abraham buried Sarah his wife in the cave of the field of Machpelah **which is** before Mamre: the same is **called** Hebron in the land of Canaan.

Genesis 23:20 And the field, and the cave that ~~*is*~~ therein, were made sure unto Abraham for a possession of a buryingplace by the sons of Heth.	And the field, and the cave that **was** therein, were made sure unto Abraham for a possession of a buryingplace by the sons of Heth. **OT1** And the field, and the cave that **were** therein, were made sure unto Abraham for a possession of a burying-place by the sons of Heth.

Genesis 24

KING JAMES VERSION	JOSEPH SMITH TRANSLATION
Genesis 24:1 AND Abraham was old, ~~*and*~~ well stricken in age: and the LORD had blessed Abraham in all things.	And **now** Abraham was old, **being** well stricken in age: and the Lord had blessed Abraham in all things.
Genesis 24:2 And Abraham said unto his eldest servant of his house, that ruled over all that he had, Put, I pray thee, thy hand under my ~~thigh~~:	And Abraham said unto his eldest servant of his house, that ruled over all that he had, Put **forth**, I pray thee, thy hand under my **hand**: **OT1** And Abraham said unto his eldest servant of his house, that ruled over all that he had, Put **forth**, I pray thee, thy hand under my **head**:
Genesis 24:3 And I will make thee swear ~~by~~ the LORD, the God of heaven, and the God of the earth, that thou shalt not take a wife unto my son of the daughters of the Canaanites, among whom I dwell:	And I will make thee swear **before** the Lord, the God of heaven, and the God of the earth, that thou shalt not take a wife unto my son of the daughters of the Canaanites, among whom I dwell:
Genesis 24:5 And the servant said unto him, ~~Peradventure~~ the woman will not be willing to follow me unto this land: ~~must~~ I needs bring thy son again unto the land from whence thou camest?	And the servant said unto him, **Perhaps** the woman will not be willing to follow me unto this land: **then** I **must** needs bring thy son again unto the land from whence thou camest?
Genesis 24:7 The LORD God of heaven, which took me from my	The Lord God of heaven, which took me from my father's house, and from

father's house, and from the land of my kindred, and which spake unto me, and that sware unto me, saying, Unto ~~thy seed~~ will I give this land; he shall send his angel before thee, and thou shalt take a wife unto my son from thence.	the land of my kindred, and which spake unto me, and that sware unto me, saying, Unto **thee** will I give this land; he shall send his angel before thee, and thou shalt take a wife unto my son from thence.
Genesis 24:8 And if the woman will not be willing to follow thee, then thou shalt be clear from this ~~my~~ oath: only bring not my son thither again.	And if the woman will not be willing to follow thee, then thou shalt be clear from this **thy** oath: only bring not my son thither again.
Genesis 24:9 And the servant put his hand under the ~~thigh~~ of Abraham his master, and ~~sware~~ to him concerning that matter.	And the servant put his hand under the **hand** of Abraham his master, and **swore** to him concerning that matter. **OT1** And the servant put his hand under the **head** of Abraham his master, and sware to him concerning that matter.
Genesis 24:10 And the servant took ten camels ~~of the camels~~ of his master, and departed; for all the goods of his master ~~*were*~~ in his hand: and he arose, and went to Mesopotamia, unto the city of Nahor.	And the servant took ten camels of his master, and departed; for all the goods of his master **was** in his hand: and he arose, and went to Mesopotamia, unto the city of Nahor.
Genesis 24:11 And he made his camels to kneel down without the city by a well of water at ~~the time of the~~ evening, ~~*even*~~ the time that women go out to draw *water*.	And he made his camels to kneel down without the city by a well of water at evening, **at** the time that women go out to draw water.
Genesis 24:12 And he said, O LORD God of my master Abraham, I pray thee, ~~send me good speed~~ this day, ~~and~~ shew kindness ~~unto~~ my master Abraham.	And he said, O Lord God of my master Abraham, I pray thee, this day, **that thou wouldst** shew kindness **to** my master Abraham**, and send me good speed**.
Genesis 24:13 Behold, I stand ~~*here*~~ by the well of water; and the daughters of the men of the city come out to draw water:	Behold, I stand by the well of water; and the daughters of the men of the city come out to draw water:

Genesis 24:14 And let it come to pass, that the damsel to whom I shall say, Let down thy pitcher, I pray thee, that I may drink; and she shall say, Drink, and I will give thy camels drink also: *let ~~the same~~ be* ~~she *that*~~ thou hast appointed for thy servant Isaac; and thereby shall I know that thou hast shewed kindness unto my master.	And let it come to pass, that the damsel to whom I shall say, Let down thy pitcher, I pray thee, that I may drink; and she shall say, Drink, and I will give thy camels drink also: let **her** be **the one whom** thou hast appointed for thy servant Isaac; and thereby shall I know that thou hast shewed kindness unto my master.
Genesis 24:16 And the damsel ~~*was*~~ very fair to look upon, ~~a virgin~~, neither had any man known her: and she went down to the well, and filled her pitcher, and came up.	And the damsel, **being a virgin,** very fair to look upon, **such as the servant of Abraham had not seen,** neither had any man known **the like unto** her: and she went down to the well, and filled her pitcher, and came up.
Genesis 24:19 And when she had done giving him drink, she said, I will draw ~~*water*~~ for thy camels also, until they have done drinking.	And when she had done giving him drink, she said, I will draw for thy camels also, until they have done drinking.
Genesis 24:20 And she hasted, and emptied her pitcher into the trough, and ran again unto the well to draw ~~*water*~~, and drew for all his camels.	And she hasted, and emptied her pitcher into the trough, and ran again unto the well to draw, and drew for all his camels.
Genesis 24:21 And the man wondering at her held his peace, ~~to wit~~ whether the LORD had made his journey prosperous or not.	And the man wondering at her held his peace, **pondering in his heart** whether the Lord had made his journey prosperous or not.
Genesis 24:22 And it came to pass, as the camels had done drinking, that the man took a ~~golden~~ earring of half a ~~shekel~~ weight, and two bracelets for her hands of ten *shekels* weight of gold;	And it came to pass, as the camels had done drinking, that the man took a **gold** earring of half a **shekels** weight, and two bracelets for her hands of ten shekels weight of gold;
Genesis 24:23 And said, Whose daughter *art* thou? tell me, I pray thee: is there room *in* thy father's house for us to lodge in?	And said, Whose daughter art thou? tell me, I pray thee: **and** is there room in thy father's house for us to lodge in?
Genesis 24:27 And he said, Blessed ~~*be*~~ the LORD God of my master Abraham, who ~~hath~~ not left ~~destitute~~ my master	And he said, Blessed **is** the Lord God of my master Abraham, who **has** not left my master **destitute** of his mercy

of his mercy and his truth: I ~~*being*~~ in the way, the LORD led me to the house of my master's brethren.	and his truth: **And when** I **was** in the way, the Lord led me to the house of my master's brethren.
Genesis 24:28 And the damsel ran, and told ~~*them of*~~ her ~~mother's house~~ these things.	And the damsel ran **to the house**, and told her mother these things.
Genesis 24:29 And Rebekah had a brother, ~~and his~~ name *was* Laban: and Laban ran out ~~unto~~ the man, unto the well.	And Rebekah had a brother, **whose** name was Laban: and Laban ran out **to** the man, unto the well.
Genesis 24:30 And it came to pass, when he saw the earring and bracelets upon his sister's hands, and when he heard the words of Rebekah his sister, saying, Thus spake the man unto me; ~~that he~~ came unto the man; and, behold, he stood by the camels at the well.	And it came to pass, when he saw the earring and bracelets upon his sister's hands, and when he heard the words of Rebekah his sister, saying, Thus spake the man unto me; **and I** came unto the man; and, behold, he stood by the camels at the well.
Genesis 24:32 And the man came into the house: and he ~~ungirded~~ his camels, and gave straw and provender for the camels, and water to wash his feet, and the men's feet that ~~*were*~~ with him.	And the man came into the house: and he **unburdened** his camels, and gave straw and provender for the camels, and water to wash his feet, and the men's feet that **came** with him.
Genesis 24:33 And there was set ~~*meat*~~ before him to eat: but he said, I will not eat, until I have told mine errand. And ~~he~~ said, Speak on.	And there was set before him **food** to eat: but he said, I will not eat, until I have told mine errand. And **Laban** said, Speak on. **OT1** And there was set before him **food** to eat: but he said, I will not eat, **till** I have told mine errand. And **Laban** said, Speak on.
Genesis 24:39 And I said unto my master, ~~Peradventure~~ the woman will not follow me.	And I said unto my master, **Perhaps** the woman will not follow me.
Genesis 24:40 And he said unto me, The LORD, before whom I walk, will send his angel with thee, and prosper	And he said unto me, The Lord, before whom I walk, will send his angel with thee, and **he will** prosper thy way; and

thy way; and thou shalt take a wife for my son of my kindred, and of my father's house:	thou shalt take a wife for my son of my kindred, and of my father's house:
Genesis 24:41 Then shalt thou be clear ~~from *this*~~ my oath, when thou comest to my kindred; and if they give ~~not~~ thee ~~*one*~~, thou shalt be clear from my oath.	Then shalt thou be clear **of** my oath, when thou comest to my kindred; and if they give thee **not a wife for my son**, thou shalt be clear from my oath.
Genesis 24:42 And I came this day unto the well, and said, O LORD God of my master Abraham, if now thou ~~do~~ prosper my way which I go:	And I came this day unto the well, and said, O Lord God of my master Abraham, if now thou **wilt** prosper my way which I go:
Genesis 24:44 And she say to me, Both drink thou, and I will also draw for thy camels: ~~*let*~~ the same ~~*be*~~ the woman whom the LORD hath appointed out for my master's son.	And **if** she say to me, Both drink thou, and I will also draw for thy camels: the same **is** the woman whom the Lord hath appointed out for my master's son.
Genesis 24:45 And before I had done speaking in ~~mine~~ heart, behold, Rebekah came forth with her pitcher on her shoulder; and she went down unto the well, and drew *water:* and I said unto her, Let me drink, I pray thee.	And before I had done speaking in **my** heart, behold, Rebekah came forth with her pitcher on her shoulder; and she went down unto the well, and drew water: and I said unto her, Let me drink, I pray thee.
Genesis 24:47 And I asked her, and said, Whose daughter *art* thou? And she said, The daughter of Bethuel, Nahor's son, whom Milcah bare unto him: and I ~~put~~ the ~~earring upon~~ her ~~face~~, and the bracelets upon her hands.	And I asked her, and said, Whose daughter art thou? And she said, The daughter of Bethuel, Nahor's son, whom Milcah bare unto him: and I **gave** the **earrings unto** her **to put into her ears**, and the bracelets upon her hands.
Genesis 24:48 And I bowed down my head, and worshipped the LORD, and blessed the LORD God of my master Abraham, ~~which~~ had led me in the right way to take my master's brother's daughter unto his son.	And I bowed down my head, and worshipped the Lord, and blessed the Lord God of my master Abraham, **who** had led me in the right way to take my master's brother's daughter unto his son.
Genesis 24:49 And now if ~~ye will~~ deal kindly and truly with my master, tell	And now if **thou wilt** deal kindly and truly with my master, tell me: and if

me: and if not, tell me; that I may turn to the right hand, or to the left.	not, tell me; that I may turn to the right hand, or to the left.
Genesis 24:53 And the servant brought forth jewels of silver, and jewels of gold, and raiment, and gave ~~*them*~~ to Rebekah: he gave also to her brother and to her mother precious things.	And the servant brought forth jewels of silver, and jewels of gold, and raiment, and gave to Rebekah: he gave also to her brother and to her mother precious things.
Genesis 24:54 And they did eat and drink, he and the men that *were* with him, and tarried all night; and they ~~rose~~ up in the morning, and he said, Send me away unto my master.	And they did eat and drink, he and the men that were with him, and tarried all night; and they **arose** up in the morning, and he said, Send me away unto my master.
Genesis 24:55 And her brother and her mother said, Let the damsel abide with us ~~*a few*~~ days, ~~at the least ten~~; after that she shall go.	And her brother and her mother said, Let the damsel abide with us **at the least ten** days; after that she shall go.
Genesis 24:56 And he said unto them, Hinder me not, seeing the LORD hath prospered my way; send me away that I may go ~~to~~ my master.	And he said unto them, Hinder me not, seeing the Lord hath prospered my way; send me away that I may go **unto** my master.
Genesis 24:60 And they blessed Rebekah, and said unto her, Thou ~~*art*~~ our sister, be thou ~~*the mother*~~ of thousands of millions, and let thy seed possess the gate of those ~~which~~ hate them.	And they blessed Rebekah, and said unto her, **O** thou our sister, be thou **blessed** of thousands of millions, and let thy seed possess the gate of those **who** hate them.
Genesis 24:63 And Isaac went out to meditate in the field at ~~the~~ eventide: and he ~~lifted~~ up his eyes, and saw, and, behold, the camels ~~*were*~~ coming.	And Isaac went out to meditate in the field at eventide: and he **lift** up his eyes, and saw, and, behold, the camels coming.
Genesis 24:64 And Rebekah ~~lifted~~ up her eyes, and when she saw Isaac, she lighted off the camel.	And Rebekah **lift** up her eyes, and when she saw Isaac, she lighted off the camel.
Genesis 24:65 For she ~~*had*~~ said unto the servant, What man *is* this that walketh in the field to meet us? And the servant ~~*had*~~ said, It *is* my master: therefore she took a vail, and covered herself.	For she said unto the servant, What man is this that walketh in the field to meet us? And the servant said, It is my master: therefore she took a vail, and covered herself.

Genesis 25

KING JAMES VERSION	JOSEPH SMITH TRANSLATION
Genesis 25:7 And these *are* the ~~days~~ of the years of Abraham's life which he lived, an hundred threescore and fifteen years.	And these are the **number** of the years of Abraham's life which he lived, an hundred threescore and fifteen years.
Genesis 25:17 And these *are* the years of the life of Ishmael, an hundred and thirty and seven years: and he gave up the ghost and died; and was gathered unto his people.	And these are the **number of the** years of the life of Ishmael, an hundred and thirty and seven years: and he gave up the ghost and died; and was gathered unto his people.
Genesis 25:21 And Isaac intreated the LORD for his wife, because she *was* barren: and the LORD was intreated of him, and Rebekah his wife conceived.	And Isaac intreated the Lord for his wife, **that she might bear children,** because she was barren: and the Lord was intreated of him, and Rebekah his wife conceived.
Genesis 25:22 And the children struggled together within her; and she said, If ~~*it be* so~~, why ~~*am* I~~ thus? And she went to enquire of the LORD.	And the children struggled together within her **womb**; and she said, If **I am with child**, why **is it** thus **with me**? And she went to enquire of the Lord.
Genesis 25:32 And Esau said, Behold, I *am* at the point ~~to die~~: and what ~~profit~~ shall this birthright ~~do to~~ me?	And Esau said, Behold, I am at the point **of dying**: and what shall this birthright **profit** me?

Genesis 26

KING JAMES VERSION	JOSEPH SMITH TRANSLATION
Genesis 26:7 And the men of the place asked *him* ~~of~~ his wife; and he said, She *is* my sister: for he feared to say, *She is* my wife; lest, ~~*said he,*~~ the men of the place should kill ~~me~~ for Rebekah; because she *was* fair to look upon.	And the men of the place asked him **concerning** his wife; and he said, She is my sister: for he feared to say, She is my wife; lest the men of the place should kill **him** for **to get** Rebekah; because she was fair to look upon.
Genesis 26:9 And Abimelech called Isaac, and said, Behold, of a surety ~~she~~ *is* thy wife: and how saidst thou, She	And Abimelech called Isaac, and said, Behold, of a surety **Rebekah** is thy wife: and how saidst thou, She is **thy**

is ~~my~~ sister? And Isaac said unto him, ~~Because~~ I said, Lest I die for her.	sister? And Isaac said unto him, I said **it because I feared**, Lest I die for her.

Genesis 28

King James Version	Joseph Smith Translation
Genesis 28:22 And this stone, which I have set *for* a pillar, shall be God's house: and of all that thou shalt give me I will surely give the tenth unto thee.	And **the place of** this stone, which I have set for a pillar, shall be **the place of** God's house: and of all that thou shalt give me I will surely give the tenth unto thee.

Genesis 29

King James Version	Joseph Smith Translation
Genesis 29:4 And Jacob said unto them, My brethren, whence *~~be~~* ye? And they said, ~~Of~~ Haran *~~are~~* ~~we~~.	And Jacob said unto them, My brethren, **from** whence **are** ye? And they said, **From** Haran.
Genesis 29:21 And Jacob said unto Laban, Give *me* my wife, for my days are fulfilled, ~~that I may go in unto her~~.	And Jacob said unto Laban, Give **unto** me my wife **that I may go and take her**, for my days **of serving thee** are fulfilled.
Genesis 29:22 And Laban gathered together all the men of the place, and made a feast.	And Laban **gave her to Jacob, and** gathered together all the men of the place, and made a feast.
Genesis 29:23 And it came to pass in the evening, that he took Leah his daughter, and brought her to ~~him~~; and ~~he~~ went in ~~unto her~~.	And it came to pass in the evening, that he took Leah his daughter, and brought her to **Jacob**; and **she** went in **and slept with him**.
Genesis 29:24 And Laban gave unto his daughter Leah Zilpah his ~~maid~~ *~~for~~* ~~an~~ handmaid.	And Laban gave unto his daughter Leah Zilpah his **handmaid, to be a** handmaid **for her**.
Genesis 29:30 And he went in also ~~unto~~ Rachel, and he loved ~~also~~ Rachel more than Leah, and served with ~~him~~ yet seven other years.	And he went in also **and he slept with** Rachel, and he loved Rachel **also** more than Leah, and served with **Laban** yet seven other years.

Genesis 30

KING JAMES VERSION	JOSEPH SMITH TRANSLATION
Genesis 30:3 And she said, Behold my maid Bilhah, go in ~~unto~~ her; and she shall bear upon my knees, that I may also have children by her.	And she said, Behold my maid Bilhah, go in **and lay with** her; and she shall bear upon my knees, that I may also have children by her.
Genesis 30:4 And she gave him Bilhah her handmaid to wife: and Jacob went in ~~unto~~ her.	And she gave him Bilhah her handmaid to wife: and Jacob went in **and lay with** her.
Genesis 30:9 When Leah saw that she had left bearing, she took Zilpah her maid, and gave her Jacob to wife.	When Leah saw that she had left bearing, she took Zilpah her maid, and gave her **unto** Jacob to wife.
Genesis 30:16 And Jacob came out of the field in the evening, and Leah went out to meet him, and said, Thou must come in ~~unto~~ me; for surely I have hired thee with my son's mandrakes. And he lay with her that night.	And Jacob came out of the field in the evening, and Leah went out to meet him, and said, Thou must come in **and lie with**[32] me; for surely I have hired thee with my son's mandrakes. And he lay with her that night.

Genesis 32

KING JAMES VERSION	JOSEPH SMITH TRANSLATION
Genesis 32:11 Deliver me, I pray thee, from the hand of my brother, from the hand of Esau: for I fear him, lest he will come and smite me, *and* the ~~mother~~ with the children.	Deliver me, I pray thee, from the hand of my brother, from the hand of Esau: for I fear him, lest he will come and smite me, and the **mothers** with the children.

32. OT1 omits "with" which must be supplied to make sense of the change.

Genesis 37

King James Version	Joseph Smith Translation
Genesis 37:2 ~~These *are*~~ the generations of Jacob. Joseph, *being* seventeen years old, was feeding the flock with his brethren; and the lad *was* with the sons of Bilhah, and with the sons of Zilpah, his father's wives: and Joseph brought unto his father their evil report.	**And this is the history of** the generations of Jacob. Joseph, being seventeen years old, was feeding the flock with his brethren; and the lad was with the sons of Bilhah, and with the sons of Zilpah, his father's wives: and Joseph brought unto his father their evil report.

Genesis 38

King James Version	Joseph Smith Translation
Genesis 38:2 And Judah saw there a daughter of a certain Canaanite, whose name *was* Shuah; and he took her, and went in ~~unto~~ her.	And Judah saw there a daughter of a certain Canaanite, whose name was Shuah; and he took her, and went in **and lay with** her.
Genesis 38:8 And Judah said unto Onan, Go ~~in unto~~ thy brother's wife, ~~and marry her~~, and raise up seed ~~to~~ thy brother.	And Judah said unto Onan, Go **and marry** thy brother's wife, and raise up seed **unto** thy brother.
Genesis 38:9 And Onan knew that the seed should not be his; and it came to pass, when he ~~went in unto~~ his brother's wife, that he ~~spilled *it* on the ground~~, lest ~~that~~ he should ~~give~~ seed ~~to~~ his brother.	And Onan knew that the seed should not be his; and it came to pass, when he **married** his brother's wife, that he **would not lie with her**, lest he should **raise up** seed **unto** his brother.
Genesis 38:16 And he turned unto her by the way, and said, Go to, I pray thee, let me come in ~~unto~~ thee; (for he knew not that she *was* his daughter in law.) And she said, What wilt thou give me, that thou mayest come in ~~unto~~ me?	And he turned unto her by the way, and said, Go to, I pray thee, let me come in **and lie with** thee; (for he knew not that she was his daughter in law.) And she said, What wilt thou give me, that thou mayest come in **and lie with** me?
Genesis 38:18 And he said, What pledge shall I give thee? And she said, Thy signet, and thy bracelets, and thy	And he said, What pledge shall I give thee? And she said, Thy signet, and thy bracelets, and thy staff that is in thine

staff that *is* in thine hand. And he gave *it* her, and came in ~~unto~~ her, and she conceived by him.	hand. And he gave it her, and came in **and slept with** her, and she conceived by him.

Genesis 39

KING JAMES VERSION	JOSEPH SMITH TRANSLATION
Genesis 39:8 But he refused, and said unto his master's wife, Behold, my master ~~wotteth~~ not what *is* with me in the house, and he hath committed all that he hath to my hand;	But he refused, and said unto his master's wife, Behold, my master **knoweth** not what is with me in the house, and he hath committed all that he hath to my hand;
Genesis 39:22 And the keeper of the prison committed to Joseph's hand all the prisoners that *were* in the prison; and whatsoever they did there, he was the ~~doer *of it*~~.	And the keeper of the prison committed to Joseph's hand all the prisoners that were in the prison; and whatsoever they did there, he was the **overseer**.

Genesis 44

KING JAMES VERSION	JOSEPH SMITH TRANSLATION
Genesis 44:15 And Joseph said unto them, What deed *is* this that ye have done? ~~wot~~ ye not that such a man as I can certainly divine?	And Joseph said unto them, What deed is this that ye have done? **knew** ye not that such a man as I can certainly divine?

Genesis 48

KING JAMES VERSION	JOSEPH SMITH TRANSLATION
Genesis 48:1 AND it came to pass after these things, that ~~*one*~~ told Joseph, Behold, thy father *is* sick: and he took with him his two sons, Manasseh and Ephraim.	And it came to pass after these things, that **it was** told Joseph **saying**, Behold, thy father is sick: and he took with him his two sons, Manasseh and Ephraim.
Genesis 48:2 And ~~*one*~~ told Jacob, and ~~said~~, Behold, thy son Joseph cometh	And **it was** told Jacob **saying, Look** and behold, thy son Joseph cometh

unto thee: and Israel strengthened himself, and sat upon the bed.	unto thee: and Israel strengthened himself, and sat upon the bed.
Genesis 48:4 And said unto me, Behold, I will make thee fruitful, and multiply thee, and I will make of thee a multitude of people; and will give this land to thy seed after thee *for* an everlasting possession.	And said unto me, Behold, I will make thee fruitful, and multiply thee, **saith the Lord;** and I will make of thee a multitude of people; and will give this land to thy seed after thee for an everlasting possession.
Genesis 48:5 And now thy two sons, Ephraim and Manasseh, which were born unto thee in the land of Egypt before I came unto thee into Egypt, *are* mine; as Reuben and Simeon, they shall be mine.	And now **of** thy two sons, Ephraim and Manasseh, which were born unto thee in the land of Egypt before I came unto thee into Egypt, **behold they** are mine, **and the God of my fathers shall bless them; even** as Reuben and Simeon, they shall **also** be **blessed, for they are** mine. **Wherefore they shall be called after my name, therefore they were called Israel.**
Genesis 48:6 And thy issue, which thou begettest after them, shall be thine, *and* shall be called after the name of their brethren in their inheritance.	And thy issue, which thou begettest after them, shall be thine, and shall be called after the name of their brethren in their inheritance **in their tribes; therefore they were called the tribes of Manasseh and of Ephraim**.

Joseph Smith Translation

And Jacob said unto Joseph, when the God of my fathers appeared unto me in Luz, in the land of Canaan; he sware unto me that he would give unto me, and unto my seed, the land for an everlasting possession,

Therefore, O my son, he hath blessed me in raising thee up to be a servant unto me, in saving my house from death,

In delivering my people, thy brethren, from famine which was sore in the land; wherefore the God of thy fathers shall bless thee, and the fruit of thy loins, that they shall be blessed above thy brethren, and above thy father's house;

For thou hast prevailed, and thy father's house has bowed down unto thee, even as it was shewn unto thee, before thou wast sold into Egypt, by the hands of thy brethren; wherefore thy brethren shall bow down unto thee from generation to generation, unto the fruit of thy loins forever;

For thou shalt be a light unto my people, to deliver them in the days of their captivity, from bondage; and to bring salvation unto them, when they are altogether bowed down under sin.

KING JAMES VERSION	JOSEPH SMITH TRANSLATION
Genesis 48:7 And as for me, when I came from Padan, Rachel died by me in the land of Canaan in the way, when yet ~~*there was*~~ but a little way to come unto Ephrath: and I buried her there in the way of Ephrath; the same *is* Beth-lehem.	And **therefore,** as for me, when I came from Padan, Rachel died by me in the land of Canaan in the way, when **we were** yet but a little way to come unto Ephrath: and I buried her there in the way of Ephrath; the same is **called** Beth-lehem.
Genesis 48:9 And Joseph said unto his father, They *are* my sons, whom God hath given me in this ~~*place*~~. And he said, Bring them, I pray thee, unto me, and I will bless them.	And Joseph said unto his father, They are my sons, whom God hath given me in this **land**. And he said, Bring them, I pray thee, unto me, and I will bless them.
Genesis 48:10 Now the eyes of Israel were dim for age, *so that* he could not see. And he brought them near unto him; and he kissed them, and embraced them.	Now the eyes of Israel were dim for age, so that he could not see **well**. And he brought them near unto him; and he kissed them, and embraced them.

Genesis 49

KING JAMES VERSION	JOSEPH SMITH TRANSLATION
Genesis 49:1 AND Jacob called unto his sons, and said, Gather yourselves together, that I may tell you ~~*that* which~~ shall befall you in the last days.	And Jacob called unto his sons, and said, Gather yourselves together, that I may tell you **what** shall befall you in the last days.

Genesis 50

KING JAMES VERSION	JOSEPH SMITH TRANSLATION
Genesis 50:24a And Joseph said unto his brethren, I die:	And Joseph said unto his brethren, I die: **and go unto my fathers; and I go**

	down to my grave with joy. The God of my father Jacob be with you, to deliver you out of affliction, in the day of your bondage; for the Lord hath visited me, and I have obtained a promise of the Lord, that out of the fruit of my loins, the Lord God will raise up a righteous branch, out of my lines. And unto thee, whom my father Jacob hath named Israel, a prophet, not the Messiah, who is called Shilo; and this prophet shall deliver my people out of Egypt, in the days of thy bondage.

JOSEPH SMITH TRANSLATION

And it shall come to pass, that they shall be scattered again, and a branch shall be broken off, and shall be carried into a far country; nevertheless they shall be remembered in the covenants of the Lord, when the Messiah cometh; for he shall be made manifest unto them in the latter days, in the spirit of power; and shall bring them out of darkness unto light; out of hidden darkness, and out of captivity unto freedom.

A seer shall the Lord my God raise up, who shall be a choice seer unto the fruit of my lines.

Thus saith the Lord God of my fathers unto me, a choice seer will I raise up out of the fruit of thy loins, and he shall be esteemed highly among the fruit of thy loins. And unto him will I give commandment, that he shall do a work for the fruit of thy loins, his brethren.

And he shall bring them to the knowledge of the covenants, which I have made with thy father; and he shall do whatsoever work I shall command him.

And I will make him great in mine eyes; for he shall do my work; and he shall be great like unto him whom I have said I would raise up unto you, to deliver my people, O house of Israel, out of the land of Egypt; for a seer will I raise up out of the fruit of thy lines, to deliver my people out of the land of Egypt; and he shall be called Moses, and by this name he shall know that he is of thy house, for he shall be nursed by the king's daughter and shall be called her son.

And again, a seer will I raise up out of the fruit of thy loins, and unto him will I give power to bring forth my word unto the seed of thy loins; and not

to the bringing forth my word only, saith the Lord, but to the convincing them of my word, which shall have already gone forth among them in the last days.

Wherefore, the fruit of thy loins shall write, and the fruit of the loins of Judah shall write; and that which shall be written by the fruit of thy loins, and also that which shall be written by the fruit of the loins of Judah shall grow together unto the confounding of false doctrines, and laying down of contentions, and establishing peace among the fruit of thy loins, and bringing them to the knowledge of their fathers in the latter days; and also to the knowledge of my covenants, saith the Lord.

And out of weakness shall be made strong, in that day when my work shall go forth among all my people, which shall restore them who are of the house of Israel in the last days.

And that seer will I bless, and they that seek to destroy him shall be confounded; for this promise I give unto you, for I will remember you from generation to generation; and his name shall be called Joseph, and it shall be after the name of his father; and he shall be like unto you; for the thing which the Lord shall bring forth by his hand, shall bring my people unto salvation.

And the Lord sware unto Joseph, that he would preserve his seed forever, saying, I will raise up Moses. And a rod shall be in his hand, and he shall gather together my people; and he shall lead them as a flock, and he shall smite the waters of the Red Sea with his rod.

And he shall have judgment, and shall write the word of the Lord, and he shall not speak many words, for I will write unto him my law, by the finger of mine own hand. And I will make a spokesman for him, and his name shall be called Aaron.

King James Version	Joseph Smith Translation
Genesis 50:24b ~~and~~ God will surely visit you, and bring you out of this land unto the land which he sware ~~to~~ Abraham, to Isaac, and to Jacob.	**And it shall be done unto thee in the last days also, even as I have sworn. Therefore, Joseph said unto his brethren,** God will surely visit you, and bring you out of this land unto the land which he sware **unto** Abraham, to Isaac, and to Jacob.
Genesis 50:25 And Joseph took an oath of the children of Israel, saying, God will surely visit you, and ye shall carry up my bones from hence.	And Joseph **confirmed many other things unto his brethren, and** took an oath of the children of Israel, saying **unto them**, God will surely visit you,

	and ye shall carry up my bones from hence.
Genesis 50:26 So Joseph died, ~~*being*~~ an hundred and ten years old: and they embalmed him, and ~~he was~~ put in a coffin in Egypt.	So Joseph died, **when he was** an hundred and ten years old: and they embalmed him, and **they** put **him** in a coffin in Egypt**; and he was kept from burial, by the children of Israel, that he might be carried up and laid in the sepulcher with his fathers, and thus they remembered the oath which they sware unto him.**

Exodus

Exodus 1	
King James Version	Joseph Smith Translation
Exodus 1:1 Now these *are* the names of the children of Israel, which came into Egypt; every man ~~and~~ his household came with Jacob.	Now these are the names of the children of Israel, which came into Egypt; every man **according to** his household **who** came with Jacob.
Exodus 3	
Exodus 3:2 And the ~~angel~~ of the LORD appeared unto him in a flame of fire ~~out of~~ the midst of a bush: and he looked, and, behold, the bush burned with fire, and the bush *was* not consumed.	And **again** the **presence** of the Lord appeared unto him in a flame of fire **in** the midst of a bush: and he looked, and, behold, the bush burned with fire, and the bush was not consumed.
Exodus 3:3 And Moses said, I will now turn aside, and see this great sight, why the bush is not ~~burnt~~.	And Moses said, I will now turn aside, and see this great sight, why the bush is not **consumed**.
Exodus 4	
Exodus 4:21 And the LORD said unto Moses, When thou goest to return into Egypt, see that thou do all those wonders before Pharaoh, which I have put in thine hand: ~~but~~ I will harden his heart, ~~that~~ he ~~shall~~ not let the people go.	And the Lord said unto Moses, When thou goest to return into Egypt, see that thou do all those wonders before Pharaoh, which I have put in thine hand: **and** I will **prosper thee, but Pharaoh will** harden his heart, **and** he **will** not let the people go.
Exodus 4:24 And it came to pass ~~by the way in the inn~~, that the LORD ~~met~~ him, and ~~sought~~ to kill him.	And it came to pass, that the Lord **appeared unto** him **as he was in the way, by the inn, the Lord was angry**

	with Moses, and **his hand was about to fall upon him** to kill him**, for he had not circumcised his son**.
Exodus 4:25 Then Zipporah took a sharp stone, and ~~cut off the foreskin of~~ her son, and cast *it* at his feet, and said, Surely a bloody husband ~~*art* thou to~~ me.	Then Zipporah took a sharp stone, and **circumcised** her son, and cast **the stone** at his feet, and said, Surely **thou art** a bloody husband **unto** me.
Exodus 4:26 ~~So he~~ let him go: ~~then~~ she said, A bloody husband ~~*thou art,* because of the circumcision~~.	**And the Lord spared Moses, and** let him go**, because Zipporah, his wife, circumcised the child. And** she said, **Thou art** a bloody husband. **And Moses was ashamed, and hid his face from the Lord, and said, I have sinned before the Lord.**
Exodus 4:27 And the Lord said to Aaron, Go into the wilderness to meet Moses. And he went, and met him in the mount of God, and kissed him.	And the Lord said to Aaron, Go into the wilderness to meet Moses. And he went, and met him in the mount of God**; in the mount where God appeared unto him**, and **Aaron** kissed him.

Exodus 5

Exodus 5:4 And the king of Egypt said unto them, Wherefore do ye, Moses and Aaron, ~~let~~ the people from their works? get you unto your burdens.	And the king of Egypt said unto them, Wherefore do ye, Moses and Aaron, **lead** the people from their works? get you unto your burdens.

Exodus 6

Exodus 6:3 And I appeared unto Abraham, unto Isaac, and unto Jacob, ~~by~~ *the* ~~*name of*~~ God Almighty, ~~but by my name~~ JEHOVAH was ~~I~~ not known ~~to~~ them.	And I appeared unto Abraham, unto Isaac, and unto Jacob**. I am** the **Lord** God Almighty, **the Lord** Jehovah**. And** was not **my name** known **unto** them**?**
Exodus 6:4 And I have also established my covenant with them, to give them the land of Canaan, the land of	**Yea,** and I have also established my covenant with them, **which I made with them,** to give them the land of Canaan,

their pilgrimage, wherein they were strangers.	the land of their pilgrimage, wherein they were strangers.
Exodus 6:8 And I will bring you in unto the land, concerning the which I did swear to give it to Abraham, to Isaac, and to Jacob; and I will give it you for an heritage: I ~~*am*~~ the LORD.	And I will bring you in unto the land, concerning the which I did swear to give it to Abraham, to Isaac, and to Jacob; and I will give it you for an heritage: I the Lord **will do it**.
Exodus 6:12 And Moses spake before the LORD, saying, Behold, the children of Israel have not hearkened unto me; how then shall Pharaoh hear me, who ~~*am*~~ of uncircumcised lips?	And Moses spake before the Lord, saying, Behold, the children of Israel have not hearkened unto me; how then shall Pharaoh hear me, who **is** of uncircumcised lips?
Exodus 6:14 These ~~*be*~~ the heads of their fathers' houses: The sons of Reuben the firstborn of Israel; Hanoch, and Pallu, Hezron, and Carmi: these ~~*be*~~ the families of Reuben.	These **are** the heads of their fathers' houses: The sons of Reuben the firstborn of Israel; Hanoch, and Pallu, Hezron, and Carmi: these **are** the families of Reuben.
Exodus 6:26 These *are* that ~~Aaron and Moses, to whom~~ the LORD said, Bring out ~~the children~~ of ~~Israel from~~ the land of Egypt according to their armies.	These are **the sons of Aaron, according to their families, and all these are the names of the children of Israel, according to the heads of their families,** that the Lord said **unto Aaron and Moses**, **They should** bring **up** out of the land of Egypt according to their armies.
Exodus 6:27 These *are* they ~~which~~ spake to Pharaoh king of Egypt, to bring out the children of Israel from Egypt: ~~these *are* that Moses and Aaron~~.	These are they **concerning whom the Lord** spake to Pharaoh king of Egypt, **that he should let them go. And he sent Moses and Aaron** to bring out the children of Israel from Egypt.
Exodus 6:28 And it came to pass on the day ~~*when*~~ the LORD spake unto Moses in the land of Egypt,	And it came to pass on the day the Lord spake unto Moses in the land of Egypt,
Exodus 6:29 That the LORD ~~spake unto~~ Moses, saying, I ~~*am*~~ the LORD: ~~speak thou~~ unto Pharaoh king of Egypt all that I say unto thee.	That the Lord **commanded** Moses **that he should speak unto Pharaoh, king of Egypt, all that I say unto thee**, saying, I the Lord **will do** unto Pharaoh king of Egypt all that I say unto thee.
Exodus 6:30 And Moses said before the LORD, Behold, I *am* of ~~uncircumcised~~	And Moses said before the Lord, Behold, I am of **stammering** lips, and

lips, and how shall Pharaoh hearken unto me?	**slow of speech;** how shall Pharaoh hearken unto me?

Exodus 7

Exodus 7:1 AND the LORD said unto Moses, See, I have made thee a ~~god~~ to Pharaoh: and Aaron thy brother shall be thy ~~prophet~~.	And the Lord said unto Moses, See, I have made thee a **prophet** to Pharaoh: and Aaron thy brother shall be thy **spokesman**.
Exodus 7:2 Thou shalt speak all that I command thee: and Aaron thy brother shall speak unto Pharaoh, that he send the children of Israel out of his land.	Thou shalt speak **unto thy brother,** all that I command thee: and Aaron thy brother shall speak unto Pharaoh, that he send the children of Israel out of his land.
Exodus 7:3 And ~~I~~ will harden ~~Pharaoh's~~ heart, and multiply my signs and my wonders in the land of Egypt.	And **Pharaoh** will harden **his** heart, **as I said unto thee;** and **thou shall** multiply my signs and my wonders in the land of Egypt.
Exodus 7:4 But Pharaoh ~~shall~~ not hearken unto you, ~~that~~ I ~~may~~ lay my hand upon Egypt, and bring forth mine armies, ~~*and*~~ my people the children of Israel, out of the land of Egypt by great judgments.	But Pharaoh **will** not hearken unto you, **therefore** I **will** lay my hand upon Egypt, and bring forth mine armies, my people the children of Israel, out of the land of Egypt by great judgments.
Exodus 7:9 When Pharaoh shall speak unto you, saying, Shew a miracle ~~for~~ you: then thou shalt say unto Aaron, Take thy rod, and cast *it* before Pharaoh, *and* it shall become a serpent.	When Pharaoh shall speak unto you, saying, Shew a miracle **that I may know** you: then thou shalt say unto Aaron, Take thy rod, and cast it before Pharaoh, and it shall become a serpent.
Exodus 7:13 And ~~he~~ hardened ~~Pharaoh's~~ heart, that he hearkened not unto them; as the LORD had said.	And **Pharaoh** hardened **his** heart, that he hearkened not unto them; as the Lord had said.

Exodus 9

Exodus 9:12 And ~~the LORD~~ hardened ~~the~~ heart ~~of Pharaoh~~, and he hearkened not unto them; as the LORD had spoken unto Moses.	And **Pharaoh** hardened **his** heart, and he hearkened not unto them; as the Lord had spoken unto Moses.

Exodus 9:17 As yet ~~exaltest thou thyself against my people,~~ that ~~thou wilt~~ not let them go?	**Therefore speak unto Pharaoh the thing which I commanded thee; who** as yet **exalteth himself** that **he will** not let them go**.**

Exodus 10

Exodus 10:1 AND the LORD said unto Moses, Go in unto Pharaoh: for ~~I have~~ hardened his heart, and the ~~heart~~ of his servants, ~~that~~ I ~~might~~ shew these my signs before him:	And the Lord said unto Moses, Go in unto Pharaoh: for **he hath** hardened his heart, and the **hearts** of his servants, **therefore** I **will** shew these my signs before him:
Exodus 10:20 But ~~the LORD~~ hardened ~~Pharaoh's~~ heart, so that he would not let the children of Israel go.	But **Pharaoh** hardened **his** heart, so that he would not let the children of Israel go.
Exodus 10:27 But ~~the LORD~~ hardened ~~Pharaoh's~~ heart, and he would not let them go.	But **Pharaoh** hardened **his** heart, and he would not let them go.

Exodus 11

Exodus 11:8 And all these ~~thy~~ servants shall come down unto me, and bow down themselves unto me, saying, Get thee out, and all the people that follow thee: and after that I will go out. ~~And he went out from Pharaoh in a great anger~~.	And all **the** servants of **Pharaoh** shall come down unto me, and bow down themselves unto me, saying, Get thee out, and all the people that follow thee: and after that I will go out.
Exodus 11:9 And the LORD said unto Moses, Pharaoh ~~shall~~ not hearken unto you; ~~that~~ my wonders ~~may~~ be multiplied in the land of Egypt.	And the Lord said unto Moses, Pharaoh **will** not hearken unto you; **therefore** my wonders **shall** be multiplied in the land of Egypt.
Exodus 11:10 And Moses and Aaron did all these wonders before Pharaoh: and ~~the LORD~~ hardened ~~Pharaoh's~~ heart, so that he would not let the children of Israel go out of his land.	And Moses and Aaron did all these wonders before Pharaoh: **and they went out from Pharaoh, and he was in a great anger,** and **Pharaoh** hardened **his** heart, so that he would not let the children of Israel go out of his land.

Exodus 12

Exodus 12:33 And the Egyptians were urgent upon the people, that they might send them out of the land in haste; for they said, We ~~*be*~~ all dead *men.*	And the Egyptians were urgent upon the people, that they might send them out of the land in haste; for they said, **We be all dead men, for** we **have found our firstborn** all dead, **therefore get ye out of the land lest we die also.**
Exodus 12:37 And the children of Israel journeyed from Rameses to Succoth, about six hundred thousand on foot ~~*that were* men, beside~~ children.	And the children of Israel journeyed from Rameses to Succoth, about six hundred thousand **men** on foot, **besides women and** children.

Exodus 14

Exodus 14:4 And ~~I~~ will harden ~~Pharaoh's~~ heart, that he shall follow after them; and I will be honoured upon Pharaoh, and upon all his host; that the Egyptians may know that I *am* the LORD. And they did so.	And **Pharaoh** will harden **his** heart, that he shall follow after them; and I will be honoured upon Pharaoh, and upon all his host; that the Egyptians may know that I *am* the Lord. And they did so.
Exodus 14:8 And ~~the LORD~~ hardened ~~the~~ heart ~~of Pharaoh king of Egypt~~, and he pursued after the children of Israel: and the children of Israel went out with an high hand.	And **Pharaoh** hardened **his** heart, and he pursued after the children of Israel: and the children of Israel went out with an high hand.
Exodus 14:17 And I, behold, I ~~will harden~~ the hearts of the Egyptians, and they shall follow them: and I will get me honour upon Pharaoh, and upon all his host, upon his chariots, and upon his horsemen.	And I, behold, I **say unto thee** the hearts of the Egyptians **shall be hardened**, and they shall follow them: and I will get me honour upon Pharaoh, and upon all his host, upon his chariots, and upon his horsemen.
Exodus 14:20 And it came between the camp of the Egyptians and the camp of Israel; and it was a cloud and darkness *to* ~~*them*~~, but it gave light by night *to* ~~*these*~~*:* so that the one came not near the other all the night.	And it came between the camp of the Egyptians and the camp of Israel; and it was a cloud and darkness to **the Egyptians**, but it gave light by night to **the Israelites**: so that the one came not near the other all the night.

Exodus 18

Exodus 18:1 WHEN Jethro, the priest of Midian, Moses' father in law, heard of all that God had done for Moses, and for Israel his people, *and* that the LORD had brought Israel out of Egypt;	When Jethro, the **high** priest of Midian, Moses' father in law, heard of all that God had done for Moses, and for Israel his people, and that the Lord had brought Israel out of Egypt;

Exodus 20

Exodus 20:23 Ye shall not make ~~with me~~ gods of silver, neither shall ye make unto you gods of gold.	Ye shall not make **unto you** gods of silver, neither shall ye make unto you gods of gold.

Exodus 21

Exodus 21:8 If she please not her master, who hath betrothed her to himself, then shall he let her be redeemed: to sell her unto a strange nation he shall have no power, seeing he hath dealt deceitfully with her.	If she please not her master, who hath betrothed her to himself, then shall he let her be redeemed: **not** to sell her unto a strange nation he shall have no power **to do this**, seeing he hath dealt deceitfully with her.
Exodus 21:20 And if a man smite his servant, or his maid, with a rod, and he die under his hand; he shall be surely ~~punished~~.	And if a man smite his servant, or his maid, with a rod, and he die under his hand; he shall be surely **put to death**.
Exodus 21:21 Notwithstanding, if he continue a day or two, he shall not be ~~punished~~: for he *is* his ~~money~~.	Notwithstanding, if he continue a day or two **and recover**, he shall not be **put to death**: for he is his **servant**.

Exodus 22

Exodus 22:18 Thou shalt not suffer a ~~witch~~ to live.	Thou shalt not suffer a **murderer** to live.
Exodus 22:28 Thou shalt not revile ~~the gods~~, nor curse the ruler of thy people.	Thou shalt not revile **against God**, nor curse the ruler of thy people.

Exodus 23	
Exodus 23:3 Neither shalt thou countenance a ~~poor~~ man in his cause.	Neither shalt thou countenance a **wicked** man in his cause.

Exodus 27	
Exodus 27: 8 Hollow with boards shalt thou make it: as it was shewed thee in the mount, so shall ~~they~~ make *it.*	Hollow with boards shalt thou make it: as it was shewed thee in the mount, so shall **thou** make it.

Exodus 32	
Exodus 32:1 AND when the people saw that Moses delayed to come down out of the mount, the people gathered themselves together unto Aaron, and said unto him, Up, make us gods, which shall go before us; for *as for* this Moses, the man that brought us up out of the land of Egypt, we ~~wot~~ not what is become of him.	And when the people saw that Moses delayed to come down out of the mount, the people gathered themselves together unto Aaron, and said unto him, Up, make us gods, which shall go before us; for as for this Moses, the man that brought us up out of the land of Egypt, we **know**[1] not what is become of him.
Exodus 32:12 Wherefore should the Egyptians speak, and say, For mischief did he bring them out, to slay them in the mountains, and to consume them from the face of the earth? Turn from thy fierce wrath, and repent of this evil ~~against thy people~~.	Wherefore should the Egyptians speak, and say, For mischief did he bring them out, to slay them in the mountains, and to consume them from the face of the earth? Turn from thy fierce wrath, and **thy people will** repent of this evil, **therefore come thou not out against them**.
Exodus 32:14 And the LORD ~~repented~~ of the evil which ~~he~~ thought to do unto ~~his~~ people.	And the Lord **said unto Moses, If they will repent** of the evil which **they have done, I will spare them, and turn away my fierce wrath; but, behold, thou shalt execute judgment upon**

1. The manuscript notes at Exodus 32:1 that "know" should replace "wot" in all places.

	all that will not repent of this evil this day. Therefore, see thou do this thing that I have commanded thee, or I will execute all that which I had thought to do unto **my** people.
Exodus 32:23 For they said unto me, Make us gods, which shall go before us: for *as for* this Moses, the man that brought us up out of the land of Egypt, we ~~wot~~ not what is become of him.	For they said unto me, Make us gods, which shall go before us: for as for this Moses, the man that brought us up out of the land of Egypt, we **know** not what is become of him.
Exodus 32:35 And the LORD plagued the people, because they ~~made~~ the calf, which Aaron made.	And the Lord plagued the people, because they **worshipped** the calf, which Aaron made.

Exodus 33

Exodus 33:1 AND the LORD said unto Moses, Depart, *and* go up hence, thou and the people which thou hast brought up out of the land of Egypt, unto the land which I sware unto Abraham, to Isaac, and to Jacob, saying, Unto thy seed will I give it:	And the Lord said unto Moses, Depart, and go up hence, thou and the people which thou hast brought up out of the land of Egypt, unto **a land flowing with milk and honey;** the land which I sware unto Abraham, to Isaac, and to Jacob, saying, Unto thy seed will I give it:
Exodus 33:3 ~~Unto a land flowing with milk and honey~~: for I will not go up in the midst of thee; for thou *art* a stiffnecked people: lest I consume thee in the way.	For I will not go up in the midst of thee; for thou art a stiffnecked people: lest I consume thee in the way.
Exodus 33:20 And he said, Thou canst not see my face: for there shall no man see me, and live.	And he said **unto Moses**, Thou canst not see my face **at this time, lest mine anger is kindled against thee also, and I destroy thee and thy people**: for there shall no man **among them** see me **at this time**, and live, **for they are exceedingly sinful, and no sinful man hath at any time, neither shall there be any sinful man at any time that shall see my face and live**.

Exodus 33:21 And the Lord said, Behold, ~~*there is* a place by me, and~~ thou shalt stand upon a rock:	And the Lord said, Behold, thou shalt stand upon a rock**, and I will prepare a place by me, for thee;**
Exodus 33:22 And it shall come to pass, while my glory passeth by, that I will put thee in a clift of the rock, and ~~will~~ cover thee with my hand while I pass by:	And it shall come to pass, while my glory passeth by, that I will put thee in a cleft[2] of the rock, and cover thee with my hand while I pass by:
Exodus 33:23 And I will take away mine hand, and thou shalt see my back parts: but my face shall not be seen.	And I will take away mine hand, and thou shalt see my back parts: but my face shall not be seen**, as at other times; for I am angry with my people, Israel**.

Exodus 34

Exodus 34:1 And the Lord said unto Moses, Hew thee two tables of ~~stone~~ like unto the first: and I will write upon ~~*these* tables~~ the words ~~that~~ were ~~in~~ the ~~first~~ tables, which thou brakest.	And the Lord said unto Moses, Hew thee two **other** tables of **stones** like unto the first: and I will write upon **them also,** the words **of the Law, according as they** were **written at the first, on** the tables, which thou brakest; **but it shall not be according to the first, for I will take away the priesthood out of their midst; therefore my holy order; and the ordinances thereof, shall not go before them; for my presence shall not go up in their midst lest I destroy them. But I will give unto them the law as at the first, but it shall be after the law of a carnal commandment; for I have sworn in my wrath, that they shall not enter into my presence, into my rest, in the days of their pilgrimage.**

2. Joseph Smith's Bible reads "cleft," whereas the 1979 LDS KJV reads "clift."

Exodus 34:2 And be ready in the morning, and come up in the morning unto mount Sinai, and present thyself there to me in the top of the mount.	**Therefore do as I have commanded thee,** and be ready in the morning, and come up in the morning unto mount Sinai, and present thyself there to me in the top of the mount.
Exodus 34:4 And ~~he~~ hewed two tables of stone like unto the first; and ~~Moses~~ rose up early in the morning, and went up unto mount Sinai, as the LORD had commanded him, and took in his hand the two tables of stone.	And **Moses** hewed two tables of stone like unto the first; and **he** rose up early in the morning, and went up unto mount Sinai, as the Lord had commanded him, and took in his hand the two tables of stone.
Exodus 34:7 Keeping mercy for thousands, forgiving iniquity and transgression and sin, and that will by no means clear *the ~~guilty~~;* visiting the iniquity of the fathers upon the children, and upon the children's children, unto the third and to the fourth *generation.*	Keeping mercy for thousands, forgiving iniquity and transgression and sin, and that will by no means clear the **rebellious***;* visiting the iniquity of the fathers upon the children, and upon the children's children, unto the third and to the fourth generation.
Exodus 34:14 For thou shalt worship no other god: for the LORD, whose name *is* ~~Jealous~~, *is* a jealous God:	For thou shalt worship no other god: for the Lord, whose name is **Jehovah**, is a jealous God:
Exodus 34:35 And the children of Israel saw the face of Moses, that the skin of Moses' face shone: and Moses put the vail upon his face again, until he went in to speak with ~~him~~.	And the children of Israel saw the face of Moses, that the skin of Moses' face shone: and Moses put the vail upon his face again, until he went in to speak with **the Lord**.

Leviticus

Leviticus 12	
King James Version	**Joseph Smith Translation**
Leviticus 12:3 And in the eighth day the ~~flesh of his foreskin~~ shall be circumcised.	And in the eighth day the **man child** shall be circumcised.
Leviticus 12:4 And she shall then continue in the ~~blood~~ of her purifying three and thirty days; she shall touch no hallowed thing, nor come into the sanctuary, until the days of her purifying be fulfilled.	And she shall then continue in the **time** of her purifying **which shall be** three and thirty days; she shall touch no hallowed thing, nor come into the sanctuary, until the days of her purifying be fulfilled.
Leviticus 12:5 But if she bear a maid child, ~~then~~ she shall be unclean two weeks, as in her separation: and she shall continue in the ~~blood~~ of her purifying threescore and six days.	But if she bear a maid child, she shall be unclean two weeks, as in her separation: and she shall continue in the **time** of her purifying threescore and six days.
Leviticus 21	
Leviticus 21:1 AND the LORD said unto Moses, Speak unto the priests the sons of Aaron, and say unto them, There shall none be defiled ~~for~~ the dead among his people:	And the Lord said unto Moses, Speak unto the priests the sons of Aaron, and say unto them, There shall none be defiled **with** the dead among his people:
Leviticus 21:11 Neither shall he go in to any dead body, nor defile himself for his father, or for his mother;	Neither shall he go in to **touch** any dead body, nor defile himself for his father, or for his mother;

Leviticus 22	
Leviticus 22:9 They shall therefore keep mine ordinance, lest they bear sin for it, and die therefore, if they profane ~~it~~: I the LORD ~~do~~ sanctify them.	They shall therefore keep mine ordinance, lest they bear sin for it, and die therefore, if they profane **not mine ordinances**: I the Lord **will** sanctify them.

Numbers

Numbers 16	
King James Version	Joseph Smith Translation
Numbers 16:10 And he hath brought thee near *to him,* and all thy brethren the sons of Levi with thee: and seek ye the priesthood also?	And he hath brought thee near to him, and all thy brethren the sons of Levi with thee: and seek ye the **high** priesthood also?
Numbers 22	
Numbers 22:20 And God came unto Balaam at night, and said unto him, If the men come to call thee, rise up, ~~*and*~~ go with them; but yet the word which I shall say unto thee, ~~that~~ shalt thou ~~do~~.	And God came unto Balaam at night, and said unto him, If the men come to call thee, rise up, **if thou wilt** go with them; but yet the word which I shall say unto thee, shalt thou **speak**.

Deuteronomy

Deuteronomy 2	
King James Version	Joseph Smith Translation
Deuteronomy 2:30 But Sihon king of Heshbon would not let us pass by him: for ~~the LORD thy God~~ hardened his spirit, and made his heart obstinate, that ~~he~~ might deliver him into thy hand, as ~~*appeareth*~~ this day.	But Sihon king of Heshbon would not let us pass by him: for **he** hardened his spirit, and made his heart obstinate, that **the Lord thy God** might deliver him into thy hand, as **he hath done** this day.
Deuteronomy 10	
Deuteronomy 10:1 AT that time the LORD said unto me, Hew thee two tables of stone like unto the first, and come up unto me ~~into~~ the mount, and make thee an ark of wood.	At that time the Lord said unto me, Hew thee two **other** tables of stone like unto the first, and come up unto me **upon** the mount, and make thee an ark of wood.
Deuteronomy 10:2 And I will write on the tables the words that were ~~in~~ the first tables which thou brakest, and thou shalt put them in the ark.	And I will write on the tables the words that were **on** the first tables which thou brakest**, save the words of the everlasting covenant of the holy priesthood**, and thou shalt put them in the ark.
Deuteronomy 14	
Deuteronomy 14:21 Ye shall not eat *of* any thing that dieth of itself: thou shalt give it unto the stranger that *is* in thy gates, that he may eat it; or thou mayest sell it unto an alien: for thou *art* an	Ye shall not eat of any thing that dieth of itself: thou shalt **not** give it unto the stranger that is in thy gates, that he may eat it; or thou mayest **not** sell it unto an alien: for thou art a holy people unto

holy people unto the LORD thy God. Thou shalt not seethe a kid in his mother's milk.	the Lord thy God. Thou shalt not seethe a kid in his mother's milk.

Deuteronomy 34

Deuteronomy 34:6 ~~And he buried~~ him in a valley in the land of Moab, over against Beth-peor: ~~but~~ no man knoweth of his sepulchre unto this day.	**For the Lord took** him **unto his fathers,** in a valley in the land of Moab, over against Beth-peor: **therefore** no man knoweth of his sepulchre unto this day.

Joshua

Joshua 11	
King James Version	Joseph Smith Translation
Joshua 11:20 For it was of the LORD to ~~harden~~ their hearts, that they should come against Israel in battle, ~~that he might destroy them utterly, *and*~~ that they might have no favour, ~~but~~ that ~~he~~ might destroy them, as the LORD commanded Moses.	For it was of the Lord to **destroy them utterly, because they hardened** their hearts, that they should come against Israel in battle, that they might have no favour, that **they** might destroy them **in battle**, as the Lord commanded Moses.

Judges

Judges 2	
King James Version	Joseph Smith Translation
Judges 2:18 And when the Lord raised them up judges, then the Lord was with the judge, and delivered them out of the hand of their enemies all the days of the judge: ~~for it repented~~ the Lord because of their groanings by reason of them that oppressed them and vexed them.	And when the Lord raised them up judges, then the Lord was with the judge, and delivered them out of the hand of their enemies all the days of the judge: the Lord **hearkened** because of their groanings by reason of them that oppressed them and vexed them.

I Samuel

1 Samuel 15	
King James Version	Joseph Smith Translation
1 Samuel 15: 11 ~~It repenteth me that~~ I have set up Saul *to be* king: for he is turned back from following me, and hath not performed my commandments. And it grieved Samuel; and he cried unto the Lord all night.	I have set up Saul to be **a** king**, and he repenteth not that he hath sinned**: for he is turned back from following me, and hath not performed my commandments. And it grieved Samuel; and he cried unto the Lord all night.
1 Samuel 15:35 And Samuel came no more to see Saul until the day of his death: nevertheless Samuel mourned for Saul: and the Lord ~~repented that~~ he had made ~~Saul~~ king over Israel.	And Samuel came no more to see Saul until the day of his death: nevertheless Samuel mourned for Saul: and the Lord **rent the kingdom from Saul, whom** he had made king over Israel.

1 Samuel 16	
1 Samuel 16:16 Let our lord now command thy servants, *which are* before thee, to seek out a man, *who is* a cunning player on an harp: and it shall come to pass, when the evil spirit ~~from~~ God is upon thee, that he shall play with his hand, and thou shalt be well.	Let our lord now command thy servants, which are before thee, to seek out a man, who is a cunning player on an harp: and it shall come to pass, when the evil spirit **which is not of** God is upon thee, that he shall play with his hand, and thou shalt be well.
1 Samuel 16:23 And it came to pass, when the *evil* spirit ~~from~~ God was upon Saul, that David took an harp, and played with his hand: so Saul was refreshed, and was well, and the evil spirit departed from him.	And it came to pass, when the evil spirit **which was not of** God was upon Saul, that David took an harp, and played with his hand: so Saul was refreshed, and was well, and the evil spirit departed from him.

1 Samuel 18

1 Samuel 18:10 And it came to pass on the morrow, that the evil spirit ~~from~~ God came upon Saul, and he prophesied in the midst of the house: and David played with his hand, as at other times: and *there was* a javelin in Saul's hand.	And it came to pass on the morrow, that the evil spirit **which was not of** God came upon Saul, and he prophesied in the midst of the house: and David played with his hand, as at other times: and there was a javelin in Saul's hand.

1 Samuel 19

1 Samuel 19:9 And the evil spirit ~~from~~ the LORD was upon Saul, as he sat in his house with his javelin in his hand: and David played with *his* hand.	And the evil spirit **which was not of** the Lord was upon Saul, as he sat in his house with his javelin in his hand: and David played with his hand.

1 Samuel 28

1 Samuel 28:9 And the woman said unto him, Behold, thou knowest what Saul hath done, how he hath cut off those that ~~have~~ familiar spirits, and the wizards, out of the land: wherefore then layest thou a snare for my life, to cause me to die?	And the woman said unto him, Behold, thou knowest what Saul hath done, how he hath cut off those that **hath** familiar spirits, and the wizards, out of the land: wherefore then layest thou a snare for my life, to cause me to die **also, who hath not a familiar spirit**?
1 Samuel 28:10 And Saul sware ~~to~~ her by the LORD, saying, *As* the LORD liveth, ~~there~~ shall no punishment happen to thee for this thing.	And Saul sware **unto** her by the Lord, saying, As the Lord liveth, **then** shall no punishment happen to thee for this thing.
1 Samuel 28:11 Then said the woman, Whom shall I bring up unto thee? And he said, Bring me up Samuel.	Then said the woman, **The words of** whom shall I bring up unto thee? And he said, Bring me up **the words of** Samuel.
1 Samuel 28:12 And when the woman saw Samuel, she cried with a loud voice: and the woman spake to Saul,	And when the woman saw **the words of** Samuel, she cried with a loud voice: and the woman spake to Saul, saying,

saying, Why hast thou deceived me? for thou *art* Saul.	Why hast thou deceived me? for thou art Saul.
1 Samuel 28:13 And the king said unto her, Be not afraid: for what sawest thou? And the woman said unto Saul, I saw ~~gods~~ ascending out of the earth.	And the king said unto her, Be not afraid: for what sawest thou? And the woman said unto Saul, I saw **the words of Samuel** ascending out of the earth. **And she said, I saw Samuel also.**
1 Samuel 28:14 And he said unto her, What form *is* he of? And she said, An old man ~~cometh~~ up; ~~and he *is*~~ covered with a mantle. And Saul perceived that it *was* Samuel, and he stooped ~~with~~ *his* face to the ground, and bowed himself.	And he said unto her, What form is he of? And she said, **I saw** an old man **coming** up, covered with a mantle. And Saul perceived that it was Samuel, and he stooped**,** his face to the ground, and bowed himself.
1 Samuel 28:15 And Samuel ~~said to~~ Saul, Why hast thou disquieted me, to bring me up? And Saul answered, I am sore distressed; for the Philistines make war against me, and God is departed from me, and answereth me no more, neither by prophets, nor by dreams: therefore I have called thee, that thou mayest make known unto me what I shall do.	And **these are the words of** Samuel **unto** Saul, Why hast thou disquieted me, to bring me up? And Saul answered, I am sore distressed; for the Philistines make war against me, and God is departed from me, and answereth me no more, neither by prophets, nor by dreams: therefore I have called thee, that thou mayest make known unto me what I shall do.

2 Samuel

2 Samuel 12	
King James Version	Joseph Smith Translation
2 Samuel 12:13 And David said unto Nathan, I have sinned against the Lord. And Nathan said unto David, The Lord also hath put away thy sin; thou shalt not die.	And David said unto Nathan, I have sinned against the Lord. And Nathan said unto David, The Lord also hath **not** put away thy sin; **that** thou shalt not die.
2 Samuel 24	
2 Samuel 24:16 And when the angel stretched out his hand upon Jerusalem to destroy it, the Lord ~~repented him of the evil, and~~ said ~~to the angel that destroyed the people~~, ~~It is enough:~~ stay now thine hand. And the angel of the Lord was by the ~~threshingplace~~ of Araunah the Jebusite.	And when the angel stretched out his hand upon Jerusalem to destroy it, the Lord said **unto him**, Stay now thine hand**, it is enough, for the people repented and the Lord stayed the hand of the angel, that he destroyed not the people**. And the angel of the Lord was by the **threshold** of Araunah the Jebusite.
2 Samuel 24:17 ~~And~~ David spake unto the Lord when he saw the angel that smote the people, and said, Lo, I have sinned, and I have done wickedly: but these sheep, what have they done? let thine hand, I pray thee, be against me, and against my father's house.	**For** David spake unto the Lord when he saw the angel that smote the people, and said, Lo, I have sinned, and I have done wickedly: but these sheep, what have they done? let thine hand, I pray thee, be against me, and against my father's house.

1 Kings

1 Kings 3

King James Version	Joseph Smith Translation
1 Kings 3:1 And Solomon made affinity with Pharaoh king of Egypt, and took Pharaoh's daughter, and brought her into the ~~city~~ of David, until he had made an end of building his own house, and the house of the Lord, and the wall of Jerusalem round about.	And **the Lord was not pleased with** Solomon**, for he** made affinity with Pharaoh king of Egypt, and took Pharaoh's daughter **to wife**, and brought her into the **house** of David, until he had made an end of building his own house, and the house of the Lord, and the wall of Jerusalem round about**; and the Lord blessed Solomon for the people's sake only**.
1 Kings 3:2 ~~Only~~ the people sacrificed in high places, because there was no house built unto the name of the Lord, until those days.	**And** the people sacrificed in high places, because there was no house built unto the name of the Lord, until those days.
1 Kings 3:3 And ~~Solomon loved~~ the Lord, walking in the statutes of David his father: ~~only~~ he sacrificed and burnt incense in high places.	And **because** the Lord **blessed Solomon as he was** walking in the statutes of David his father**, he began to love the Lord; and** he sacrificed and burnt incense in high places**, and he called on the name of the Lord**.
1 Kings 3:4 And the king went to Gibeon to sacrifice there; for ~~that~~ *was* ~~the~~ great high place: a thousand burnt offerings ~~did Solomon offer upon that altar~~.	And the king went to Gibeon to sacrifice there; for **Gibeon** was **in a** great high place: **and Solomon offered upon that altar, in Gibeon,** a thousand burnt offerings.
1 Kings 3:5 ~~In Gibeon~~ the Lord appeared ~~to Solomon~~ in a dream by night: and ~~God~~ said, Ask what I shall give thee.	**And** the Lord **God hearkened unto Solomon, and** appeared **unto him** in a dream by night: and said, Ask what I shall give thee.

1 Kings 3:6 And Solomon said, Thou hast shewed unto thy servant David my father great ~~mercy~~, according ~~as~~ he walked before thee in truth, and in righteousness, and in uprightness of heart with thee; and thou hast kept for him this great kindness, that thou hast given him a son to sit on his throne, ~~as *it is*~~ this day.

And Solomon said, Thou hast shewed unto thy servant David my father great **things**, according **to thy mercy, when** he walked before thee in truth, and in righteousness, and in uprightness of heart with thee; and thou hast kept for him this great kindness, that thou hast given him a son to sit on his throne, this day.

1 Kings 3:7 And now, O Lord my God, thou hast made thy servant king instead of David my father: and I ~~*am but* a little child: I~~ know not *how* to go out or come in.

And now, O Lord my God, thou hast made thy servant king instead of David my father**, over thy people**: and I know not how to **lead them, to** go out or come in **before them**.

1 Kings 3:8 And thy servant *is* in the midst of thy people ~~which~~ thou hast chosen, a great people, that cannot be numbered nor counted for multitude.

And thy servant **am as a little child,** in the midst of thy people **whom** thou hast chosen, a great people, that cannot be numbered nor counted for multitude.

1 Kings 3:9 Give therefore thy servant an understanding heart to judge thy people, that I may discern between good and bad: for who is able to judge this thy so great a people?

Give therefore thy servant an understanding heart to judge thy people, that I may discern between good and bad: for who is able to judge this thy **people,** so great a people?

1 Kings 3:12 Behold, I have done according to thy ~~words~~: lo, I have given thee a wise and an understanding heart; so that there was none like thee before thee, neither after thee shall any arise like unto thee.

Behold, I have done according to thy **word**: lo, I have given thee a wise and an understanding heart; so that there was none **made king over Israel** like **unto** thee before thee, neither after thee shall any arise like unto thee.

1 Kings 3:14 And if thou wilt walk in my ways, to keep my statutes and my commandments, ~~as thy father David did walk,~~ then I will lengthen thy days.

And if thou wilt walk in my ways, to keep my statutes and my commandments, then I will lengthen thy days, **and thou shalt not walk in unrighteousness as did thy father, David**.

1 Kings 11

1 Kings 11:4 For it came to pass, when Solomon was old, ~~*that*~~ his wives turned away his heart after other gods: and his heart was not perfect with the LORD his God, as ~~*was*~~ the heart of David his father.	For it came to pass, when Solomon was old, his wives turned away his heart after other gods: and his heart was not perfect with the Lord his God, **and it became** as the heart of David his father.
1 Kings 11:6 And Solomon did evil in the sight of the LORD, and went not fully after the LORD, ~~as *did* David his father~~.	And Solomon did evil in the sight of the Lord, **as David his father,** and went not fully after the Lord.
1 Kings 11:33 Because that they have forsaken me, and have worshipped Ashtoreth the goddess of the Zidonians, Chemosh the god of the Moabites, and Milcom the god of the children of Ammon, and have not walked in my ways, to do *that which is* right in mine eyes, and ~~*to keep*~~ my statutes and my judgments, as *did* David his father.	Because that they have forsaken me, and have worshipped Ashtoreth the goddess of the Zidonians, Chemosh the god of the Moabites, and Milcom the god of the children of Ammon, and have not walked in my ways, to do that which is right in mine eyes, and my statutes and my judgments, **and his heart is become** as David his father**; and he repenteth not as did David his father, that I may forgive him**.
1 Kings 11:34 Howbeit I will not take the whole kingdom out of his hand: but I will make him prince all the days of his life for David my servant's sake, whom I chose, because he kept my ~~commandments~~ and my statutes:	Howbeit I will not take the whole kingdom out of his hand: but I will make him prince all the days of his life for David my servant's sake, whom I chose, because he kept my **commandment** and my statutes **in that day**:
1 Kings 11:35 But I will take the kingdom out of his son's hand, and will give it unto ~~thee~~, ~~*even*~~ ten tribes.	But I will take the kingdom out of his son's hand, and will give it unto **the** ten tribes.
1 Kings 11:37 And I will take thee, and thou ~~shalt~~ reign according to all that thy soul desireth, and ~~shalt~~ be king over Israel.	And I will take thee, and thou **shall** reign according to all that thy soul desireth, and **shall** be king over Israel.
1 Kings 11:38 And it shall be, if thou wilt hearken unto all that I command thee, and wilt walk in my ways, and	And it shall be, if thou wilt hearken unto all that I command thee, and wilt walk in my ways, and do right in my

do ~~*that is*~~ right in my sight, to keep my statutes and my commandments, as David my servant did; that I will be with thee, and build thee a sure house, as I built for David, and ~~will~~ give Israel unto thee.	sight, to keep my statutes and my commandments, as David my servant did **in the day** that **I blessed him**; I will be with thee, and build thee a sure house, as I built for David, and give Israel unto thee.
1 Kings 11:39 And I will ~~for this~~ afflict the seed of David, but not for ever.	**And for the transgression of David, and also for the people, I have rent the kingdom,** and **for this** I will afflict the seed of David, but not for ever.

1 Kings 13

1 Kings 13:18 He said unto him, I *am* a prophet also as thou ~~*art*~~; and an angel spake unto me by the word of the LORD, saying, Bring him back with thee into thine house, that he may eat bread and drink water. ~~*But*~~ he lied unto him.	He said unto him, I am a prophet also **even** as thou; and an angel spake unto me by the word of the Lord, saying, Bring him back with thee into thine house, that he may eat bread and drink water**, that I may prove him; and** he lied **not** unto him.

1 Kings 14

1 Kings 14:8 And rent the kingdom away from the house of David, and gave it thee: ~~and *yet*~~ thou hast not been as my servant David, ~~who kept my commandments, and who~~ followed me with all his heart, to do ~~*that only which was*~~ right in mine eyes;	And rent the kingdom away from the house of David, and gave it thee: **because he kept not my commandments, but** thou hast not been as my servant David, **when he** followed me with all his heart, **only** to do right in mine eyes;

1 Kings 15

1 Kings 15:3 And he walked in all the sins of his father, which he had done before him: and his heart was not perfect with the LORD his God, as the ~~heart of~~ David his father.	And he walked in all the sins of his father, which he had done before him: and his heart was not perfect with the Lord his God, as the **Lord commanded** David his father.

1 Kings 15:5 Because David did ~~*that which was*~~ right in the eyes of the LORD, and turned not aside from ~~*any thing*~~ that he commanded him all the days of his life, save only in the matter of Uriah the Hittite.	Because David did right in the eyes of the Lord, and turned not aside from **all** that he commanded him**; to sin against the Lord; but repented of the evil** all the days of his life, save only in the matter of Uriah the Hittite**, wherein the Lord cursed him**.
1 Kings 15:11 And Asa did ~~*that which was*~~ right in the eyes of the LORD, as ~~*did*~~ David his father.	And Asa did right in the eyes of the Lord, as **he commanded** David his father.
1 Kings 15:12 And he took away the sodomites out of the land, and removed all the idols that his fathers had made.	And he took away the sodomites out of the land, and removed all the idols that his fathers had made**, and it pleased the Lord**.

1 Kings 18

1 Kings 18:37 Hear me, O LORD, hear me, that this people may know that thou *art* the LORD God, and ~~*that*~~ thou ~~hast turned~~ their heart back again.	Hear me, O Lord, hear me, that this people may know that thou art the Lord God, and thou **mayest turn** their heart back again.

2 Kings

2 Kings 1

King James Version	Joseph Smith Translation
2 Kings 1:10 And Elijah answered and said to the captain of fifty, If I *be* a man of God, then let fire come down ~~from~~ heaven, and consume thee and thy fifty. And there came down fire from heaven, and consumed him and his fifty.	And Elijah answered and said to the captain of fifty, If I be a man of God, then let fire come down **out of** heaven, and consume thee and thy fifty. And there came down fire from heaven, and consumed him and his fifty.
2 Kings 1:12 And Elijah answered and said unto them, If I *be* a man of God, let fire come down from heaven, and consume thee and thy fifty. And the fire of God came down ~~from~~ heaven, and consumed him and his fifty.	And Elijah answered and said unto them, If I be a man of God, let fire come down from heaven, and consume thee and thy fifty. And the fire of God came down **out of** heaven, and consumed him and his fifty.
2 Kings 1:14 Behold, there came fire down ~~from~~ heaven, and burnt up the two captains of the former fifties with their fifties: therefore let my life now be precious in thy sight.	Behold, there came fire down **out of** heaven, and burnt up the two captains of the former fifties with their fifties: therefore let my life now be precious in thy sight.

2 Kings 8

King James Version	Joseph Smith Translation
2 Kings 8:10 And Elisha said unto him, Go, say unto him, Thou mayest certainly recover: howbeit the LORD hath shewed me that he shall surely die.	And Elisha said unto him, **Thou wilt** go, **and** say unto him, Thou mayest certainly recover: howbeit the Lord hath shewed me that he shall surely die.

1 Chronicles

1 Chronicles 10

King James Version	Joseph Smith Translation
1 Chronicles 10:13 So Saul died for his transgression which he committed against the Lord, *even* against the word of the Lord, which he kept not, and also for asking ~~*counsel* of *one that had*~~ a familiar spirit, to enquire *of it;*	So Saul died for his transgression which he committed against the Lord, even against the word of the Lord, which he kept not, and also for asking **for** a familiar spirit, to enquire of it;[1]

1 Chronicles 21

King James Version	Joseph Smith Translation
1 Chronicles 21:15 And ~~God sent an~~ angel unto Jerusalem to destroy it: ~~and as he was destroying, the Lord beheld, and he repented him of the evil,~~ and said to the angel ~~that destroyed, It is enough~~, stay now thine hand. ~~And the angel of~~ the Lord stood by the threshingfloor of Ornan the Jebusite.	And **the** angel **stretched forth his hand** unto Jerusalem to destroy it: and **God** said to the angel, Stay now thine hand, **it is enough, for as he was destroying,** the Lord **beheld Israel, that he repented him of the evil; therefore the Lord stayed the angel that destroyed, as he** stood by the threshingfloor of Ornan the Jebusite.
1 Chronicles 21:20 And Ornan turned back, and saw the angel; and ~~his four sons with him~~ hid themselves. ~~Now Ornan was threshing wheat.~~	**Now Ornan was threshing wheat, and his four sons with him,** and Ornan turned back, and saw the angel; and **they** hid themselves.

1. The exact wording of this change is ambiguous. OT2 crosses out the italicized words "counsel... one that had," but then records "or–for" as the text to be inserted. It appears that "or" should read "of" as in the phrase "counsel of one that had" and that the Prophet intended "for" to replace "of" instead of "or" as the scribe recorded it.

2 Chronicles

2 Chronicles 2	
King James Version	Joseph Smith Translation
2 Chronicles 2:3 And Solomon sent to Huram the king of Tyre, saying, As thou didst deal with David my father, and didst send him cedars to build him an house to dwell therein, *~~even so deal with me~~*.	And Solomon sent to Huram the king of Tyre, saying, As thou didst deal with David my father, and didst send him cedars to build him an house to dwell therein.[1]
2 Chronicles 2:4 Behold, I build an house to the name of the LORD my God, to dedicate *it* to him, *and* to burn before him sweet incense, and for the continual shewbread, and for the burnt offerings morning and evening, on the sabbaths, and on the new moons, and on the solemn feasts of the LORD our God. This *~~is an~~ ordinance* for ever ~~to Israel~~.	**Therefore** behold, I build an house to the name of the Lord my God, to dedicate it to him, and to burn before him sweet incense, and for the continual shewbread, and for the burnt offerings morning and evening, on the sabbaths, and on the new moons, and on the solemn feasts of the Lord our God. **And** this ordinance **shall be kept in Israel** for ever.
2 Chronicles 2:5 And the house which I build *~~is~~* great: for great *is* our God above all gods.	And the house which I build **shall be a** great **house**: for great is **the Lord** our God above all gods.
2 Chronicles 2:7 Send me now therefore a man cunning to work in gold, and in silver, and in brass, and in iron, and in purple, and crimson, and blue, and that ~~can~~ skill to grave with the	Send me now therefore a man cunning to work in gold, and in silver, and in brass, and in iron, and in purple, and crimson, and blue, and that **have** skill to grave with the cunning men that

1. The final phrase of 2 Chronicles 2:3 is crossed out in the Prophet's marked Bible, thus suggesting that he intended to remove it to ease the transition into the next verse.

cunning men that *are* with me in Judah and in Jerusalem, whom David my father did provide.	are with me in Judah and in Jerusalem, whom David my father did provide.
2 Chronicles 2:8 Send me also cedar trees, fir trees, and algum trees, out of Lebanon: for I know that thy servants ~~can~~ skill to cut timber in Lebanon; and, behold, my servants ~~*shall be*~~ with thy servants,	Send me also cedar trees, fir trees, and algum trees, out of Lebanon: for I know that thy servants **have** skill to cut timber in Lebanon; and, behold, my servants **I will send** with thy servants,

2 Chronicles 18

2 Chronicles 18:20 Then there came out a spirit, and stood before the LORD, and said, I will entice him. And the LORD said unto him, Wherewith?	Then there came out **[of]**[2] **them** a **lying** spirit, and stood before the Lord, and said, I will entice him. And the Lord said unto him, Wherewith?
2 Chronicles 18:21 And he said, I will go out, and be a lying spirit in the mouth of all his prophets. And *the LORD* said, Thou shalt entice *him,* and thou shalt also prevail: go out, and do *even* so.	And he said, I will go out, and be a lying spirit in the mouth of all his prophets. And the Lord said, Thou shalt entice him, and thou shalt also prevail: go out, and do even so **for all these have sinned against me**.
2 Chronicles 18:22 Now therefore, behold, the LORD hath ~~put~~ a lying spirit in the mouth of these thy prophets, and the LORD hath spoken evil against thee.	Now therefore, behold, the Lord hath **found** a lying spirit in the mouth of these thy prophets, and the Lord hath spoken evil against thee.

2 Chronicles 20

2 Chronicles 20:2 Then there came some that told Jehoshaphat, saying, There cometh a great multitude against thee from beyond the sea on this side Syria; and, behold, they ~~*be*~~ in Hazazon-tamar, which ~~*is*~~ En-gedi.	Then there came some that told Jehoshaphat, saying, There cometh a great multitude against thee from beyond the sea on this side Syria; and, behold, they **are** in Hazazon-tamar, which **was called** En-gedi.

2. The word "of" is omitted in OT2.

2 Chronicles 20:6 And said, O LORD God of our fathers, ~~*art* not~~ thou God in heaven? and rulest ~~*not* thou~~ over all the kingdoms of the heathen? and in ~~thine~~ hand ~~*is there not*~~ power and might, so that none is able to withstand thee?	And said, O Lord God of our fathers, thou God **who art** in heaven? and rulest over all the kingdoms of the heathen? and in **thy** hand **thou hast** power and might, so that none is able to withstand thee?
2 Chronicles 20:7 ~~*Art* not~~ thou our God, ~~*who*~~ didst drive out the inhabitants of this land before thy people Israel, and gavest it to the seed of Abraham thy friend for ever?	Thou our God, didst drive out the inhabitants of this land before thy people Israel, and gavest it to the seed of Abraham thy friend for ever.
2 Chronicles 20:11 Behold, ~~*I say, how*~~ they reward us, ~~to~~ come to cast us out of thy possession, which thou hast given us to inherit.	Behold, they reward us **not**, **but have** come to cast us out of thy possession, which thou hast given us to inherit.
2 Chronicles 20:17 Ye shall not ~~*need*~~ to fight in this ~~*battle*~~*:* set yourselves, stand ye *still,* and see the salvation of the LORD with you, O Judah and Jerusalem: fear not, nor be dismayed; to morrow go out against them: for the LORD *will be* with you.	Ye shall not **go** to fight in this **day**: set yourselves, stand ye still, and see the salvation of the Lord with you, O Judah and Jerusalem: fear not, nor be dismayed; to morrow go out against them: for the Lord will be with you.

2 Chronicles 22

2 Chronicles 22:2 ~~Forty~~ and ~~two~~ years old *was* Ahaziah when he began to reign, and he reigned one year in Jerusalem. His mother's name also *was* Athaliah the daughter of Omri.	**Two** and **twenty** years old was Ahaziah when he began to reign, and he reigned one year in Jerusalem. His mother's name also was Athaliah the daughter of Omri.

2 Chronicles 24

2 Chronicles 24:9 And they made a proclamation through Judah and Jerusalem, to bring in to the LORD the collection ~~*that*~~ Moses the servant of God *laid* upon Israel in the wilderness.	And they made a proclamation through Judah and Jerusalem, to bring in to the Lord the collection **of** Moses the servant of God laid upon Israel in the wilderness.

2 Chronicles 24:22 Thus Joash the king remembered not the kindness which Jehoiada his father had done to him, but slew his son. And when he died, he said, The LORD look upon ~~*it*~~, and require ~~*it*~~.	Thus Joash the king remembered not the kindness which Jehoiada his father had done to him, but slew his son. And when he died, he said, The Lord look upon **me**, and require **me**.

2 Chronicles 25

2 Chronicles 25:18 And Joash king of Israel sent to Amaziah king of Judah, saying, The thistle that ~~*was*~~ in Lebanon sent to the cedar that ~~*was*~~ in Lebanon, saying, Give thy daughter to my son to wife: and there passed by a wild beast that *was* in Lebanon, and trode down the thistle.	And Joash king of Israel sent to Amaziah king of Judah, saying, The thistle that **grew** in Lebanon sent to the cedar that **grew** in Lebanon, saying, Give thy daughter to my son to wife: and there passed by a wild beast that was in Lebanon, and trode down the thistle.

2 Chronicles 34

2 Chronicles 34:16 And Shaphan carried the book to the king, and brought the king ~~word~~ back again, saying, All that was committed to thy servants, they do ~~*it*~~.	And Shaphan carried the book to the king, and brought **the word of** the king back again, saying, All that was committed to thy servants, they do.

Nehemiah

Nehemiah 6

King James Version	Joseph Smith Translation
Nehemiah 6:11 And I said, Should such a man as I flee? and who *is* ~~*there*~~, that, ~~*being*~~ as I ~~*am*~~, would go into the temple to save his life? I will not go in.	And I said, Should such a man as I flee? and who is **mine enemy**, that, **such a man** as I would go into the temple to save his life? I will not go in.
Nehemiah 6:13 Therefore ~~*was*~~ he hired, ~~that I should be afraid~~, and do so, and sin, and *that* they might have ~~*matter*~~ for an evil report, that they might reproach me.	Therefore **should I be afraid of him,** he hired**?** And do so **as he said**, and sin, and that they might have **me** for an evil report, that they might reproach me.

Nehemiah 7

King James Version	Joseph Smith Translation
Nehemiah 7:10 The children of Arah, ~~six~~ hundred ~~fifty~~ and ~~two~~.	The children of Arah, **seven** hundred **seventy** and **five**.
Nehemiah 7:11 The children of Pahath-moab, of the children of Jeshua and Joab, two thousand and eight hundred *and* ~~eighteen~~.	The children of Pahath-moab, of the children of Jeshua and Joab, two thousand and eight hundred and **twelve**.
Nehemiah 7:13 The children of Zattu, ~~eight~~ hundred forty and five.	The children of Zattu, **nine** hundred forty and five.
Nehemiah 7:15 The children of ~~Binnui~~, six hundred forty and ~~eight~~.	The children of **Bani**, six hundred forty and **two**.
Nehemiah 7:16 The children of Bebai, six hundred twenty and ~~eight~~.	The children of Bebai, six hundred twenty and **three**.
Nehemiah 7:17 The children of Azgad, ~~two~~ thousand ~~three~~ hundred twenty and two.	The children of Azgad, **a** thousand **two** hundred twenty and two.

Nehemiah 7:18 The children of Adonikam, six hundred ~~threescore~~ and ~~seven~~.	The children of Adonikam, six hundred **sixty** and **six**.
Nehemiah 7:19 The children of Bigvai, two thousand ~~threescore~~ and ~~seven~~.	The children of Bigvai, two thousand **fifty** and **six**.
Nehemiah 7:20 The children of Adin, ~~six~~ hundred fifty and ~~five~~.	The children of Adin, **four** hundred fifty and **four**.
Nehemiah 7:22 The children of Hashum, ~~three~~ hundred twenty and ~~eight~~.	The children of Hashum, **two** hundred twenty and **three**.
Nehemiah 7:23 The children of Bezai, three hundred twenty and ~~four~~.	The children of Bezai, three hundred twenty and **three**.
Nehemiah 7:24 The children of ~~Hariph~~, an hundred and twelve.	The children of **Jorah**, an hundred and twelve.
Nehemiah 7:32 The men of Beth-el and Ai, ~~an~~ hundred twenty and three.	The men of Beth-el and Ai, **two** hundred twenty and three.
Nehemiah 7:37 The children of Lod, Hadid, and Ono, seven hundred twenty and ~~one~~.	The children of Lod, Hadid, and Ono, seven hundred twenty and **five**.
Nehemiah 7:44 The singers: the children of Asaph, an hundred ~~forty~~ and eight.	The singers **of** the children of Asaph, an hundred **twenty** and eight.
Nehemiah 7:45 The porters: the children of Shallum, the children of Ater, the children of Talmon, the children of Akkub, the children of Hatita, the children of Shobai, an hundred thirty and ~~eight~~.	The porters: the children of Shallum, the children of Ater, the children of Talmon, the children of Akkub, the children of Hatita, the children of Shobai, an hundred thirty and **nine**.
Nehemiah 7:62 The children of Delaiah, the children of Tobiah, the children of Nekoda, six hundred ~~forty~~ and two.	The children of Delaiah, the children of Tobiah, the children of Nekoda, six hundred **fifty** and two.

Nehemiah 10	
Nehemiah 10:29 They clave to their brethren, their nobles, and entered ~~into a curse, and~~ into an oath, ~~to~~ walk in God's law, which was given by Moses the servant of God, and to observe and do all the commandments of the LORD ~~our Lord~~, and his judgments and ~~his~~ statutes;	They clave to their brethren, their nobles, and entered into an oath, **that a curse should come upon them if they did not** walk in God's law, which was given by Moses the servant of God, and to observe and do all the commandments of the Lord **their God**, and his judgments and statutes;
Nehemiah 10:30 And that ~~we~~ would not give ~~our~~ daughters unto the people of the land, nor take ~~their~~ daughters for ~~our~~ sons:	And that **they** would not give **their** daughters unto the people of the land, nor take **the** daughters **of the people** for **their** sons:

Job

Job 1	
King James Version	Joseph Smith Translation
Job 1:6 Now there was a day when the ~~sons~~ of God came to present themselves before the LORD, and Satan came also among them.	Now there was a day when the **children** of God came to present themselves before the Lord, and Satan came also among them.
Job 2	
Job 2:1 AGAIN there was a day when the ~~sons~~ of God came to present themselves before the LORD, and Satan came also among them to present himself before the LORD.	Again there was a day when the **children** of God came to present themselves before the Lord, and Satan came also among them to present himself before the Lord.

Psalms

Psalm 10

King James Version	Joseph Smith Translation
Psalm 10:6 He hath said in his heart, I shall not be moved: ~~for *I shall*~~ never ~~*be*~~ in adversity.	**For** he hath said in his heart, I shall not be moved: never in adversity.
Psalm 10:7 His mouth is full of cursing and deceit and fraud: under his tongue ~~*is*~~ mischief and vanity.	His mouth is full of cursing and deceit and **his heart is full of** fraud: **and** under his tongue, mischief and vanity.
Psalm 10:10 He croucheth, *and* humbleth himself, that the poor may fall by his ~~strong ones~~.	He croucheth, **to the strong ones** and humbleth himself, that the poor may fall by his **devices**.
Psalm 10:13 ~~Wherefore doth~~ the wicked contemn God? he ~~hath said~~ in his heart, Thou wilt not require ~~*it*~~.	The wicked contemn God? **Wherefore** he **doth say** in his heart, Thou wilt not require **iniquity at my hand**.
Psalm 10:14 Thou hast seen ~~*it;*~~ for thou beholdest mischief and spite, to requite ~~*it*~~ with thy hand: the poor committeth himself unto thee; thou art the helper of the fatherless.	**O Lord,** thou hast seen **all this**; for thou beholdest mischief and spite, to requite with thy hand: the poor committeth himself unto thee; thou art the helper of the fatherless.
Psalm 10:15 Break ~~thou~~ the arm of the wicked and the evil ~~*man:*~~ seek out his wickedness ~~*till*~~ thou find none.	**O Lord, thou wilt** break the arm of the wicked and **of** the evil: **and** seek out his wickedness **until** thou find none **that remain**.
Psalm 10:16 The LORD ~~*is*~~ King for ever and ever: the ~~heathen are perished~~ out of his land.	**And** the Lord **shall be** King for ever and ever **over his people**: **for** the **wicked shall perish** out of his land.

Psalm 11

Psalm 11:1 IN ~~the~~ LORD put ~~I~~ my trust: ~~How~~ say ~~ye to my~~ soul, Flee ~~*as a*~~ ~~bird to your~~ mountain?	In **that day thou shalt come, O** Lord **and I will** put my trust **in thee, thou shalt say unto thy people, for my ear hath heard thy voice**: **thou shalt** say **unto every** soul, Flee **unto my** mountain**, and the righteous shall flee like a bird that is let go from the snare of the fowler.**
Psalm 11:2 For, ~~lo~~, the wicked bend *their* bow, they make ready their arrow upon the string, that they may privily shoot at the upright in heart.	For the wicked bend their bow, **lo** they make ready their arrow upon the string, that they may privily shoot at the upright in heart **to destroy their foundation**.
Psalm 11:3 ~~If~~ the foundations be destroyed, what can ~~the righteous~~ do?	**But** the foundations **of the wicked shall** be destroyed, **and** what can **they** do?
Psalm 11:4 The LORD ~~*is in*~~ his holy temple, ~~the LORD's~~ throne *is* in heaven: his eyes behold, his eyelids try, the children of men.	**For** the Lord **when he shall come into** his holy temple, **sitting upon God's** throne in heaven: his eyes **shall pierce the wicked.** Behold, his eyelids **shall** try, the children of men**, and he shall redeem the righteous, and they shall be tried**.
Psalm 11:5 The LORD ~~trieth~~ the righteous: but the wicked and him that loveth violence his soul hateth.	The Lord **loveth** the righteous: but the wicked and him that loveth violence his soul hateth.
Psalm 11:6 Upon the wicked he shall rain snares, fire and brimstone, and an horrible tempest: ~~*this shall be*~~ the portion of their cup.	Upon the wicked he shall rain snares, fire and brimstone, and an horrible tempest: the portion of their cup.

Psalm 12

Psalm 12:1 HELP, LORD; for the godly man ~~ceaseth; for~~ the faithful fail from among the children of men.	**In that day thou shalt** help, **O** Lord, **the poor and the meek of the earth**; for the godly man **shall cease to be**

	found and the faithful fail from among the children of men.
Psalm 12:2 They speak vanity every one with his neighbour: *with* flattering lips ~~*and*~~ with a double heart do they speak.	They **shall** speak vanity every one with his neighbour: with flattering lips, with a double heart do they speak.
Psalm 12:3 The LORD shall cut off all flattering lips, ~~*and*~~ the tongue that speaketh proud things:	**But** the Lord shall cut off all flattering lips, the tongue that speaketh proud things:
Psalm 12:4 Who have said, With our tongue will we prevail; our lips *are* our own: who ~~*is*~~ lord over us?	Who have said, With our tongue will we prevail; our lips are our own: who **shall be** lord over us?
Psalm 12:5 For the oppression of the poor, for the sighing of the needy, ~~now will I arise, saith~~ the LORD; ~~I will set *him*~~ in safety ~~*from him that*~~ puffeth at him.	**Therefore, thus saith the Lord, I will arise in that day, I will stand upon the earth, and I will judge the earth** for the oppression of the poor, for the sighing of the needy; **and their cry hath entered into mine ear, therefore** the Lord **shall sit in judgment, upon all those who say in their hearts, We all sit** in safety **and** puffeth at him.
Psalm 12:6 The words of the LORD ~~*are*~~ pure ~~words: *as*~~ silver tried in a furnace of earth, purified seven times.	**These are** the words of the Lord**, yea** pure **word like** silver tried in a furnace of earth, purified seven times.
Psalm 12:7 Thou shalt ~~keep them~~, O LORD, thou shalt preserve them from ~~this generation~~ for ever.	Thou shalt **save thy people**, O Lord, **thou shalt keep them;** thou shalt preserve them from **the wickedness of these generations** for ever.
Psalm 12:8 The wicked walk on every side, ~~when~~ the vilest men are exalted.	The wicked walk on every side, **and** the vilest men are exalted**; but in the day of their pride thou shalt visit them**.

Psalm 13

Psalm 13:1 *How* long ~~wilt thou forget me~~, O LORD? ~~for ever~~? how long wilt thou hide thy face from me?	How long O Lord**, wilt thou withdraw thyself from me**? how long wilt thou hide thy face from me **that I may not see thee**? **wilt thou forget me, and**

	cast me off from thy presence for ever?
Psalm 13:2 How long shall I take counsel in my soul, ~~*having*~~ ~~sorrow~~ in my heart daily? how long shall mine enemy be exalted over me?	How long shall I take counsel in my soul, **sorrowing** in my heart daily? how long shall mine enemy be exalted over me?
Psalm 13:3 Consider ~~*and*~~ ~~hear~~ me, O LORD my God: lighten mine eyes, lest I sleep the ~~*sleep*~~ ~~of~~ death;	Consider me, O Lord **and hear my cry O** my God: **and** lighten mine eyes, lest I sleep the death **of the ungodly**;
Psalm 13:4 Lest mine enemy say, I have prevailed against him; ~~*and*~~ those that trouble me rejoice when I am moved.	Lest mine enemy say, I have prevailed against him**.** Those that trouble me rejoice when I am moved.

Psalm 14

Psalm 14:1 THE fool hath said in his heart, *There is* no God. They are corrupt, they have done abominable works, ~~*there is*~~ none ~~that~~ doeth good.	The fool hath said in his heart, **There is no man that hath seen God, because he sheweth himself not unto us, therefore** there is no God. **Behold** they are corrupt, they have done abominable works, **and** none **of them** doeth good.
Psalm 14:2 The LORD ~~looked~~ down from heaven upon the children of men, to see if there ~~were~~ any that ~~did~~ understand, ~~*and*~~ ~~seek~~ God.	The Lord **look** down from heaven upon the children of men, **and by his voice said unto his servant, seek ye among the children of men,** to see if there **are** any that **do** understand God.
Psalm 14:3 They are all gone aside, they are ~~*all*~~ together become filthy: ~~*there is*~~ none that ~~doeth~~ good, no, not one.	**And he opened his mouth unto the Lord, and said, behold, all these who say they are thine. The Lord answered and said,** They are all gone aside, they are together become filthy: **Thou canst behold** none **of these** that **are doing** good, no, not one.
Psalm 14:4 Have ~~all the~~ workers of iniquity no knowledge? who eat up my people ~~*as*~~ they eat bread, and call not upon the LORD.	**All they** have **for their teachers are** workers of iniquity **and there is** no knowledge **in them. They are they** who eat up my people, they eat bread, and call not upon the Lord.

Psalm 14:5 ~~There were~~ they in great fear: for God ~~*is*~~ in the generation of the righteous.	They **are** in great fear: for God **dwells** in the generation of the righteous**, he is the counsel of the poor, because they are ashamed of the wicked, and flee unto the Lord for their refuge**.
Psalm 14:6 ~~Ye have shamed~~ the counsel of the poor, because the LORD *is* his refuge.	**They are ashamed of** the counsel of the poor, because the Lord is his refuge.
Psalm 14:7 Oh that the salvation of Israel ~~*were come* out of~~ Zion! when the LORD bringeth back the captivity of his people, Jacob shall rejoice, ~~*and*~~ Israel shall be glad.	Oh that **Zion were established out of heaven,** the salvation of Israel. **O Lord, when wilt thou establish** Zion? When the Lord bringeth back the captivity of his people, Jacob shall rejoice, Israel shall be glad.

Psalm 15

Psalm 15:1 LORD, who shall abide in thy tabernacle? who shall dwell in thy holy hill?	Lord, who shall abide in thy tabernacle? who shall dwell in thy holy hill **of Zion**?
Psalm 15:4 In whose eyes a vile person is contemned; but he honoureth them that fear the LORD. ~~*He that*~~ sweareth to ~~*his own*~~ hurt, and changeth not.	In whose eyes a vile person is contemned; but he honoureth them that fear the Lord; sweareth **not falsely** to hurt **any man**, and changeth not.

Psalm 16

Pslams 16:2 ~~*O my soul,*~~ thou hast said unto ~~the LORD~~, Thou *art* ~~my~~ Lord: my goodness ~~*extendeth* not to~~ thee;	Thou hast said unto **me**, Thou art **the** Lord**, my God**: my goodness **is extended unto** thee;
Psalm 16:3 ~~*But*~~ to the saints that ~~*are*~~ in the earth, and ~~*to*~~ the excellent, in whom *is* all my delight.	**And** to **all** the saints that **dwell** in the earth, and the excellent, in whom is all my delight.
Psalm 16:4 Their sorrows shall be multiplied ~~*that*~~ hasten ~~*after*~~ another *god:* their drink offerings of blood will	**And the wicked, there is no delight in them;** their sorrows shall be multiplied **upon all those who** hasten **for to**

I not ~~offer~~, nor take up their names into my lips.	**seek** another god: their drink offerings of blood will I not **accept**, nor take up their names into my lips.
Psalm 16:5 ~~The~~ LORD ~~*is*~~ the portion of mine inheritance and of my cup: thou maintainest my lot.	**Therefore thou** Lord **art** the portion of mine inheritance and of my cup: thou maintainest my lot.

Psalm 17

Psalm 17:1 ~~HEAR the~~ right, O LORD, attend unto my cry, give ear unto my prayer, ~~*that goeth*~~ not out of feigned lips.	**Give me** right **word**, O Lord, **speak and thy servant shall hear thee;** attend unto my cry, **and** give ear unto my prayer. **I come** not **unto thee** out of feigned lips.
Psalm 17:3 Thou hast proved ~~mine~~ heart; thou hast visited *me* in the night; thou hast tried me, ~~*and*~~ shalt find nothing; I am purposed ~~*that*~~ my mouth shall not transgress.	Thou hast proved **my** heart; thou hast visited me in the night; thou hast tried me, **thou** shalt find nothing **evil in me, for** I am purposed, my mouth shall not transgress.
Psalm 17:4 Concerning the works of men, by the word of thy lips I have kept ~~*me from*~~ the paths of the destroyer.	Concerning the works of men, by the word of thy lips I have kept **out of** the paths of the destroyer.
Psalm 17:6 I have called upon thee, for thou wilt hear me, O God: incline thine ear unto me, ~~*and hear* my speech~~.	I have called upon thee, for thou wilt hear me, O God, **my speech; and** incline thine ear unto me.
Psalm 17:7 Shew thy marvellous lovingkindness, O thou that savest ~~by thy right hand~~ them which put their trust *in thee* from those that rise up ~~*against them*~~.	Shew thy marvellous lovingkindness, O thou that savest them which put their trust in thee. **By thy right hand,** from those that rise up.
Psalm 17:12 Like as a lion ~~*that*~~ is greedy of his prey, and as it were a young lion lurking in secret places.	Like as a lion is greedy of his prey, and as it were a young lion lurking in secret places.
Psalm 17:13 Arise, O LORD, disappoint him, cast him down: deliver my soul from the wicked, ~~*which is*~~ thy sword:	Arise, O Lord, disappoint him, cast him down: deliver my soul from the wicked, **by** thy sword:

<table>
<tr><td>Psalm 17:14 From men <s>which are</s> thy hand, O LORD, from men of the world, <s>which have</s> their portion in <s>this</s> life, and whose belly thou fillest with thy <s>hid treasure</s>: they are full of children, and leave the rest of their <s>substance</s> to their babes.</td><td>From men by thy strong hand, yea O Lord, from men of the world, for their portion is in their life, and whose belly thou fillest with thy good things: they are full of children, and they die and leave the rest of their inheritance to their babes.</td></tr>
<tr><td colspan="2">Psalm 18</td></tr>
<tr><td>Psalm 18:3 I will call upon the LORD, <s>who</s> is worthy to be praised: so shall I be saved from mine enemies.</td><td>I will call upon the Lord, for he is worthy to be praised: so shall I be saved from mine enemies.</td></tr>
<tr><td>Psalm 18:30 <s>As for</s> God, <s>his way is</s> perfect: the word of the LORD is tried: <s>he</s> is a buckler to all those <s>that</s> trust in him.</td><td>O God, thy ways are perfect: the word of the Lord is tried: is a buckler to all those who trust in him.</td></tr>
<tr><td>Psalm 18:32 <s>It is</s> God that girdeth me with strength, and maketh my way perfect.</td><td>Our God that girdeth me with strength, and maketh my way perfect.</td></tr>
<tr><td>Psalm 18:41 They cried, but <s>there was</s> none to save <s>them: even</s> unto the LORD, but he answered them not.</td><td>They cried, but found none to save; unto the Lord, but he answered them not.</td></tr>
<tr><td colspan="2">Psalm 19</td></tr>
<tr><td>Psalm 19:3 <s>There is</s> no speech nor language, <s>where</s> their voice is not heard.</td><td>No speech nor language can be, if their voice is not heard.</td></tr>
<tr><td>Psalm 19:13 Keep back thy servant also from presumptuous <s>sins</s>; let them not have dominion over me: then shall I be upright, and I shall be innocent from the great transgression.</td><td>Keep back thy servant also from presumptuous acts; let them not have dominion over me: then shall I be upright, and I shall be innocent from the great transgression.</td></tr>
</table>

Psalm 22	
Psalm 22:1 MY God, ~~my God,~~ why hast thou forsaken me? ~~*why art thou so* far from helping me, *and from*~~ the words of my roaring?	My God, why hast thou forsaken me? **My God, hear** the words of my roaring**; thou are far from helping me.**
Psalm 22:2 O my God, I cry in the daytime, but thou ~~hearest~~ not; and in the night season, and am not silent.	O my God, I cry in the daytime, but thou **answerest** not; and in the night season, and am not silent.
Psalm 22:3 But thou *art* holy, ~~*O thou*~~ that inhabitest the praises of Israel.	But thou art holy, that inhabitest **the heavens; thou art worthy of** the praises of Israel.
Psalm 22:6 But I ~~*am*~~ a worm, and no man; a reproach of men, and despised of the people.	But I**,** a worm, and **loved of** no man; a reproach of men, and despised of the people.
Psalm 22:10 I was cast upon thee from the womb: thou ~~*art*~~ my God from my mother's ~~belly~~.	I was cast upon thee from the womb: thou **wast** my God from my mother's **breasts**.
Psalm 22:12 Many ~~bulls~~ have compassed me: strong ~~*bulls*~~ of Bashan have beset me ~~round~~.	Many **armies** have compassed me: strong **armies** of Bashan have beset me **around**.
Psalm 22:13 They gaped upon me *with* their ~~mouths~~, ~~*as*~~ a ravening and a roaring lion.	They gaped upon me with their **mouth**, **like** a[1] ravening and a roaring lion.
Psalm 22:21 Save me from the lion's mouth: for thou hast heard me from the horns of the unicorns.	Save me from the lion's mouth: for thou hast heard me **speak** from **the secret places of the wilderness, through** the horns of the unicorns.
Psalm 22:31 They shall come, and shall declare his righteousness unto a people that shall be born, ~~that~~ he hath done ~~*this*~~.	They shall come, and shall declare his righteousness unto a people that shall be born, that he hath done **what** he hath done.

1. The word "a" is missing in OT2.

Psalm 24

Psalm 24:7 Lift up your heads, O ye ~~gates~~; and be ye ~~lift~~ up, ~~ye everlasting doors; and the King of glory shall come in~~.	Lift up your heads, O ye **generations of Jacob**; and be ye **lifted** up.
Psalm 24:8 ~~Who *is* this King of glory~~? The Lord strong and mighty, the Lord mighty in battle.	**And** the Lord strong and mighty, the Lord mighty in battle, **who is the king of glory, shall establish you forever. And he will roll away the heavens; and will come down to redeem his people; to make you an everlasting name; to establish you upon his everlasting rock**.
Psalm 24:9 Lift up your heads, O ye ~~gates~~; ~~even~~ lift *them* up, ye everlasting ~~doors~~; and the King of glory shall come ~~in~~.	Lift up your heads, O ye **generations of Jacob**; lift up **your heads**, ye everlasting **generations**; and **the Lord of Hosts, the King of Kings; even** the King of glory shall come **unto you; and shall redeem his people, and shall establish them in righteousness**.
Psalm 24:10 ~~Who is this King of glory? The Lord of hosts, he *is* the King of glory.~~ Selah.	Selah.

Psalm 27

Psalm 27:3 Though an host should encamp against me, my heart shall not fear: though war should rise against me, in this ~~*will*~~ I ~~*be*~~ confident.	Though an host should encamp against me, my heart shall not fear: though war should rise against me, in this I **am** confident.
Psalm 27:13 ~~*I had fainted,* unless I had believed to see the goodness of the Lord in the land of the living.~~	**Thou wouldest deliver my soul into hell, thou didst say unto me,**

Psalm 30

Psalm 30:5 For his anger ~~*endureth but*~~ a moment; in his favour ~~*is*~~ life: weeping may endure for a night, but joy *cometh* in the morning.	For his anger **kindleth against the wicked; they repent, and in** a moment **it is turned away, and they are** in his favour**, and he giveth them** life: **Therefore,** weeping may endure for a night, but joy cometh in the morning.
Psalm 30:9 ~~What profit *is there* in my blood~~, when I go down to the pit? ~~Shall~~ the dust praise thee? shall ~~it~~ declare thy truth?	When I go down to the pit**, my blood shall return to** the dust**. I will** praise thee; **my soul** shall declare thy truth **for what profit am I, if I do it not**?
Psalm 30:12 To the end that *my* glory ~~may~~ sing praise to thee, and not be silent. O LORD my God, I will give thanks unto thee for ever.	To the end that my **soul may give** glory **to thy name, and** sing praise to thee, and not be silent. O Lord my God, I will give thanks unto thee for ever.

Psalm 32

Psalm 32:1 BLESSED ~~*is he*~~ *whose* ~~transgression *is*~~ forgiven, ~~*whose* sin *is*~~ covered.	Blessed **are they** whose **transgressions are** forgiven, **and who have no sins to be** covered.
Psalm 32:3 When I kept silence, my bones waxed old through my ~~roaring~~ all the day long.	When I kept silence, **my spirit failed within me. When I opened my mouth,** my bones waxed old through my **speaking** all the day long.
Psalm 32:4 For day and night thy ~~hand~~ was heavy upon me: my moisture is turned into the drought of summer. Selah.	For day and night thy **spirit** was heavy upon me: my moisture is turned into the drought of summer. Selah.
Psalm 32:8 I will instruct thee and teach thee in the way which thou shalt go: I will guide thee with mine eye.	**Thou has said,** I will instruct thee and teach thee in the way which thou shalt go: I will guide thee with mine eye.

Psalm 33

Psalm 33:1 REJOICE in the LORD, O ye righteous: ~~*for*~~ praise is comely for the upright.	Rejoice in the Lord, O ye righteous: **to** praise **the Lord** is comely for the upright **in heart**.
Psalm 33:2 Praise the LORD with ~~harp~~: sing unto him with the psaltery *and* an instrument ~~of~~ ten strings.	Praise the Lord with **thy voice**: sing unto him with the psaltery and **harp,** an instrument **with** ten strings.
Psalm 33:4 For the word of the LORD is ~~right~~; and all his works *are done* in truth.	For the word of the Lord is **given to the upright**; and all his works are done in truth.
Psalm 33:9 For he spake, and it was ~~*done*~~; he commanded, and it stood fast.	For he spake, and it was **finished**; he commanded, and it stood fast.
Psalm 33:12 Blessed *is* the ~~nation whose God *is* the LORD~~; *and* the people *whom* ~~he~~ hath chosen for his own inheritance.	Blessed **are** the **nations,** and the people whom **the Lord God** hath chosen for his own inheritance.
Psalm 33:19 To deliver their soul from death, and to keep them alive in famine.	To deliver their soul from death, and to keep them alive in **a time of** famine.

Psalm 35

Psalm 35:12 They rewarded me evil for good *to* the spoiling ~~of~~ my soul.	They rewarded me evil for good **for the purpose of** the spoiling my soul.

Psalm 36

Psalm 36:1 THE transgression ~~of the wicked~~ saith ~~within my heart~~, *that there is* no fear of God before ~~his~~ eyes.	The **wicked, who live in** transgression, saith **in their hearts, There is no condemnation; for** there is no fear of God before **their** eyes.
Psalm 36:2 For ~~he flattereth himself~~ in ~~his~~ own eyes, until ~~his iniquity be~~ found to be hateful.	For **they flatter themselves** in **their** own eyes, until **their iniquities are** found to be hateful.

Psalm 36:3 The words of ~~his~~ mouth *are* iniquity and deceit: ~~he~~ hath left off to be wise, *and* to do good.	The words of **their** mouth are **full of** iniquity and deceit: **the wicked man** hath left off to be wise, and to do good.
Psalm 36:4 He deviseth mischief upon his bed; he setteth himself in a way *that is* not good; ~~he abhorreth not evil~~.	He deviseth mischief upon his bed; he setteth himself in a way that is not good.
Psalm 36:5 ~~Thy mercy~~, O LORD, *is* in the heavens; *and* ~~thy faithfulness *reacheth*~~ unto the clouds.	O Lord, **thou art** in the heavens; **they are full of thy mercy.** And **the thoughts of a righteous man ascendeth up** unto **thee, whose throne is far above** the clouds.
Psalm 36:6 Thy righteousness *is* like the great mountains; thy ~~judgments *are*~~ a great deep: O LORD, thou preservest man and beast.	**He is filled with** thy righteousness like the great mountains; **and with** thy **judgment like** a great deep: O Lord, thou preservest man and beast.
Psalm 36:12 ~~There~~ are the workers of iniquity ~~fallen~~: they ~~are~~ cast down, and shall not be able to rise.	**They** are the workers of iniquity**, and shall fall**: they **shall be** cast down, and shall not be able to rise.

Psalm 37

Psalm 37:38 But the transgressors shall be destroyed together: the end of the wicked shall be cut off.	But the transgressors shall be destroyed together: the end of the wicked **shall come, and they** shall be cut off.

Psalm 38

Psalm 38:7 For my loins are filled with a loathsome ~~*disease:*~~ and ~~*there is*~~ no soundness in my flesh.	For my loins are filled with a loathsome **distress**: and no soundness **is found** in my flesh.
Psalm 38:8 I am feeble and ~~sore~~ broken: I have ~~roared~~ by reason of the disquietness of my heart.	I am feeble and broken**, and very sore**: I have **wept** by reason of the disquietness of my heart.
Psalm 38:11 My lovers and my friends stand aloof ~~from~~ my sore; and my kinsmen stand afar off.	My lovers and my friends stand aloof **because of** my sore; and my kinsmen stand afar off.

Psalm 39

Psalm 39:9 I was dumb, ~~I~~ opened not my mouth; because thou didst ~~*it*~~.	I was dumb, **and** opened not my mouth; because thou didst **chasten me**.
Psalm 39:10 Remove thy stroke away from me: I ~~am~~ consumed by the blow of ~~thine~~ hand.	Remove thy stroke away from me: **or** I **shall be** consumed by the blow of **thy** hand.

Psalm 41

Psalm 41:3 The LORD will strengthen him upon the bed of languishing: thou wilt make all his bed ~~in his~~ sickness.	The Lord will strengthen him upon the bed of languishing: thou wilt make all his **pains to cease, when he is laid in his** bed **of** sickness.

Psalm 42

Psalm 42:2 My soul thirsteth for God, for the living God: when shall I come and appear before God?	My soul thirsteth for **to see** God, for **to see** the living God: when shall I come and appear before **thee, O** God?
Psalm 42:3 My tears have been ~~my meat~~ day and night, while ~~they~~ continually say unto me, Where *is* thy God?	My tears have been **poured out unto thee** day and night, while **mine enemies** continually say unto me, Where is thy God?
Psalm 42:4 When I remember these ~~*things*~~, I pour out my soul ~~in me~~: for I had gone with the multitude, I went with them to the house of God, with the voice of joy and praise, with ~~a~~ multitude that kept holyday.	When I remember these **mine enemies**, I pour out my soul **unto thee**: for I had gone with the multitude, I **also** went with them to the house of God, with the voice of joy and praise, with **the** multitude that kept holyday.

Psalm 46

Psalm 46:1 GOD *is* our refuge and strength, a ~~very~~ present help in trouble.	God is our refuge and strength, a present help in trouble.

Psalm 46:2 Therefore will not ~~we~~ fear, though the earth be removed, and though the mountains be carried into the midst of the sea;	Therefore **we** will not fear, though the earth **shall** be removed, and though the mountains **shall** be carried into the midst of the sea;
Psalm 46:3 ~~*Though*~~ the ~~waters~~ thereof roar ~~*and* be~~ troubled, ~~*though*~~ the mountains shake with the swelling thereof. ~~Selah.~~	**And** the **water** thereof roar**, being** troubled, **and** the mountains shake with the swelling thereof.
Psalm 46:4 *There* ~~*is*~~ a river, the ~~streams~~ whereof shall make glad the city of God, the holy ~~*place*~~ of the ~~tabernacles~~ of the most High.	**Yet** there **shall be** a river, the **stream** whereof shall make glad the city of God, the holy of the **tabernacle** of the most High.
Psalm 46:5 God ~~*is*~~ in the midst of her; she shall not be moved: God shall help her, ~~*and that*~~ right early.	**For Zion shall come, and** God **shall be** in the midst of her; she shall not be moved: God shall help her right early.
Psalm 46:6 The heathen ~~raged, the~~ kingdoms ~~were~~ moved: ~~he uttered~~ his voice, the earth melted.	The heathen **shall be enraged**, **and their** kingdoms **shall be** moved: **and the Lord shall utter** his voice, **and** the earth **shall be** melted.
Psalm 46:7 The Lord of hosts ~~*is*~~ with us; the God of Jacob ~~*is*~~ our refuge. Selah.	The Lord of hosts**, who shall be** with us; the God of Jacob our refuge. Selah.
Psalm 46:8 Come, behold the works of the Lord, what desolations he ~~hath made~~ in the earth.	Come, behold the works of the Lord, what desolations he **shall make** in the earth **in the latter days**.
Psalm 46:10 Be still, and know that I *am* God: I will be exalted among the heathen, I will be exalted in the earth.	**And saith unto the nations,** Be still, and know that I am God: I will be exalted among the heathen, I will be exalted in the earth.
Psalm 46:11 The Lord of hosts ~~*is*~~ with us; the God of Jacob ~~*is*~~ our refuge. ~~Selah~~.	The Lord of hosts **shall be** with us; the God of Jacob our refuge.

Psalm 49

Psalm 49:7 None ~~*of them*~~ can by any means redeem his brother, nor give to God a ransom for him:	None can by any means redeem his brother, nor give to God a ransom for him:

Psalm 49:8 (~~For the redemption of their soul *is* precious, and it ceaseth for ever~~:)	**Verse omitted**
Psalm 49:9 That he should still live for ever, ~~*and*~~ not see corruption.	That he should still live for ever, **that it ceaseth** not **forever to** see corruption. **For the redemption of their souls are through God, and precious.**
Psalm 49:10 For he seeth ~~*that*~~ wise men die, likewise the fool and the brutish person perish, and leave their wealth to others.	For he seeth wise men die, likewise the fool and the brutish person perish, and leave their wealth to others.
Psalm 49:11 Their inward thought ~~*is, that*~~ their houses ~~*shall continue*~~ for ever, ~~*and*~~ their dwelling places to all generations; ~~they call *their*~~ lands after their own names.	Their inward thought **of** their houses for ever, their dwelling places to all generations; lands **they called** after their own names**, and they are honorable**.
Psalm 49:12 Nevertheless man ~~*being*~~ in honour abideth not: he is like the beasts *that* perish.	Nevertheless man in honour abideth not: he is **also** like the beasts that perish.
Psalm 49:13 This their way ~~*is*~~ their folly: yet their posterity approve their sayings. Selah.	This **I speak of them who walk in** their way, **and forsaketh the Almighty in** their folly: yet their posterity approve their sayings. Selah.
Psalm 50	
Psalm 50:21 These *things* hast thou done, and I kept silence; thou thoughtest that I was altogether ~~*such an one*~~ as thyself: ~~*but*~~ I will reprove thee, and set ~~*them*~~ in order before thine eyes.	These things hast thou done, and I kept silence; thou thoughtest that I was altogether as thyself: I will reprove thee, and set **covenants** in order before thine eyes.
Psalm 50:22 Now consider this, ye that forget God, lest I tear *you* in pieces, and ~~*there be*~~ none ~~to~~ deliver.	Now consider this, ye that forget God, lest I tear you in pieces, and none **can** deliver.

Psalm 52

Psalm 52:7 Lo, ~~*this is*~~ the man ~~*that*~~ made not God his strength; but trusted in the abundance of his riches, *and* strengthened himself in his wickedness.	Lo, the man **who** made not God his strength; but trusted in the abundance of his riches, and strengthened himself in his wickedness.
Psalm 52:9 I will praise thee for ever, because thou hast done ~~*it*: and~~ I will wait on thy name; for ~~*it is*~~ good before thy saints.	I will praise thee for ever, because thou hast done **wonderful work.** I will wait on thy name; for **thou art** good before thy saints.

Psalm 53

Psalm 53:1 THE fool hath said in his heart, *There is* no God. Corrupt ~~are~~ they, ~~and~~ have done abominable iniquity: *there* ~~*is*~~ none that doeth good.	The fool hath said in his heart, There is no God. **Such are** corrupt**, and** they have done abominable iniquity: there **are** none that doeth good.
Psalm 53:3 Every one of them is gone back: they are altogether become filthy; ~~*there is* none that doeth good, no, not one~~.	Every one of them is gone back: they are altogether become filthy;
Psalm 53:4 ~~Have~~ the workers of iniquity no knowledge? ~~who~~ eat up my people *as* they eat bread: they have not called upon God.	The workers of iniquity **have** no knowledge; **they** eat up my people as they eat bread: they have not called upon God. **There is none that doeth good, no not one.**
Psalm 53:5 ~~There were~~ they in great fear, ~~*where* no fear was~~: for God hath scattered the bones of him that encampeth *against* ~~thee~~: thou hast put ~~*them*~~ to shame, because ~~God~~ hath despised them.	They **were** in great fear, for God hath scattered the bones of him that encampeth against **him. O Lord,** thou hast put to shame **those who have said in their hearts, there was no fear**, because **thou** hath despised them.
Psalm 53:6 Oh that the salvation of Israel ~~*were come*~~ out of Zion! When God bringeth back the captivity of his people, Jacob shall rejoice, ~~*and*~~ Israel shall be glad.	Oh that **Zion were come,** the salvation of Israel, **for** out of Zion **shall they be judged**, when God bringeth back the captivity of his people, **and** Jacob shall rejoice, Israel shall be glad.

Psalm 55

Psalm 55:6 And I said, Oh that I had wings like a dove! *for then* would ~~I~~ fly away, and be at rest.	And I said, Oh that I had wings like a dove! for then **I** would fly away, and be at rest.
Psalm 55:12 For *it was* not an enemy *that* reproached me; ~~then I could have borne *it:*~~ neither ~~*was it*~~ he that hated me *that* did magnify *himself* against me; then I would have hid myself from him:	For it was not an enemy that reproached me; neither he that hated me that did magnify himself against me; **if so** then **I could have born it:** I would have hid myself from him:
Psalm 55:13 But *it was* ~~thou~~, a man mine equal, my guide, and mine acquaintance.	But it was a man **of** mine equal, my guide, and mine acquaintance.
Psalm 55:20 ~~He hath~~ put forth ~~his hands~~ against such as be at peace with ~~him~~: ~~he hath~~ broken ~~his~~ covenant.	**They have** put forth **their hand** against such as be at peace with **them**: **they have** broken **the Lord's** covenant.
Psalm 55:21 *The words* of ~~his~~ mouth were smoother than butter, but war *was* in ~~his~~ heart: ~~his~~ words were softer than oil, yet ~~*were*~~ they drawn swords.	The words of **their** mouth were smoother than butter, but war was in **their** heart: **their** words were softer than oil, yet they **have** drawn swords.

Psalm 56

Psalm 56:3 What ~~time I~~ am afraid, I will trust in thee.	What**!** am **I** afraid, I will trust in thee.

Psalm 82

Psalm 82:2 How long will ye judge unjustly, and accept the persons of the wicked? Selah.	How long will ye **suffer them to** judge unjustly, and accept the persons of the wicked? Selah.

Psalm 90

Psalm 90:13 Return, O LORD, how long? and let ~~it~~ repent ~~thee~~ concerning ~~thy servants~~.	Return **us**, O Lord, how long **wilt thou hide thy face from they servants**? and let **them** repent **of all their hard speeches thy have spoken** concerning **thee**.

Psalm 102

Psalm 102:18 This shall be written for the generation to come: and the people which shall be ~~created~~ shall praise the LORD.	This shall be written for the generation to come: and the people which shall be **gathered** shall praise the Lord.

Psalm 104

Psalm 104:26 There go the ships: ~~*there is* that leviathan, *whom*~~ thou hast made to play therein.	There go the ships: **and** thou hast made **leviathan** to play therein.

Psalm 105

Psalm 105:42 For he remembered his holy promise, ~~*and*~~ Abraham his servant.	For he remembered his holy promise **unto** Abraham his servant.

Psalm 106

Psalm 106:4 Remember me, O LORD, with the favour ~~*that thou bearest unto*~~ thy people: O visit me with thy salvation;	Remember me, O Lord, with the favour **of** thy people: O visit me with thy salvation;

Psalm 106:7 Our fathers understood not thy wonders in Egypt; they remembered not the multitude of thy mercies; but provoked ~~*him*~~ at the sea, ~~*even*~~ at the Red sea.	Our fathers understood not thy wonders in Egypt; they remembered not the multitude of thy mercies; but provoked **thee** at the sea, at the Red sea.
Psalm 106:45 And he remembered for them his covenant, and ~~repented~~ according to the multitude of his mercies.	And he remembered for them his covenant, and **spared his people** according to the multitude of his mercies.

Psalm 109

Psalm 109:3 They compassed me about also with words of hatred; and fought against me without a cause.	They compassed me about**; they spake against me** also with words of hatred; and fought against me without a cause.
Psalm 109:4 ~~For~~ my love they are my adversaries: ~~but~~ I ~~*give myself unto*~~ prayer.	**And notwithstanding** my love they are my adversaries: **yet** I **will continue in** prayer **for them**.
Psalm 109:6 Set thou a wicked man over ~~him~~: and let Satan stand at his right hand.	Set thou a wicked man over **them**: and let Satan stand at his right hand.
Psalm 109:7 When ~~he~~ shall be judged, let him be condemned: and let ~~his~~ prayer become sin.	When **they** shall be judged, let **them** be condemned: and let **their** prayer become sin.
Psalm 109:8 Let ~~his~~ days be few; ~~*and*~~ let another take ~~his~~ office.	Let **their** days be few; let another take **their** office.
Psalm 109:9 Let ~~his~~ children be fatherless, and ~~his wife a widow~~.	Let **their** children be fatherless, and **their wives widows**.
Psalm 109:10 Let ~~his~~ children be continually vagabonds, and beg: let them seek ~~*their bread*~~ also out of their desolate places.	Let **their** children be continually vagabonds, and beg: let them seek also out of their desolate places.
Psalm 109:11 Let the extortioner catch all that ~~he hath~~; and let the ~~strangers~~ spoil ~~his~~ labour.	Let the extortioner catch all that **they have**; and let the **stranger** spoil **their** labour.
Psalm 109:12 Let there be none to extend mercy unto ~~him~~: neither let there be any to favour ~~his~~ fatherless children.	Let there be none to extend mercy unto **them**: neither let there be any to favour **their** fatherless children.

Psalm 109:13 Let ~~his~~ posterity be cut off; ~~*and*~~ in the generation following let their ~~name~~ be blotted out.	Let **their** posterity be cut off; in the generation following**, O** let their **names** be blotted out.
Psalm 109:14 Let the iniquity of ~~his~~ fathers be remembered ~~with~~ the LORD; and let not the sin of ~~his mother~~ be blotted out.	Let the iniquity of **their** fathers be remembered **before** the Lord; and let not the sin of **their mothers** be blotted out.
Psalm 109:16 Because ~~that he~~ remembered not to shew mercy, but persecuted the poor and needy man, that ~~he~~ might even slay the broken in heart.	Because **they** remembered not to shew mercy, but persecuted the poor and needy man, that **they** might even slay the broken in heart.
Psalm 109:17 As ~~he~~ loved cursing, so let it come ~~unto him~~: as ~~he~~ delighted not in blessing, so let it be far from ~~him~~.	As **they** loved cursing, so let it come **upon them**: as **they** delighted not in blessing, so let it be far from **them**.
Psalm 109:18 As ~~he~~ clothed ~~himself~~ with cursing like as with ~~his garment~~, so let it come into ~~his~~ bowels like water, and like oil into ~~his~~ bones.	As **they** clothed **themselves** with cursing like as with **their garments**, so let it come into **their** bowels like water, and like oil into **their** bones.
Psalm 109:19 Let it be unto ~~him~~ as ~~the~~ garment ~~*which*~~ covereth ~~him~~, and for a girdle wherewith ~~he is~~ girded continually.	Let it be unto **them** as **a** garment covereth **them**, and for a girdle wherewith **they are** girded continually.
Psalm 109:20 ~~*Let*~~ this *be* the reward of mine adversaries from the LORD, and of them ~~that~~ speak evil against my soul.	This **shall** be the reward of mine adversaries from the Lord, and of them **who** speak evil against my soul.
Psalm 109:21 But do thou ~~for~~ me, O GOD ~~the Lord~~, for thy name's sake: because thy mercy *is* good, deliver thou me.	But do thou **deliver** me, O **Lord, my** God, for thy name's sake: because thy mercy is good, **therefore** deliver thou me.

Psalm 110

Psalm 110:6 He shall judge among the heathen, he shall fill ~~*the places*~~ with ~~the~~ dead bodies; he shall wound the heads over many countries.	He shall judge among the heathen, he shall fill **these streets** with **their** dead bodies; he shall wound the heads over many countries.

Psalm 112

Psalm 112:1 PRAISE ye the LORD. Blessed *is* the man ~~*that*~~ feareth the LORD, ~~*that*~~ delighteth greatly in his commandments.	Praise ye the Lord. Blessed is the man **who** feareth the Lord, **and** delighteth greatly in his commandments.
Psalm 112:8 His heart *is* established, he shall not be afraid, until he see ~~*his desire*~~ upon his enemies.	His heart is established, he shall not be afraid, until he see **judgment executed** upon his enemies.

Psalm 115

Psalm 115:1 NOT unto us, O LORD, not unto us, but unto thy name ~~give~~ glory, for thy mercy, ~~*and*~~ for thy truth's sake.	Not unto us, O Lord, not unto us, but unto thy name **be** glory, for thy mercy **be** for thy truth's sake.
Psalm 115:9 O Israel, trust thou in the LORD: he *is* ~~their~~ help and ~~their~~ shield.	O Israel, trust thou in the Lord: he is **thy** help and **thy** shield.
Psalm 115:10 O house of Aaron, trust in the LORD: he *is* ~~their~~ help and ~~their~~ shield.	O house of Aaron, trust in the Lord: he is **thy** help and **thy** shield.
Psalm 115:11 Ye that fear the LORD, trust in the LORD: he *is* ~~their~~ help and ~~their~~ shield.	Ye that fear the Lord, trust in the Lord: he is **your** help and **your** shield.

Psalm 119

Psalm 119:15 I will meditate ~~in~~ thy precepts, and have respect unto thy ways.	I will meditate **upon** thy precepts, and have respect unto thy ways.
Psalm 119:20 My ~~soul~~ breaketh for ~~the longing *that it hath* unto~~ thy ~~judgments~~ at all times.	My **heart** breaketh for **my soul longeth after** thy **judgment** at all times.
Psalm 119:21 Thou hast rebuked the proud ~~*that*~~ *are* cursed, which do err from thy commandments.	Thou hast rebuked the proud**, they** are cursed, which do err from thy commandments.

Psalm 119:33 Teach me, O LORD, the way of thy statutes; and I shall keep it ~~*unto*~~ the end.	Teach me, O Lord, the way of thy statutes; and I shall keep it **to** the end.
Psalm 119:48 My hands also will I lift up unto thy commandments, which I have loved; and I will meditate ~~in~~ thy statutes.	My hands also will I lift up unto thy commandments, which I have loved; and I will meditate **upon** thy statutes.
Psalm 119:78 Let the proud be ashamed; for they dealt perversely with me without a cause: *but* I will meditate ~~in~~ thy precepts.	Let the proud be ashamed; for they dealt perversely with me without a cause: but I will meditate **upon** thy precepts.
Psalm 119:109 My soul *is* continually in ~~my~~ hand: ~~yet do~~ I not forget thy law.	My soul is continually in **thy** hand: **and** I **do** not forget thy law.
Psalm 119:126 ~~*It is*~~ time ~~for *thee,*~~ LORD, to work: *for* they have made void thy law.	**And the** time, **O** Lord, **for me** to work: for they have made void thy law.
Psalm 119:130 The entrance of thy words giveth light; ~~it giveth~~ understanding unto the simple.	The entrance of thy words giveth light; **they give** understanding unto the simple.

Psalm 121

Psalm 121:3 ~~He will not suffer thy foot to be moved: he that keepeth thee will not slumber~~.	**Behold, he that keepeth Israel shall neither slumber nor sleep.**
Psalm 121:4 Behold, he that keepeth Israel shall neither slumber nor sleep.	**He will not suffer thy foot to be moved: he that keepeth thee will not slumber**.

Psalm 124

Psalm 124:1 ~~If *it had* not *been* the LORD who was on our side~~, now may Israel say;	Now may Israel say;

Psalm 124:2 If ~~*it had* not *been*~~ the LORD ~~who~~ was on our side, when men rose up against us:	If the Lord was **not** on our side, when men rose up against us:

Psalm 125

Psalm 125:1 THEY that trust in the LORD ~~*shall be* as~~ mount Zion, ~~*which*~~ cannot be removed, *but* abideth for ever.	They that trust in the Lord **in** mount Zion, cannot be removed, but abideth for ever.
Psalm 125:4 Do good, O LORD, unto ~~*those that be*~~ good, and ~~to *them that are*~~ upright in their hearts.	Do good, O Lord, unto **the** good, and **unto the** upright in their hearts.

Psalm 135

Psalm 135:14 For the LORD will judge his people, and he will repent himself concerning his servants.	For the Lord will judge his people, and he will **not** repent himself concerning his servants.[2]
Psalm 135:21 Blessed be the LORD out of Zion, ~~which dwelleth at~~ Jerusalem. Praise ye the LORD.	Blessed be the Lord out of Zion, **blessed be the Lord out of** Jerusalem. Praise ye the Lord.

Psalm 137

Psalm 137:5 If I forget thee, O Jerusalem, let my right hand forget ~~*her*~~ *cunning*.	If I forget thee, O Jerusalem, let my right hand forget **its** cunning.

2. The Prophet did not note where "not" should appear in the verse.

Psalm 138	
Psalm 138:8 The LORD will perfect ~~*that which* concerneth~~ me: ~~thy mercy~~, O LORD, ~~*endureth*~~ for ever: forsake ~~not~~ the works of thine own hands.	The Lord will perfect me **in knowledge, concerning his kingdom. I will praise thee**, O Lord, for ever: **for thou art merciful, and wilt not** forsake the works of thine own hands.

Psalm 139	
Psalm 139:16 Thine eyes did see my substance, yet being unperfect; and in thy book all ~~*my members*~~ were written, *which* in continuance were fashioned, when *as yet* ~~*there was*~~ none of them.	Thine eyes did see my substance, yet being unperfect; and in thy book all I knew were written, which in continuance were fashioned, when as yet **I knew** none of them.

Psalm 141	
Psalm 141:5 ~~Let~~ the righteous smite me; *it* ~~*shall be*~~ a kindness: and ~~let him~~ reprove me; *it shall be* an excellent oil, ~~*which*~~ shall not ~~break~~ my ~~head~~: for yet my prayer also *shall be* in their calamities.	**When** the righteous smite me **with the word of the Lord,** it **is** a kindness: and **when they** reprove me; it shall be an excellent oil, **and** shall not **destroy** my **faith,** for yet my prayer also shall be **for them. I delight not** in their calamities.

Psalm 146	
Psalm 146:8 The LORD openeth *the eyes of* the blind: the LORD raiseth them ~~that are~~ bowed down: the LORD loveth the righteous:	The Lord openeth the eyes of the blind: the Lord raiseth **the** bowed down: the Lord loveth the righteous:

Proverbs

Proverbs 16	
King James Version	Joseph Smith Translation
Proverbs 16:29 A violent man enticeth his neighbour, and leadeth him into ~~the~~ way *that is* not good.	A violent man enticeth his neighbour, and leadeth him into **a** way that is not good.
Proverbs 18	
Proverbs 18:22 *Whoso* findeth a wife ~~findeth a good *thing*, and obtaineth~~ favour of the LORD.	Whoso findeth a **good** wife, **hath obtained** favour of the Lord.
Proverbs 22	
Proverbs 22:12 The eyes of the LORD preserve knowledge, ~~and~~ he overthroweth the words of the transgressor.	**For** the eyes of the Lord preserve knowledge, **but** he overthroweth the words of the transgressor.

Isaiah

Isaiah 2	
King James Version	Joseph Smith Translation
Isaiah 2:2 And it shall come to pass in the last days, ~~*that*~~ the mountain of the Lord's house shall be established in the top of the mountains, and shall be exalted above the hills; and all nations shall flow unto it.	And it shall come to pass in the last days, **when** the mountain of the Lord's house shall be established in the top of the mountains, and shall be exalted above the hills; and all nations shall flow unto it.
Isaiah 2:5 O house of Jacob, come ye, and let us walk in the light of the Lord.	O house of Jacob, come ye, and let us walk in the light of the Lord**, yea, come for ye have all gone astray, every one to his wicked ways**.
Isaiah 2:6 Therefore thou hast forsaken thy people the house of Jacob, because they be replenished from the east, and ~~*are*~~ soothsayers like the Philistines, and they please themselves in the children of strangers.	Therefore, **O Lord,** thou hast forsaken thy people the house of Jacob, because they be replenished from the east, and **hearken unto** soothsayers like the Philistines, and they please themselves in the children of strangers.
Isaiah 2:9 And the mean man boweth down, and the great man humbleth himself: therefore forgive ~~them~~ not.	And the mean man boweth down, and the great man humbleth himself **not**: therefore forgive **him** not.
Isaiah 2:10 Enter into the rock, and hide thee in the dust, for fear of the Lord, and ~~for the glory of~~ his majesty.	**O ye wicked ones,** enter into the rock, and hide thee in the dust, for **the** fear of the Lord, and his majesty **shall smite thee**.
Isaiah 2:11 The lofty looks of man shall be humbled, and the haughtiness of ~~men~~ shall be bowed down, and the Lord alone shall be exalted in that day.	**And it shall come to pass that** the lofty looks of man shall be humbled, and the haughtiness of **man** shall be bowed down, and the Lord alone shall be exalted in that day.

Isaiah 2:12 For the day of the Lord of hosts ~~*shall be*~~ upon every *one* ~~*that is*~~ proud and lofty, and upon every *one* ~~*that*~~ *is* lifted up; and he shall be brought low:	For the day of the Lord of hosts **soon cometh upon all nations; yea,** upon every one; **yea, upon the** proud and lofty, and upon every one **who** is lifted up; and he shall be brought low:
Isaiah 2:13 And upon all the cedars of Lebanon, ~~*that*~~ *are* high and lifted up, and upon all the oaks of Bashan,	**Yea,** and **the day of the Lord shall come** upon all the cedars of Lebanon, **for they** are high and lifted up, and upon all the oaks of Bashan,
Isaiah 2:14 And upon all the high mountains, and upon all the hills ~~*that*~~ *are* lifted up,	And upon all the high mountains, and upon all the hills, **and upon all the nations which** are lifted up,
Isaiah 2:15 And upon every high tower, and upon every fenced wall,	**And upon every people,** and upon every high tower, and upon every fenced wall,
Isaiah 2:16 And upon all the ships of Tarshish, and upon all pleasant pictures.	**And upon all the ships of the sea,** and upon all the ships of Tarshish, and upon all pleasant pictures.
Isaiah 2:19 And they shall go into the holes of the rocks, and into the caves of the earth, for fear of the Lord, and ~~for~~ the glory of his majesty, when he ariseth to shake terribly the earth.	And they shall go into the holes of the rocks, and into the caves of the earth, for **the** fear of the Lord **shall come upon them**, and the glory of his majesty **shall smite them**, when he ariseth to shake terribly the earth.
Isaiah 2:20 In that day a man shall cast his idols of silver, and his idols of gold, which ~~they~~ made ~~*each one*~~ for himself to worship, to the moles and to the bats;	In that day a man shall cast his idols of silver, and his idols of gold, which **he hath** made for himself to worship, to the moles and to the bats;
Isaiah 2:21 To go into the clefts of the rocks, and into the tops of the ragged rocks, for fear of the Lord, and ~~for~~ the ~~glory of his~~ majesty, when he ariseth to shake terribly the earth.	To go into the clefts of the rocks, and into the tops of the ragged rocks, for **the** fear of the Lord **shall come upon them;** and the majesty **of the Lord shall smite them**, when he ariseth to shake terribly the earth.

Isaiah 3

Isaiah 3:1 FOR, behold, the Lord, the LORD of hosts, doth take away from Jerusalem and from Judah the stay and the staff, the whole ~~stay~~ of bread, and the whole stay of water,	For, behold, the Lord, the Lord of hosts, doth take away from Jerusalem and from Judah the stay and the staff, the whole **staff** of bread, and the whole stay of water,
Isaiah 3:4 And I will give children *to be* their princes, and babes shall rule over them.	And I will give children **unto them** to be their princes, and babes shall rule over them.
Isaiah 3:6 When a man shall take hold of his brother of the house of his father, *saying,* Thou hast clothing, be thou our ruler, and *let* this ruin ~~*be*~~ under thy hand:	When a man shall take hold of his brother of the house of his father, saying, Thou hast clothing, be thou our ruler, and **shall say,** let **not** this ruin **come** under thy hand:
Isaiah 3:7 In that day shall he swear, saying, I will not be an healer; for in my house *is* neither bread nor clothing: make me not a ruler of the people.	In that day shall he swear, saying, I will not be an healer; for in my house **there** is neither bread nor clothing: make me not a ruler of the people.
Isaiah 3:8 For Jerusalem is ruined, and Judah is fallen: because their ~~tongue~~ and their doings ~~*are*~~ against the LORD, to provoke the eyes of his glory.	For Jerusalem is ruined, and Judah is fallen: because their **tongues** and their doings **have been** against the Lord, to provoke the eyes of his glory.
Isaiah 3:9 The shew of their countenance doth witness against them; and ~~they~~ declare their sin as Sodom, they hide *it* ~~not~~. Woe unto their soul! for they have rewarded evil unto themselves.	The shew of their countenance doth witness against them; and **doth** declare their sin **to be even** as Sodom, they **can not** hide it. Woe unto their soul! for they have rewarded evil unto themselves.
Isaiah 3:10 Say ~~ye to~~ the righteous, that *it* ~~*shall be*~~ well *with* ~~*him*~~*:* for they shall eat the fruit of their doings.	Say **unto** the righteous, that it **is** well with **them**: for they shall eat the fruit of their doings.
Isaiah 3:11 Woe unto the wicked! ~~*it shall be*~~ ~~ill~~ ~~*with him*~~*:* for the reward of ~~his hands~~ shall be ~~given him~~.	Woe unto the wicked! **For they shall perish,** for the reward of **their hand** shall be **upon them**.
Isaiah 3:12 ~~*As for*~~ my people, children *are* their oppressors, and women rule	**And** my people, children are their oppressors, and women rule over **thee**.

over ~~them~~. O my people, they which lead thee cause *thee* to err, and destroy the way of thy paths.	O my people, they which lead thee cause thee to err, and destroy the way of thy paths.
Isaiah 3:14 The LORD will enter into judgment with the ancients of his people, and the princes thereof: for ye have eaten up the vineyard; the spoil of the poor ~~*is*~~ in your houses.	The Lord will enter into judgment with the ancients of his people, and the princes thereof: for ye have eaten up the vineyard **and** the spoil of the poor in your houses.
Isaiah 3:26 And her gates shall lament and mourn; and she ~~*being*~~ desolate shall sit upon the ground.	And her gates shall lament and mourn; and she **shall be** desolate [**and**[1]] shall sit upon the ground.

Isaiah 4

Isaiah 4:2 In that day shall the branch of the LORD be beautiful and glorious, and the fruit of the earth *shall be* excellent and comely ~~for~~ them that are escaped of Israel.	In that day shall the branch of the Lord be beautiful and glorious, and the fruit of the earth shall be excellent and comely **to** them that are escaped of Israel.
Isaiah 4:3 And it shall come to pass, *that* ~~*he that is*~~ left in Zion, and ~~*he that*~~ remaineth in Jerusalem, shall be called holy, *even* every one that is written among the living in Jerusalem:	And it shall come to pass, **they** that **are** left in Zion, and remaineth in Jerusalem, shall be called holy, even every one that is written among the living in Jerusalem:
Isaiah 4:5 And the LORD will create upon every dwelling place of mount Zion, and upon her assemblies, a cloud and smoke by day, and the shining of a flaming fire by night: for upon all the glory *shall be* a defence.	And the Lord will create upon every dwelling place of mount Zion, and upon her assemblies, a cloud and smoke by day, and the shining of a flaming fire by night: for upon all the glory **of Zion** shall be a defence.
Isaiah 4:6 And there shall be a tabernacle for a shadow in the daytime from the heat, and for a place of refuge, and ~~for~~ a covert from storm and from rain.	And there shall be a tabernacle for a shadow in the daytime from the heat, and for a place of refuge, and a covert from storm and from rain.

1. OT2 does not contain the conjunction "and."

Isaiah 5

Isaiah 5:1 ~~Now~~ will I sing to my wellbeloved a song of my beloved touching his vineyard. My wellbeloved hath a vineyard in a very fruitful hill:	**And then** will I sing to my wellbeloved a song of my beloved touching his vineyard. My wellbeloved hath a vineyard in a very fruitful hill:
Isaiah 5:4 What could have been done more to my vineyard, that I have not done in it? wherefore, when I looked that it should bring forth grapes, brought ~~it~~ forth wild grapes?	What could have been done more to my vineyard, that I have not done in it? wherefore, when I looked that it should bring forth grapes, **it** brought forth wild grapes?
Isaiah 5:5 And now go to; I will tell you what I will do to my vineyard: I will take away the hedge thereof, and it shall be eaten up; *and* break down the wall thereof, and it shall be trodden down:	And now go to; I will tell you what I will do to my vineyard: I will take away the hedge thereof, and it shall be eaten up; and **I will** break down the wall thereof, and it shall be trodden down:
Isaiah 5:7 For the vineyard of the LORD of hosts *is* the house of Israel, and the men of Judah his pleasant plant: and he looked for judgment, ~~but~~ behold oppression; for righteousness, but behold a cry.	For the vineyard of the Lord of hosts is the house of Israel, and the men of Judah his pleasant plant: and he looked for judgment, **and** behold oppression; for righteousness, but behold a cry.
Isaiah 5:8 Woe unto them that join house to house, ~~*that* lay field to field,~~ till *there be* no place, that they may be placed alone in the midst of the earth!	Woe unto them that join house to house, till there **can** be no place, that they may be placed alone in the midst of the earth!
Isaiah 5:9 In mine ears *said* the LORD of hosts, Of a truth many houses shall be desolate, ~~*even*~~ great and fair, without inhabitant.	In mine ears said the Lord of hosts, Of a truth many houses shall be desolate, **and** great and fair **cities** without inhabitant.
Isaiah 5:11 Woe unto them that rise up early in the morning, *that* they may follow strong drink; that continue until night, ~~till~~ wine inflame them!	Woe unto them that rise up early in the morning, that they may follow strong drink; that continue until night, **and** wine inflame them!
Isaiah 5:21 Woe unto ~~*them that are*~~ wise in their own eyes, and prudent in their own sight!	Woe unto **the** wise in their own eyes, and prudent in their own sight!

Isaiah 5:22 Woe unto ~~*them that are*~~ mighty to drink wine, and men of strength to mingle strong drink:	Woe unto **the** mighty to drink wine, and men of strength to mingle strong drink:
Isaiah 5:28 Whose arrows ~~*are*~~ sharp, and all their bows bent, their horses' hoofs shall be counted like flint, and their wheels like a whirlwind:	Whose arrows **shall be** sharp, and all their bows bent, **and** their horses' hoofs shall be counted like flint, and their wheels like a whirlwind:
Isaiah 5:30 And in that day they shall roar against them like the roaring of the sea: and if ~~*one*~~ look unto the land, behold darkness *and* sorrow, and the light is darkened in the heavens thereof.	And in that day they shall roar against them like the roaring of the sea: and if **they** look unto the land, behold darkness and sorrow, and the light is darkened in the heavens thereof.

Isaiah 6

Isaiah 6:7 And he laid *it* upon my mouth, and said, Lo, this ~~hath~~ touched thy lips; and thine iniquity is taken away, and thy sin purged.	And he laid it upon my mouth, and said, Lo, this **has** touched thy lips; and thine iniquity is taken away, and thy sin purged.
Isaiah 6:9 And he said, Go, and tell this people, Hear ye indeed, but understand not; and see ye indeed, but ~~perceive~~ not.	And he said, Go, and tell this people, Hear ye indeed, but **they** understand not; and see ye indeed, but **they perceived** not.
Isaiah 6:10 Make the heart of this people fat, and make their ears heavy, and shut their eyes; lest they see with their eyes, and hear with their ears, and understand with their ~~heart~~, and convert, and be healed.	Make the heart of this people fat, and make their ears heavy, and shut their eyes; lest they see with their eyes, and hear with their ears, and understand with their **hearts**, and convert, and be healed.
Isaiah 6:11 Then said I, Lord, how long? And he ~~answered~~, Until the cities be wasted without inhabitant, and the houses without man, and the land be utterly desolate,	Then said I, Lord, how long? And he **said**, Until the cities be wasted without inhabitant, and the houses without man, and the land be utterly desolate,
Isaiah 6:12 And the Lord have removed men far away, and *there be* a great forsaking in the midst of the land.	And the Lord have removed men far away, and **for** there **shall** be a great forsaking in the midst of the land.

Isaiah 6:13 But yet in it *shall be* a tenth, and ~~*it*~~ shall return, and shall be eaten: as a teil tree, and as an oak, whose substance *is* in them, when they cast *their leaves: so* the holy seed *shall be* the substance thereof.	But yet in it **there** shall be a tenth, and **they** shall return, and shall be eaten: as a teil tree, and as an oak, whose substance is in them, when they cast their leaves: so the holy seed shall be the substance thereof.

Isaiah 7

Isaiah 7:6 Let us go up against Judah, and vex it, and let us make a breach therein for us, and set a king in the midst of it, ~~*even*~~ the son of Tabeal:	Let us go up against Judah, and vex it, and let us make a breach therein for us, and set a king in the midst of it, **yea** the son of Tabeal:
Isaiah 7:14 Therefore the Lord himself shall give you a sign; Behold, a virgin shall conceive, and bear a son, and shall call his name Immanuel.	Therefore the Lord himself shall give you a sign; Behold, a virgin shall conceive, and **shall** bear a son, and shall call his name Immanuel.
Isaiah 7:15 Butter and honey shall he eat, that he may know to refuse the evil, and choose the good.	Butter and honey shall he eat, that he may know to refuse the evil, and **to** choose the good.
Isaiah 7:18 And it shall come to pass in that day, *that* the LORD shall hiss for the fly that *is* in the uttermost ~~part of the rivers~~ of Egypt, and for the bee that *is* in the land of Assyria.	And it shall come to pass in that day, that the Lord shall hiss for the fly that is in the uttermost of Egypt, and for the bee that is in the land of Assyria.
Isaiah 7:23 And it shall come to pass in that day, ~~*that*~~ every place shall be, where there were a thousand vines at a thousand silverlings, ~~it~~ shall *even* be for briers and thorns.	And it shall come to pass in that day, every place shall be, where there were a thousand vines at a thousand silverlings, **which** shall even be for briers and thorns.
Isaiah 7:25 And *on* all hills that shall be digged with the mattock, there shall not come thither the fear of briers and thorns: but it shall be for the sending forth of oxen, and ~~for~~ the treading of lesser cattle.	And on all hills that shall be digged with the mattock, there shall not come thither the fear of briers and thorns: but it shall be for the sending forth of oxen, and the treading of lesser cattle.

Isaiah 8

Isaiah 8:1 MOREOVER the LORD said unto me, Take thee a great roll, and write in it with a man's pen concerning Maher-shalal-hash-baz.	Moreover **the word of** the Lord said unto me, Take thee a great roll, and write in it with a man's pen concerning Maher-shalal-hash-baz.
Isaiah 8:4 For ~~before~~ the child shall have knowledge to cry, My father, and my mother, the riches of Damascus and the spoil of Samaria shall be taken away before the king of Assyria.	For **behold** the child shall **not** have knowledge to cry, My father, and my mother, **before** the riches of Damascus and the spoil of Samaria shall be taken away before the king of Assyria.
Isaiah 8:19 And when they shall say unto you, Seek unto them that have familiar spirits, and unto wizards that peep, and ~~that~~ mutter: should not a people seek unto their God? for the living to the dead?	And when they shall say unto you, Seek unto them that have familiar spirits, and unto wizards that peep, and mutter: should not a people seek unto their God? for the living to **hear from** the dead?
Isaiah 8:20 To the law and to the testimony: if they speak not according to this word, *it is* because *there is* no light in them.	To the law and to the testimony: **and** if they speak not according to this word, it is because there is no light in them.
Isaiah 8:22 And they shall look unto the earth; and behold trouble and darkness, dimness of anguish; and ~~*they*~~ *shall be* driven to darkness.	And they shall look unto the earth; and behold trouble and darkness, dimness of anguish; and shall be driven to darkness.

Isaiah 9

Isaiah 9:1 NEVERTHELESS the dimness *shall* not *be* such as *was* in her vexation, when at the first he lightly afflicted the land of Zebulun and the land of Naphtali, and afterward did more grievously afflict *her by* the way of the sea, beyond Jordan, in Galilee of the nations.	Nevertheless the dimness shall not be such as was in her vexation, when at the first he lightly afflicted the land of Zebulun and the land of Naphtali, and afterward did more grievously afflict her by the way of the **Red** sea, beyond Jordan, in Galilee of the nations.
Isaiah 9:3 Thou hast multiplied the nation, *and* ~~not~~ increased the joy: they	Thou hast multiplied the nation, and increased the joy: they joy before thee

joy before thee according to the joy in harvest, *and* as *men* rejoice when they divide the spoil.	according to the joy in harvest, and as men rejoice when they divide the spoil.
Isaiah 9:7 Of the increase of *his* government and peace *there* ~~*shall be*~~ no end, upon the throne of David, and upon his kingdom, to order it, and to establish it with judgment and with justice from henceforth even for ever. The zeal of the LORD of hosts will perform this.	Of the increase of his government and peace there **is** no end, upon the throne of David, and upon his kingdom, to order it, and to establish it with judgment and with justice from henceforth even for ever. The zeal of the Lord of hosts will perform this.
Isaiah 9:8 The Lord sent ~~a~~ word ~~into~~ Jacob, and it hath lighted upon Israel.	The Lord sent **his** word **unto** Jacob, and it hath lighted upon Israel.
Isaiah 9:9 And all the people shall know, *even* Ephraim and the inhabitant of Samaria, that say in the pride and stoutness of heart,	And all the people shall know, even Ephraim and the inhabitant of Samaria, that say in the pride and **in the** stoutness of heart,
Isaiah 9:17 Therefore the Lord shall have no joy in their young men, neither shall have mercy on their fatherless and widows: for every one ~~*is*~~ an hypocrite and an evildoer, and every mouth speaketh folly. For all this his anger is not turned away, but his hand *is* stretched out still.	Therefore the Lord shall have no joy in their young men, neither shall have mercy on their fatherless and widows: for every one **of them** an hypocrite and an evildoer, and every mouth speaketh folly. For all this his anger is not turned away, but his hand is stretched out still.

Isaiah 10

Isaiah 10:7 Howbeit he meaneth not so, neither doth his heart think so; but ~~*it is*~~ in his heart to destroy and cut off nations not a few.	Howbeit he meaneth not so, neither doth his heart think so; but in his heart **it is** to destroy and cut off nations not a few.
Isaiah 10:10 As my hand hath ~~found~~ the kingdoms of the idols, and whose graven images did excel them of Jerusalem and of Samaria;	As my hand hath **founded** the kingdoms of the idols, and whose graven images did excel them of Jerusalem and of Samaria;
Isaiah 10:11 Shall I not, as I have done unto Samaria and her idols, so do to Jerusalem and her idols?	Shall I not, as I have done unto Samaria and **to** her idols, so do to Jerusalem and her idols?

Isaiah 10:12 Wherefore it shall come to pass, ~~*that*~~ when the Lord hath performed his whole work upon mount Zion and ~~on~~ Jerusalem, I will punish the fruit of the stout heart of the king of Assyria, and the glory of his high looks.	Wherefore it shall come to pass, when the Lord hath performed his whole work upon mount Zion and **upon** Jerusalem, I will punish the fruit of the stout heart of the king of Assyria, and the glory of his high looks.
Isaiah 10:13 For he saith, By the strength of my hand ~~I have done *it*,~~ and by my wisdom; for I am prudent: and I have ~~removed~~ the ~~bounds~~ of the people, and have robbed their treasures, and I have put down the inhabitants like a valiant *man:*	For he saith, By the strength of my hand, and by my wisdom, **I have done these things**; for I am prudent: and I have **moved** the **borders** of the people, and have robbed their treasures, and I have put down the inhabitants like a valiant man:
Isaiah 10:21 The remnant shall return, *even* the remnant of Jacob, unto the mighty God.	The remnant shall return, **yea** even the remnant of Jacob, unto the mighty God.
Isaiah 10:23 For the Lord GOD of hosts shall make a consumption, even determined, in ~~the midst of~~ all the land.	For the Lord God of hosts shall make a consumption, even determined, in all the land.

Isaiah 11

Isaiah 11:15 And the LORD shall utterly destroy the tongue of the Egyptian sea; and with his mighty wind shall ~~he~~ shake his hand over the river, and shall smite it in the seven streams, and make *men* go over dryshod.	And the Lord shall utterly destroy the tongue of the Egyptian sea; and with his mighty wind **he** shall shake his hand over the river, and shall smite it in the seven streams, and make men go over dryshod.

Isaiah 13

Isaiah 13:2 Lift ye up a banner upon the high mountain, exalt ~~the~~ voice unto them, shake the hand, that they may go into the gates of the nobles.	Lift ye up a banner upon the high mountain, exalt **my** voice unto them, shake the hand, that they may go into the gates of the nobles.[2]
Isaiah 13:3 I have commanded my sanctified ones, I have also called my mighty ones for mine anger, ~~*even*~~ them that rejoice in my highness.	I have commanded my sanctified ones, I have also called my mighty ones for mine anger **is not upon** them that rejoice in my highness.
Isaiah 13:4 The noise of ~~a~~ multitude in the mountains, like as of a great people; a tumultuous noise of the kingdoms of nations gathered together: the LORD of hosts mustereth the host of the battle.	The noise of **the** multitude in the mountains, like as of a great people; a tumultuous noise of the kingdoms of nations gathered together: the Lord of hosts mustereth the host of the battle.
Isaiah 13:5 They come from a far country, from the end of heaven, ~~*even*~~ the LORD, and the weapons of his indignation, to destroy the whole land.	They come from a far country, from the end of heaven, **yea** the Lord, and the weapons of his indignation, to destroy the whole land.
Isaiah 13:7 Therefore shall all hands be faint, ~~and~~ every man's heart shall melt:	Therefore shall all hands be faint, every man's heart shall melt:
Isaiah 13:15 Every one that is found shall be thrust through; and every one that is joined ~~*unto them*~~ shall fall by the sword.	Every one that is found **proud** shall be thrust through; and every one that is joined **to the wicked** shall fall by the sword.
Isaiah 13:22 And the wild beasts of the islands shall cry in their desolate houses, and dragons in *their* pleasant palaces: and her time *is* near to come, and her days shall not be prolonged.	And the wild beasts of the islands shall cry in their desolate houses, and dragons in their pleasant palaces: and her time is near to come, and her days shall not be prolonged. **For I will destroy her speedily; yea, for I will be merciful unto my people, but the wicked shall perish.**

2. The marked Bible does not indicate where "my" should be placed in the verse.

Isaiah 14

Isaiah 14:2 And the people shall take them, and bring them to their place: and the house of Israel shall possess them in the land of the LORD for servants and handmaids: and they shall take them captives, whose captives they were; and they shall rule over their oppressors.	And the people shall take them, and bring them to their place: **yea, from far, unto the ends of the earth. And they shall return to their lands of promise;** and the house of Israel shall possess them in the land of the Lord for servants and handmaids: and they shall take them captives, whose captives they were; and they shall rule over their oppressors.
Isaiah 14:3 And it shall come to pass in ~~the~~ day that the LORD shall give thee rest from thy sorrow, and from thy fear, and from the hard bondage wherein thou wast made to serve,	And it shall come to pass in **that** day that the Lord shall give thee rest from thy sorrow, and from thy fear, and from the hard bondage wherein thou wast made to serve,
Isaiah 14:4 That thou shalt take up this proverb against the king of Babylon, and say, How hath the oppressor ceased! the golden city ceased!	**And it shall come to pass in that day,** that thou shalt take up this proverb against the king of Babylon, and say, How hath the oppressor ceased! the golden city ceased!
Isaiah 14:5 The LORD hath broken the staff of the wicked, ~~*and*~~ the ~~sceptre~~ of the rulers.	The Lord hath broken the staff of the wicked, the **sceptres** of the rulers.
Isaiah 14:8 Yea, the fir trees rejoice at thee, *and* the cedars of Lebanon, *saying,* Since thou art laid down, no feller is come up against us.	Yea, the fir trees rejoice at thee, and **also** the cedars of Lebanon, saying, Since thou art laid down, no feller is come up against us.
Isaiah 14:16 They that see thee shall narrowly look upon thee, *and* consider thee, ~~*saying,*~~ *Is* this the man that made the earth to tremble, that did shake kingdoms;	They that see thee shall narrowly look upon thee, and **shall** consider thee, **and shall say**, Is this the man that made the earth to tremble, that did shake kingdoms;
Isaiah 14:17 ~~*That*~~ made the world as a wilderness, and destroyed the cities thereof; ~~*that*~~ opened not the house of his prisoners?	**And** made the world as a wilderness, and destroyed the cities thereof; **and** opened not the house of his prisoners?

Isaiah 14:18 All the kings of the nations, *~~even~~* all of them, lie in glory, every one in his own house.	All the kings of the nations, **yea,** all of them, lie in glory, every one in his own house.
Isaiah 14:19 But thou art cast out of thy grave like an abominable branch, *and* *~~as~~* the ~~raiment~~ of those that are slain, thrust through with a sword, that go down to the stones of the pit; as a carcase trodden under feet.	But thou art cast out of thy grave like an abominable branch, and the **remnant** of those that are slain, thrust through with a sword, that go down to the stones of the pit; as a carcase trodden under feet.
Isaiah 14:21 Prepare slaughter for his children for the ~~iniquity~~ of their fathers; that they do not rise, nor possess the land, nor fill the face of the world with cities.	Prepare slaughter for his children for the **iniquities** of their fathers; that they do not rise, nor possess the land, nor fill the face of the world with cities.

Isaiah 16

Isaiah 16:6 We have heard of the pride of Moab; *~~he is~~* ~~very proud:~~ *~~even~~* of his haughtiness, and his pride, and his wrath: *~~but~~* his lies *~~shall~~* ~~not~~ *~~be~~* ~~so~~.	We have heard of the pride of Moab; of his haughtiness, and his pride, **for he is very proud,** and his wrath: his lies **and all his evil works.**

Isaiah 23

Isaiah 23:10 Pass through thy land as a river, O daughter of Tarshish: *there is* no more strength.	Pass through thy land as a river, O daughter of Tarshish: there is no more strength **unto thee.**[3]

Isaiah 29

Isaiah 29:2 Yet I will distress Ariel, and there shall be heaviness and sorrow: ~~and~~ it shall be unto ~~me as~~ Ariel.	Yet I will distress Ariel, and there shall be heaviness and sorrow: **for thus hath the Lord said unto me,** it shall be unto Ariel.

3. OT2 clearly contains "thee," which is to be added to the verse. The marked Bible contains a notation at the end of the verse that appears to read "unto," thus indicating where "thee" should be placed in the verse.

Isaiah 29:3 ~~And~~ I will camp against ~~thee~~ round about, and will lay siege against ~~thee~~ with a mount, and I will raise forts against ~~thee~~.	**That** I **the Lord** will camp against **her** round about, and will lay siege against **her** with a mount, and I will raise forts against **her**.
Isaiah 29:4 And ~~thou~~ shalt be brought down, *and* ~~shalt~~ speak out of the ground, and ~~thy~~ speech shall be low out of the dust, and ~~thy~~ voice shall be, as of one that hath a familiar spirit, out of the ground, and ~~thy~~ speech shall whisper out of the dust.	And **she** shalt be brought down, and **shall** speak out of the ground, and **her** speech shall be low out of the dust, and **her** voice shall be, as of one that hath a familiar spirit, out of the ground, and **her** speech shall whisper out of the dust.
Isaiah 29:5 Moreover the multitude of ~~thy~~ strangers shall be like small dust, and the multitude of the terrible ones *shall be* as chaff that passeth away: yea, it shall be at an instant suddenly.	Moreover the multitude of **her** strangers shall be like small dust, and the multitude of the terrible ones shall be as chaff that passeth away: yea, it shall be at an instant suddenly.
Isaiah 29:6 ~~Thou shalt~~ be visited of the LORD of hosts with thunder, and with earthquake, and great noise, with storm and tempest, and the flame of devouring fire.	**For they shall** be visited of the Lord of hosts with thunder, and with earthquake, and great noise, with storm and tempest, and the flame of devouring fire.
Isaiah 29:8 It shall ~~even~~ be as ~~when an~~ hungry *man* dreameth, and, behold, he eateth; but he awaketh, and his soul is empty: or ~~as when~~ a thirsty man dreameth, and, behold, he drinketh; but he awaketh, and, behold, *he is* faint, and his soul hath appetite: so shall the multitude of all the nations be, that fight against mount Zion.	**Yea,** it shall be **unto them, even** as **unto a** hungry man **who** dreameth, and, behold, he eateth; but he awaketh, and his soul is empty: or **like unto** a thirsty man **who** dreameth, and, behold, he drinketh; but he awaketh, and, behold, he is faint, and his soul hath appetite: **yea, even** so shall the multitude of all the nations be, that fight against mount Zion.
Isaiah 29:9 Stay yourselves, and wonder; cry ~~ye~~ out, and cry: ~~they are~~ drunken, but not with wine; ~~they~~ stagger, but not with strong drink.	**For behold, all ye that do iniquity,** stay yourselves and wonder**, for ye shall** cry out, and cry: **yea, ye shall be** drunken but not with wine**, ye shall** stagger but not with strong drink.
Isaiah 29:10 For the LORD hath poured out upon you the spirit of deep sleep, ~~and hath~~ closed your eyes: the	For **behold,** the Lord hath poured out upon you the spirit of deep sleep**. For behold, ye have** closed your eyes, **and**

prophets and your rulers, the seers hath he covered.	**ye have rejected** the prophets; and your rulers, **and** the seers hath he covered **because of your iniquities. And it shall come to pass that the Lord God shall bring forth unto you the words of a book, and they shall be the words of them which have slumbered. And behold the book shall be sealed; and in the book shall be a revelation from God, from the beginning of the world to the ending thereof. Wherefore, because of the things which are sealed up, the things which are sealed shall not be delivered in the day of the wickedness and abominations of the people. Wherefore the book shall be kept from them. But the book shall be delivered unto a man, and he shall deliver the words of the book, which are the words of those which have slumbered in the dust, and he shall deliver these words unto another; but the words which are sealed he shall not deliver, neither shall he deliver the book. For the book shall be sealed by the power of God, and the revelation which was sealed shall be kept in the book until the own due time of the Lord, that they may come forth; for behold, they reveal all things from the foundation of the world unto the end thereof. And the day cometh that the words of the book which were sealed shall be read upon the house tops; and they shall be read by the power of Christ; and all things shall be revealed unto the children of men which ever have been among the children of men, and which ever will be even unto the end of the earth. Wherefore, at that day when the book shall be delivered unto the man of whom I have**

	spoken, the book shall be hid from the eyes of the world, that the eyes of none shall behold it save it be that three witnesses shall behold it, by the power of God, besides him to whom the book shall be delivered; and they shall testify to the truth of the book and the things therein. And there is none other which shall view it, save it be a few according to the will of God, to bear testimony of his word unto the children of men; for the Lord God hath said that the words of the faithful should speak as if it were from the dead. Wherefore, the Lord God will proceed to bring forth the words of the book; and in the mouth of as many witnesses as seemeth him good will he establish his word; and wo be unto him that rejecteth the word of God!
Isaiah 29:11 ~~And the vision of all is become unto you as the~~ words ~~of a book that is~~ sealed, ~~which *men*~~ deliver to ~~one that is~~ learned, saying, Read this, I pray thee: and ~~he saith~~, I cannot; ~~for~~ it ~~*is* sealed~~:	**But behold, it shall come to pass that the Lord God shall say unto him to whom he shall deliver the book: Take these** words **which are not** sealed **and** deliver **them** to **another, that he may show them unto the** learned, saying**:** Read this, I pray thee**.** And **the learned shall say: Bring hither the book, and I will read them. And now, because of the glory of the world and to get gain will they say this, and not for the glory of God. And the man shall say: I cannot bring the book, for it is sealed. Then shall the learned say:** I cannot **read** it.
Isaiah 29:12 ~~And~~ the book ~~is delivered~~ to him that is not learned, ~~saying~~, Read ~~this, I pray thee: and he saith, I am not learned~~.	**Wherefore it shall come to pass, that the Lord God will deliver again** the book **and the words thereof** to him that is not learned**; and the man that is not learned shall say: I am not learned. Then shall the Lord God say unto him: The learned shall not read**

	them, for they have rejected them, and I am able to do mine own work; wherefore thou shalt read **the words which I shall give unto thee. Touch not the things which are sealed, for I will bring them forth in mine own due time; for I will show unto the children of men that I am able to do mine own work. Wherefore, when thou hast read the words which I have commanded thee, and obtained the witnesses which I have promised unto thee, then shalt thou seal up the book again, and hide it up unto me, that I may preserve the words which thou hast not read, until I shall see fit in mine own wisdom to reveal all things unto the children of men. For behold, I am God; and I am a God of miracles; and I will show unto the world that I am the same yesterday, today, and forever; and I work not among the children of men save it be according to their faith.**
Isaiah 29:13 ~~Wherefore~~ the Lord ~~said~~, Forasmuch as this people draw near *me* with their mouth, and with their ~~lips~~ do honour me, but have removed their ~~heart~~ far from me, and their fear ~~toward~~ me is taught by the ~~precept~~ of men:	**And again it shall come to pass that** the Lord **shall say unto him that shall read the words that shall be delivered him:** Forasmuch as this people draw near **unto** me with their mouth, and with their lip do honour me, but have removed their **hearts** far from me, and their fear **towards** me is taught by the **precepts** of men—
Isaiah 29:14 Therefore, ~~behold~~, I will proceed to do a marvellous work among this people, ~~*even*~~ a marvellous work and a wonder: for the wisdom of their wise ~~*men*~~ shall perish, and the understanding of their prudent ~~*men*~~ shall be hid.	Therefore, I will proceed to do a marvelous work among this people, **yea,** a marvelous work and a wonder, for the wisdom of their wise **and learned** shall perish, and the understanding of their prudent shall be hid.
Isaiah 29:15 Woe unto them that seek deep to hide their counsel from the	**And** woe unto them that seek deep to hide their counsel from the Lord**!** And

Lord, and their works are in the dark, and they say, Who seeth us? and who knoweth us?	their works are in the dark**;** and they say**:** Who seeth us**,** and who knoweth us?
Isaiah 29:16 Surely your turning of things upside down shall be esteemed as the potter's clay: for shall the work say of him that made it, He made me not? or shall the thing framed say of him that framed it, He had no understanding?	**And they also say:** Surely, your turning of things upside down shall be esteemed as the potter's clay**. But behold, I will show unto them, saith the Lord of Hosts, that I know all their works.** For shall the work say of him that made it, he made me not? Or shall the thing framed say of him that framed it, he had no understanding?
Isaiah 29:17 ~~*Is*~~ it not yet a very little while, and Lebanon shall be turned into a fruitful field, and the fruitful field shall be esteemed as a forest?	**But behold, saith the Lord of Hosts: I will show unto the children of men that** it **is** not yet a very little while and Lebanon shall be turned into a fruitful field**;** and the fruitful field shall be esteemed as a forest.
Isaiah 29:19 The meek also shall increase *their* joy in the Lord, and the poor among men shall rejoice in the Holy One of Israel.	**And** the meek also shall increase**, and** their joy **shall be** in the Lord, and the poor among men shall rejoice in the Holy One of Israel.
Isaiah 29:20 For the terrible one is brought to nought, and the scorner is consumed, and all that watch for iniquity are cut off:	For **assuredly as the Lord liveth they shall see that** the terrible one is brought to naught, and the scorner is consumed, and all that watch for iniquity are cut off**;**
Isaiah 29:21 That make a man an offender for a word, and lay a snare for him that reproveth in the gate, and turn aside the just for a thing of nought.	**And they** that make a man an offender for a word, and lay a snare for him that reproveth in the gate, and turn aside the just for a thing of naught.
Isaiah 29:23 But when he seeth his children, the work of ~~mine~~ hands, in the midst of him, they shall sanctify my name, and sanctify the Holy One of Jacob, and shall fear the God of Israel.	But when he seeth his children, the work of **my** hands, in the midst of him, they shall sanctify my name, and sanctify the Holy One of Jacob, and shall fear the God of Israel.

Isaiah 32

Isaiah 32:14 Because the palaces shall be forsaken; the multitude of the ~~city~~ shall be ~~left~~; the forts and towers shall be for dens for ever, a joy of wild asses, a pasture of flocks;	Because the palaces shall be forsaken; the multitude of the **houses** shall be **desolate**; the forts and towers shall be for dens for ever, a joy of wild asses, a pasture of flocks;

Isaiah 33

Isaiah 33:2 O LORD, be gracious unto us; we have waited for thee: be thou their arm every morning, ~~our~~ salvation also in the time of trouble.	O Lord, be gracious unto us; we have waited for thee: be thou their arm every morning, **their** salvation also in the time of trouble.
Isaiah 33:18 Thine heart shall meditate terror. Where *is* the scribe? where *is* the receiver? where *is* he that counted the towers?	Thine heart shall meditate **in** terror. Where is the scribe? where is the receiver? where is he that counted the towers?

Isaiah 34

Isaiah 34:7 And the ~~unicorns~~ shall come down with them, and the bullocks with the bulls; and their land shall be soaked with blood, and their dust made fat with fatness.	And the **Re-em**[4] shall come down with them, and the bullocks with the bulls; and their land shall be soaked with blood, and their dust made fat with fatness.
Isaiah 34:16 Seek ye out of the book of the LORD, and read: no one of these shall fail, none shall want ~~her~~ mate: for my mouth it hath commanded, and ~~his~~ spirit it hath gathered them.	Seek ye out of the book of the Lord, and read **the names written therein**: no one of these shall fail, none shall want **their** mate: for my mouth it hath commanded, and **my** spirit it hath gathered them.
Isaiah 34:17 And ~~he hath~~ cast the lot for them, and ~~his hand hath~~ divided it	And **I have** cast the lot for them, and **I have** divided it unto them by line: they

4. It is unclear whether this is an intentional change or a scribal error.

unto them by line: they shall possess it for ever, from generation to generation shall ~~they~~ dwell therein.	shall possess it for ever, from generation to generation **they** shall dwell therein.

Isaiah 35

Isaiah 35:8 And an highway shall be there, ~~and~~ a way, and it shall be called The way of holiness; the unclean shall not pass over it; but it *shall be* for those: the wayfaring men, though fools, shall not err *therein.*	And an highway shall be there, **for** a way **shall be cast up**, and it shall be called The way of holiness; the unclean shall not pass over **upon** it; but it shall be **cast up** for those **who are clean, and** the wayfaring men, though **they are accounted** fools, shall not err therein.

Isaiah 36

Isaiah 36:5 I say, ~~*sayest thou,* (but *they are but* vain~~ words) *I have* counsel and strength for war: now on whom dost thou trust, that thou rebellest against me?	I say, **Thy** words **are but vain, when thou sayest,** I have counsel and strength for war: now on whom dost thou trust, that thou rebellest against me?

Isaiah 37

Isaiah 37:17 Incline thine ear, O LORD, and hear; open thine eyes, O LORD, and see: and hear all the words of Sennacherib, which hath sent to reproach the living God.	Incline thine ear, O Lord, and hear; open thine eyes, O Lord, and see: and hear all the words of Sennacherib, which **he** hath sent to reproach the living God.
Isaiah 37:32 For out of Jerusalem shall go forth a remnant, and they that escape out of mount Zion: the zeal of the LORD of hosts shall do this.	For out of Jerusalem shall go forth a remnant, and they that escape out of **Jerusalem shall come up upon** mount Zion: the zeal of the Lord of hosts shall do this.
Isaiah 37:36 Then the angel of the LORD went forth, and smote in the camp of the Assyrians a hundred and	Then the angel of the Lord went forth, and smote in the camp of the Assyrians a hundred and fourscore and five

fourscore and five thousand: and when they arose early in the morning, behold, they *were* all dead corpses.	thousand: and when they **who were left** arose early in the morning, behold, they were all dead corpses.

Isaiah 38

Isaiah 38:15 What shall I say? he hath both spoken unto me, and himself hath ~~done *it*:~~ I shall go softly all my years in the bitterness of my soul.	What shall I say? he hath both spoken unto me, and himself hath **healed me**: I shall go softly all my years **that I may not walk** in the bitterness of my soul.
Isaiah 38:16 O Lord, ~~by these *things* *men* live, and in all these *things* *is*~~ the life of my spirit: so wilt thou recover me, and make me to live.	O Lord, **thou who art** the life of my spirit**, in whom I live**: so wilt thou recover me, and make me to live; **and in all these things I will praise thee**.
Isaiah 38:17 Behold, ~~for peace~~ I had great bitterness: but thou hast in love to my soul ~~*delivered it*~~ from the pit of corruption: for thou hast cast all my sins behind thy back.	Behold, I had great bitterness **instead of peace**: but thou hast in love to my soul **saved me** from the pit of corruption: for thou hast cast all my sins behind thy back.

Isaiah 42

Isaiah 42:19 Who *is* blind, ~~but my servant? or~~ deaf, ~~as my messenger *that* I sent? who *is* blind as *he that is*~~ perfect, ~~and blind as~~ the LORD's servant?	**For I will send my servant unto you** who **are** blind**; yea, a messenger to open the eyes of the blind, and unstop the ears of the** deaf**; And they shall be made** perfect **notwithstanding their blindness, if they will hearken unto the messenger,** the Lord's servant**.**
Isaiah 42:20 Seeing many things, but thou observest not; opening the ears, but ~~he heareth~~ not.	**Thou art a people,** seeing many things, but thou observest not; opening the ears **to hear,** but **thou hearest** not.
Isaiah 42:21 The LORD is well pleased for his righteousness' sake; he will magnify the law, and make *it* honourable.	The Lord is **not** well pleased **with such a people, but** for his righteousness' sake he will magnify the law and make it honorable.

Isaiah 42:22 ~~But this *is*~~ a people robbed and spoiled; ~~*they are*~~ all of them snared in holes, and they ~~are~~ hid in prison houses: they ~~are~~ for a prey, and none delivereth; for a spoil, and none saith, Restore.	**Thou art** a people robbed and spoiled; **thine enemies,** all of them, **have** snared **thee** in holes, and they **have** hid **thee** in prison houses: they **have taken thee** for a prey, and none delivereth; for a spoil, and none saith, Restore.
Isaiah 42:23 Who among ~~you~~ will give ear ~~to this? *who* will~~ hearken and hear for the time to come?	Who among **them** will give ear **unto thee, or** hearken and hear **thee** for the time to come?
Isaiah 42:24 Who gave Jacob for a spoil, and Israel to the robbers? did not the Lord, he against whom ~~we~~ have sinned? for they would not walk in his ways, neither were they obedient unto his law.	**And** who gave Jacob for a spoil, and Israel to the robbers? did not the Lord, he against whom **they** have sinned? for they would not walk in his ways, neither were they obedient unto his law.
Isaiah 42:25 Therefore he hath poured upon ~~him~~ the fury of his anger, and the strength of battle: and ~~it hath~~ set ~~him~~ on fire round about, yet ~~he~~ knew not; and it burned ~~him~~, yet ~~he~~ laid *it* not to heart.	Therefore he hath poured upon **them** the fury of his anger, and the strength of battle: and **they have** set **them** on fire round about, yet **they** knew not; and it burned **them**, yet **they** laid it not to heart.

Isaiah 46

Isaiah 46:7 They bear him upon the shoulder, they carry him, and set him in his place, and he standeth; from his place shall he not remove: yea, ~~*one*~~ shall cry unto him, yet can he not answer, nor save him out of his trouble.	They bear him upon the shoulder, they carry him, and set him in his place, and he standeth; from his place shall he not remove: yea, **they** shall cry unto him, yet can he not answer, nor save him out of his trouble.

Isaiah 49

Isaiah 49:23 And kings shall be thy nursing fathers, and their queens thy nursing mothers: they shall bow down to thee with *their* ~~face~~ toward the earth, and lick up the dust of thy feet; and	And kings shall be thy nursing fathers, and their queens thy nursing mothers: they shall bow down to thee with their **faces** toward the earth, and lick up the dust of thy feet; and thou shalt know

thou shalt know that I *am* the LORD: for they shall not be ashamed that wait for me.	that I am the Lord: for they shall not be ashamed that wait for me.
Isaiah 49:25 But thus saith the LORD, Even the captives of the mighty shall be taken away, and the prey of the terrible shall be delivered: for I will contend with ~~him~~ that contendeth with thee, and I will save thy children.	But thus saith the Lord, Even the captives of the mighty shall be taken away, and the prey of the terrible shall be delivered: **for the mighty God shall deliver his covenant people.** For **thus saith the Lord,** I will contend with **them** that contendeth with thee, and I will save thy children.

Isaiah 50

Isaiah 50:1 THUS saith the LORD, Where *is* the bill of your mother's divorcement, whom ~~I~~ have put away? or which of my creditors ~~*is it*~~ to whom I have sold you? Behold, for your iniquities have ye sold yourselves, and for your transgressions is your mother put away.	**Yea for** thus saith the Lord, **Have I put thee away, or have I cast thee off forever? For thus saith the Lord**, Where *is* the bill of your mother's divorcement, **to** whom I have put **thee** away? or **to** which of my creditors **have I sold you; yea,** to whom have **I** sold you? Behold, for your iniquities have ye sold yourselves, and for your transgressions is your mother put away.
Isaiah 50:2 Wherefore, when I ~~came,~~ ~~*was*~~ *there* no man? when I called, ~~*was*~~ *there* none to answer? Is my hand shortened at all, that it cannot redeem? or have I no power to deliver? behold, at my rebuke I dry up the sea, I make ~~the rivers~~ a wilderness: their fish ~~stinketh~~, because ~~*there is* no water~~, and ~~dieth for~~ thirst.	Wherefore, when I **come** there was no man**;** when I called, **yea** there **was** none to answer**. O house of Israel,** is my hand shortened at all, that it cannotredeem? or have I no power to deliver? behold, at my rebuke I dry up the sea, I make **their river** a wilderness: **and** their fish **to stink**, because **the waters are dried up**, and **they die because of** thirst.
Isaiah 50:4 The Lord GOD hath given me the tongue of the learned, that I should know how to speak a word in season ~~to *him that is*~~ weary: he ~~wakeneth~~ morning by morning,	The Lord God hath given me the tongue of the learned, that I should know how to speak a word in season **unto thee, O house of Israel, when ye are** weary: he **waketh** morning by

he ~~wakeneth~~ mine ear to hear as the learned.	morning, he **waketh** mine ear to hear as the learned.
Isaiah 50:5 The Lord GOD hath ~~opened~~ mine ear, and I was not rebellious, neither turned away back.	The Lord God hath **appointed** mine ear, and I was not rebellious, neither turned away back.
Isaiah 50:6 I gave my back to the ~~smiters~~, and my cheeks to them that plucked off the hair: I hid not my face from shame and spitting.	I gave my back to the **smiter**, and my cheeks to them that plucked off the hair: I hid not my face from shame and spitting.
Isaiah 50:8 ~~*He is*~~ near ~~that~~ justifieth me; who will contend with me? let us stand together: who *is* mine adversary? let him come near ~~to~~ me.	**And the Lord** is near **and he** justifieth me; who will contend with me? let us stand together: who is mine adversary? let him come near me**, and I will smite him with the strength of my mouth**.
Isaiah 50:9 ~~Behold~~, the Lord GOD will help me; ~~who *is* he *that*~~ shall condemn me? ~~lo, they~~ all shall wax old as a garment; the moth shall eat them up.	**For** the Lord God will help me; **and all they which** shall condemn me? **behold** all **they** shall wax old as a garment; **and** moth shall eat them up.
Isaiah 50:11 Behold, all ye that ~~kindle a~~ fire, that compass *yourselves* about with sparks: walk in the light of your fire, and in the sparks *~~that~~* ye have kindled. This shall ye have of mine hand; ye shall lie down in sorrow.	Behold, all ye that **kindleth** fire, that compass yourselves about with sparks: walk in the light of your fire, and in the sparks **which** ye have kindled. This shall ye have of mine hand; ye shall lie down in sorrow.

Isaiah 51

Isaiah 51:1 HEARKEN ~~to~~ me, ye that follow after righteousness, ye that seek the LORD: look unto the rock *whence* ye ~~are~~ hewn, and to the hole of the pit *whence* ye are digged.	Hearken **unto** me, ye that follow after righteousness, ye that seek the Lord: look unto the rock **from** whence ye **were** hewn, and to the hole of the pit **from** whence ye are digged.
Isaiah 51:4 Hearken unto me, my people; and give ear unto me, O my nation: for a law shall proceed from me, and I will make my judgment to rest for a light of the people.	Hearken unto me, my people; and give ear unto me, O my nation: for a law shall proceed from me, and I will make my judgment to rest for a light **thing** of the people.

Isaiah 51:7 Hearken unto me, ye that know righteousness, the people in whose heart ~~*is*~~ my law; fear ye not the reproach of men, neither be ye afraid of their revilings.	Hearken unto me, ye that know righteousness, the people in whose heart **I have written** my law; fear ye not the reproach of men, neither be ye afraid of their revilings.
Isaiah 51:11 Therefore the redeemed of the LORD shall return, and come with singing unto Zion; and everlasting joy *shall be* upon their head: they shall obtain gladness and joy; ~~*and*~~ sorrow and mourning shall flee away.	Therefore the redeemed of the Lord shall return, and come with singing unto Zion; and everlasting joy **and holiness** shall be upon their head: they shall obtain gladness and joy; sorrow and mourning shall flee away.
Isaiah 51:12 I, ~~*even*~~ I, *am* he that comforteth you: who *art* thou, that thou shouldest be afraid of a man *that* shall die, and of the son of man *which* shall be made *as* grass;	I **am he, yea**, I am he that comforteth you: **behold** who art thou, that thou shouldest be afraid of a man that shall die, and of the son of man which shall be made as grass;
Isaiah 51:16 And I have put my words in thy mouth, and I have covered thee in the shadow of mine hand, that I may plant the heavens, and lay the foundations of the earth, and say unto Zion, Thou *art* my people.	And I have put my words in thy mouth, and I have covered thee in the shadow of mine hand, that I may plant the heavens, and lay the foundations of the earth, and say unto Zion, **behold** thou art my people.
Isaiah 51:18 ~~*There is*~~ none to guide her among all the sons *whom* she hath brought forth; neither *is there any* that taketh her by the hand of all the sons *that* she hath brought up.	**And** none to guide her among all the sons whom she hath brought forth; neither is there any that taketh her by the hand of all the sons that she hath brought up.
Isaiah 51:19 These two ~~*things*~~ are come unto thee; who shall be sorry for thee? desolation, and destruction, and the famine, and the sword: by whom shall I comfort thee?	These two **sons** are come unto thee; who shall be sorry for thee? **thy** desolation, and destruction, and the famine, and the sword: **and** by whom shall I comfort thee?
Isaiah 51:20 Thy sons have fainted, they lie at the head of all the streets, as a wild bull in a net: they are full of the fury of the LORD, the rebuke of thy God.	Thy sons have fainted **save these two**, they lie at the head of all the streets, as a wild bull in a net: they are full of the fury of the Lord, the rebuke of thy God.

Isaiah 52

Isaiah 52:6 Therefore my people shall know my name: ~~therefore *they shall know*~~ in that day that I *am* he that doth speak: behold, *it is* I.	Therefore my people shall know my name: **yea,** in that day that **they shall know that** I am he that doth speak: behold, it is I.
Isaiah 52:7 How beautiful upon the mountains are the feet of him that bringeth good tidings, that publisheth peace; that bringeth good tidings of good, that publisheth salvation; that saith unto Zion, Thy God reigneth!	**And then shall they say,** How beautiful upon the mountains are the feet of him that bringeth good tidings **unto them**, that publisheth peace; that bringeth good tidings **unto them** of good, that publisheth salvation; that saith unto Zion, Thy God reigneth!
Isaiah 52:15 So shall he ~~sprinkle~~ many nations; the kings shall shut their mouths at him: for *that* which had ~~not~~ been told them shall they see; and *that* which they had not heard shall they consider.	So shall he **gather** many nations; the kings shall shut their mouths at him: for that which had been told them shall they see; and that which they had not heard shall they consider.

Isaiah 54

Isaiah 54:10 For the mountains shall depart, and the hills be removed; but my kindness shall not depart from thee, neither shall the covenant of my ~~peace~~ be removed, saith the Lord that hath mercy on thee.	For the mountains shall depart, and the hills be removed; but my kindness shall not depart from thee, neither shall the covenant of my **people** be removed, saith the Lord that hath mercy on thee.
Isaiah 54:15 Behold, they shall surely gather together, ~~*but*~~ not by me: whosoever shall gather together against thee shall fall for thy sake.	Behold, they shall surely gather together **against thee**, not by me: whosoever shall gather together against thee shall fall for thy sake.

Isaiah 60

Isaiah 60:22 A little one shall become a thousand, and a small one a strong nation: I the LORD will hasten it in ~~his~~ time.	A little one shall become a thousand, and a small one a strong nation: I the Lord will hasten it in **my** time.

Isaiah 62

Isaiah 62:4 Thou shalt no more be termed Forsaken; neither shall thy land any more be termed Desolate: but thou shalt be called ~~Hephzi-bah~~, and thy land ~~Beulah~~: for the LORD delighteth in thee, and thy land shall be married.	Thou shalt no more be termed Forsaken; neither shall thy land any more be termed Desolate: but thou shalt be called **Delightful**, and thy land **Union**: for the Lord delighteth in thee, and thy land shall be married.
Isaiah 62:5 For *as* a young man marrieth a virgin, *so* shall thy ~~sons~~ marry thee: and *as* the bridegroom rejoiceth over the bride, *so* shall thy God rejoice over thee.	For as a young man marrieth a virgin, so shall thy **God** marry thee: and as the bridegroom rejoiceth over the bride, so shall thy God rejoice over thee.

Isaiah 63

Isaiah 63:17 O LORD, why hast thou ~~made~~ us to err from thy ways, *and* ~~hardened~~ our heart from thy fear? Return for thy servants' sake, the tribes of thine inheritance.	O Lord, why hast thou **suffered** us to err from thy ways, and **to harden** our heart from thy fear? Return for thy servants' sake, the tribes of thine inheritance.

Isaiah 64

Isaiah 64:5 Thou meetest him that ~~rejoiceth and~~ worketh righteousness, *those that* ~~remember~~ thee in thy ways: ~~behold~~, ~~thou art wroth; for we have sinned~~: in ~~those~~ is continuance, and ~~we~~ shall be saved.	Thou meetest him that worketh righteousness, **and rejoiceth him** that **remembers** thee in thy ways: in **righteousness there** is continuance, and **such** shall be saved.

Isaiah 64:6 But we are all as an unclean *thing,* and all our righteousnesses *are* as filthy rags; and we all do fade as a leaf; and our iniquities, like the wind, have taken us away.	But **we have sinned,** we are all as an unclean thing, and all our righteousnesses are as filthy rags; and we all do fade as a leaf; and our iniquities, like the wind, have taken us away.
Isaiah 64:7 And ~~*there is*~~ none ~~that~~ calleth upon thy name, that stirreth up himself to take hold of thee: for thou hast hid thy face from us, and hast consumed us, because of our iniquities.	And none calleth upon thy name, that stirreth up himself to take hold of thee: for thou hast hid thy face from us, and hast consumed us, because of our iniquities.

Isaiah 65

Isaiah 65:1 I AM ~~sought~~ of *them that* ~~asked not *for*~~ *me;* I am found of *them that* sought me not: I said, Behold me, ~~behold~~ me, unto a nation *that* ~~was~~ not called by my name.	I am **found** of them **who seek after me; I give unto all them** that **ask of** me; I am **not** found of them that sought me not **or that enquireth not after me**: I said **unto my servant**, Behold me, **look upon** me, **I will send you** unto a nation that **are** not called by my name.
Isaiah 65:2 I have spread out my hands all the day ~~unto~~ a ~~rebellious~~ people, ~~which~~ walketh in ~~a way *that was*~~ not good, after their own thoughts;	**For** I have spread out my hands all the day **to** a people, **who** walketh **not** in **my ways and their works are evil and** not good, **and they walk** after their own thoughts;
Isaiah 65:4 Which remain among the graves, and lodge in the monuments, which eat swine's flesh, and broth of abominable ~~*things is in*~~ their vessels;	Which remain among the graves, and lodge in the monuments, which eat swine's flesh, and broth of abominable **beasts and pollute** their vessels;
Isaiah 65:20 There shall be no more thence an infant of days, nor an old man that hath not filled his ~~days~~: for the child shall die an hundred years old; but the sinner ~~*being*~~ an hundred years old shall be accursed.	**In those days** there shall be no more thence an infant of days, nor an old man that hath not filled his **day**: for the child shall **not** die**, but live to be** an hundred years old; but the sinner **living to be** an hundred years old shall be accursed.

Jeremiah

Jeremiah 2	
King James Version	Joseph Smith Translation
Jeremiah 2:24 A wild ass used to the wilderness, *that* snuffeth up the wind at her pleasure; in her occasion who can turn her away? all they that seek her will ~~not~~ weary themselves; in her month they shall find her.	A wild ass used to the wilderness, that snuffeth up the wind at her pleasure; in her occasion who can turn her away? all they that seek her will weary themselves; in her month they shall **not** find her.
Jeremiah 18	
Jeremiah 18:8 If that nation, against whom I have pronounced, turn from their evil, I will ~~repent of~~ the evil that I thought to do unto them.	If that nation, against whom I have pronounced, turn from their evil, I will **withhold** the evil that I thought to do unto them.
Jeremiah 18:10 If it do evil in my sight, that it obey not my voice, then I will ~~repent of~~ the good, wherewith I said I would benefit them.	If it do evil in my sight, that it obey not my voice, then I will **withhold** the good, wherewith I said I would benefit them.
Jeremiah 18:14 Will ~~*a man*~~ leave the snow of Lebanon ~~*which cometh* from the rock of the field? *or*~~ shall the cold flowing waters that come from another place be forsaken?	Will **you not** leave the snow **of the fields** of Lebanon; shall **not** the cold flowing waters that come from another place **from the rock** be forsaken?
Jeremiah 25	
Jeremiah 25:31 A noise shall come ~~*even*~~ to the ends of the earth; for the Lord hath a controversy with the	A noise shall come to the ends of the earth; for the Lord hath a controversy with the nations, he will plead with

nations, he will plead with all flesh; he will give ~~them *that are*~~ wicked to the sword, saith the LORD.	all flesh; he will give **the** wicked to the sword, saith the Lord.

Jeremiah 26

Jeremiah 26:3 If so be they will hearken, and turn every man from his evil way, ~~that I may~~ repent ~~me of~~ the evil, which I purpose to do unto them because of the evil of their doings.	If so be they will hearken, and turn every man from his evil way, **and** repent, **I will turn away** the evil, which I purpose to do unto them because of the evil of their doings.
Jeremiah 26:5 To hearken to the words of my servants the prophets, whom I sent unto you, ~~both rising~~ up early, and sending *them,* ~~but ye have not hearkened~~;	To hearken to the words of my servants the prophets, whom I sent unto you, **commanding them to rise** up early, and sending them;
Jeremiah 26:6 Then will I make this house like Shiloh, and will make this city a curse to all the nations of the earth.	Then will I make this house like Shiloh, and will make this city a curse to all the nations of the earth; **for ye have not hearkened unto my servants, the prophets**.
Jeremiah 26:13 Therefore now amend your ways and your doings, and obey the voice of the LORD your God; and ~~the LORD will~~ repent ~~him of~~ the evil that he hath pronounced against you.	Therefore now amend your ways and your doings, and obey the voice of the Lord your God; and repent, **and the Lord will turn away** the evil that he hath pronounced against you.
Jeremiah 26:18 Micah the Morasthite prophesied in the days of Hezekiah king of Judah, and spake to all the people of Judah, saying, Thus saith the LORD of hosts; Zion shall be plowed *like* a field, and Jerusalem shall become heaps, and the mountain of the house as the high places of a forest.	Micah the Morasthite prophesied in the days of Hezekiah king of Judah, and spake to all the people of Judah, saying, Thus saith the Lord of hosts; Zion shall be plowed like a field, and Jerusalem shall become heaps, and the mountain of the house **of the Lord** as the high places of a forest.
Jeremiah 26:19 Did Hezekiah king of Judah and all Judah put him at all to death? did he not fear the LORD, and besought the LORD, and ~~the LORD~~ repented ~~him of~~ the evil which he had	Did Hezekiah king of Judah and all Judah put him at all to death? did he not fear the Lord, and besought the Lord, and repented**, and the Lord turned away** the evil which he had

pronounced against them? Thus might ~~we~~ procure great evil against our souls.	pronounced against them? Thus **by putting Jeremiah to death we** might procure great evil against our souls.
Jeremiah 26:20 ~~And~~ there was ~~also~~ a man that ~~prophesied in the name of the LORD~~, Urijah the son of Shemaiah of Kirjath-jearim, who prophesied against this city and against this land according to all the words of Jeremiah:	**But** there was a man **among the priests, rose up and said,** that, Urijah the son of Shemaiah of Kirjath-jearim, **prophesied in the name of the Lord,** who **also** prophesied against this city and against this land according to all the words of Jeremiah:

Jeremiah 27

Jeremiah 27:7 And all nations shall serve him, and his son, and his son's son, until the very time of ~~his land~~ come: and ~~then~~ many nations and great kings shall serve themselves of ~~him~~.	And all nations shall serve him, and his son, and his son's son, until the very time of **their end** come: and **after that** many nations and great kings shall serve themselves of **them**.

Jeremiah 29

Jeremiah 29:19 Because they have not hearkened to my words, saith the LORD, which I sent unto them by my servants the prophets, ~~rising up~~ early and sending *them;* but ~~ye~~ would not hear, saith the LORD.	Because they have not hearkened to my words, saith the Lord, which I sent unto them by my servants the prophets, **commanding them to rise** early and sending them*;* but **you** would not hear, saith the Lord.

Jeremiah 30

Jeremiah 30:12 For thus saith the LORD, Thy bruise *is* incurable, ~~*and*~~ thy ~~wound *is*~~ grievous.	For thus saith the Lord, Thy bruise is **not** incurable, **although** thy **wounds are** grievous.
Jeremiah 30:13 ~~*There is*~~ none to plead thy cause, that thou mayest be bound up: thou ~~hast~~ no healing medicines.	Is **there** none to plead thy cause, that thou mayest be bound up: **hast** thou no healing medicines**?**

Jeremiah 30:14 All thy lovers ~~have~~ forgotten thee; they seek thee ~~not;~~ for I have wounded thee with the wound of an enemy, with the chastisement of a cruel one, for the multitude of thine iniquity; *because* thy sins ~~were~~ increased.	**Have** all thy lovers forgotten thee; **do** they **not** seek thee**?** For I have wounded thee with the wound of an enemy, with the chastisement of a cruel one, for the multitude of thine iniquity; because thy sins **are** increased.
Jeremiah 30:15 Why criest thou for thine affliction? thy sorrow ~~*is*~~ incurable for the multitude of thine ~~iniquity~~: *because* thy sins ~~were~~ increased, I have done these things unto thee.	Why criest thou for thine affliction? **Is** thy sorrow incurable**? It was** for the multitude of thine **iniquities**: **and** because thy sins **are** increased, I have done these things unto thee.
Jeremiah 30:16 ~~Therefore~~ all they that devour thee shall be devoured; and all thine adversaries, every one of them, shall go into captivity; and they that spoil thee shall be a spoil, and all that prey upon thee will I give for a prey.	**But** all they that devour thee shall be devoured; and all thine adversaries, every one of them, shall go into captivity; and they that spoil thee shall be a spoil, and all that prey upon thee will I give for a prey.

Jeremiah 33

Jeremiah 33:11 The voice of joy, and the voice of gladness, the voice of the bridegroom, and the voice of the bride, the voice of them that shall say, Praise the Lord of hosts: for the Lord *is* good; for his mercy *endureth* for ever: ~~*and* of~~ them that shall bring the sacrifice of praise into the house of the Lord. For I will cause to return the captivity of the land, as at the first, saith the Lord.	The voice of joy, and the voice of gladness, the voice of the bridegroom, and the voice of the bride, the voice of them that shall say, Praise the Lord of hosts: for the Lord is good; for his mercy endureth for ever: **unto** them that shall bring the sacrifice of praise into the house of the Lord. For I will cause to return the captivity of the land, as at the first, saith the Lord.

Jeremiah 34

Jeremiah 34:15 ~~And~~ ye were now turned, and had done right in my sight, in proclaiming liberty every man to his neighbour; and ye had made a covenant before me in the house which is called by my name:	**But** ye were now turned, and had done right in my sight, in proclaiming liberty every man to his neighbour; and ye had made a covenant before me in the house which is called by my name:

Jeremiah 35

Jeremiah 35:14 The words of Jonadab the son of Rechab, that he commanded his sons not to drink wine, are performed; for unto this day they drink none, but obey their father's commandment: notwithstanding I have spoken unto you, ~~rising~~ early and speaking; but ye hearkened not unto me.	The words of Jonadab the son of Rechab, that he commanded his sons not to drink wine, are performed; for unto this day they drink none, but obey their father's commandment: notwithstanding I have spoken unto you, **commanding you to rise** early and speaking **to you**; but ye hearkened not unto me.
Jeremiah 35:15 I have sent also unto you all my servants the prophets, ~~rising~~ up early and sending *them,* saying, Return ye now every man from his evil way, and amend your doings, and go not after other gods to serve them, and ye shall dwell in the land which I have given to you and to your fathers: but ye have not inclined your ear, nor hearkened unto me.	I have sent also unto you all my servants the prophets, **commanding them to rise** up early and sending them, saying, Return ye now every man from his evil way, and amend your doings, and go not after other gods to serve them, and ye shall dwell in the land which I have given to you and to your fathers: but ye have not inclined your ear, nor hearkened unto me.

Jeremiah 36

Jeremiah 36:30 Therefore thus saith the LORD ~~of~~ Jehoiakim king of Judah; He shall have none to sit upon the throne of David: and his dead body shall be cast out in the day to the heat, and in the night to the frost.	Therefore thus saith the Lord **unto** Jehoiakim king of Judah; He shall have none to sit upon the throne of David: and his dead body shall be cast out in the day to the heat, and in the night to the frost.

Jeremiah 37

Jeremiah 37:16 ~~When~~ Jeremiah was entered into the dungeon, and into the cabins, and ~~Jeremiah had~~ remained there many days;	**And** Jeremiah was entered into the dungeon, and into the cabins, and **he** remained there many days;

Jeremiah 42

Jeremiah 42:10 If ~~ye~~ will still abide in this land, then will I build you, and not pull ~~*you*~~ down, and I will plant you, and not pluck ~~*you*~~ up: ~~for~~ I ~~repent me of~~ the evil that I have done unto you.	If **you** will still abide in this land, then will I build you, and not pull down, and I will plant you, and not pluck up: **and** I **will turn away** the evil that I have done unto you.
Jeremiah 42:14 Saying, No; but we will go into the land of Egypt, where we shall see no war, nor hear the sound of the trumpet, nor have hunger of bread; and there will we dwell:	Saying, No; but we will go into the land of Egypt, where we shall see no war, nor hear the sound of the trumpet, nor have hunger **for want** of bread; and there will we dwell:
Jeremiah 42:21 And *now* I have this day declared ~~*it*~~ to you; ~~but~~ ye have not obeyed the voice of the LORD your God, nor any *thing* for the which he hath sent me unto you.	And now I have this day declared to you; **that** ye have not obeyed the voice of the Lord your God, nor any thing for the which he hath sent me unto you.

Jeremiah 44

Jeremiah 44:4 Howbeit I sent unto you all my servants the prophets, ~~rising~~ early and sending *them,* saying, Oh, do not this abominable thing that I hate.	Howbeit I sent unto you all my servants the prophets, **commanding them to rise** early and sending them, saying, Oh, do not this abominable thing that I hate.

Ezekiel

King James Version	Joseph Smith Translation
Ezekiel 14	
Ezekiel 14:9 And if the prophet be deceived when he hath spoken a thing, I the LORD have deceived that prophet, ~~and~~ I will stretch out my hand upon him, and will destroy him from the midst of my people Israel.	And if the prophet be deceived when he hath spoken a thing, I the Lord have **not** deceived that prophet, **therefore** I will stretch out my hand upon him, and will destroy him from the midst of my people Israel.
Ezekiel 18	
Ezekiel 18:32 For I have no pleasure in the death of him that dieth, saith the Lord GOD: wherefore turn ~~*yourselves*~~, and live ~~ye~~.	For I have no pleasure in the death of him that dieth, saith the Lord God: wherefore turn **ye** and live.
Ezekiel 19	
Ezekiel 19:10 Thy mother *is* like a vine ~~in thy blood~~, planted by the waters: she was fruitful and full of branches by reason of many waters.	Thy mother is like a vine, planted by the waters: she was fruitful and full of branches by reason of many waters.
Ezekiel 20	
Ezekiel 20:30 Wherefore say unto the house of Israel, Thus saith the Lord GOD; Are ~~ye~~ polluted after the manner of your fathers? and commit ~~ye~~ whoredom after their abominations?	Wherefore say unto the house of Israel, Thus saith the Lord God; **ye** are polluted after the manner of your fathers? and **ye** commit whoredom after their abominations?

Ezekiel 23

Ezekiel 23:17 And the Babylonians came to her into the bed of love, and they defiled her with their whoredom, and she was polluted with them, and her mind was alienated from them.

And the Babylonians came to her into the bed of love, and they defiled her with their whoredom, and she was polluted with them, and her mind was alienated from **me by** them.

Ezekiel 23:22 Therefore, O Aholibah, thus saith the Lord GOD; Behold, I will raise up thy lovers against thee, ~~from~~ whom thy mind is alienated, and I will bring them against thee on every side;

Therefore, O Aholibah, thus saith the Lord God; Behold, I will raise up thy lovers against thee, **by** whom thy mind is alienated **from me**, and I will bring them against thee on every side;

Ezekiel 23:28 For thus saith the Lord GOD; Behold, I will deliver thee into the hand of *them* whom thou hatest, into the hand of *them* ~~*from*~~ whom thy mind is alienated:

For thus saith the LORD GOD; Behold, I will deliver thee into the hand of them whom thou hatest, into the hand of them **by** whom thy mind is alienated:

Ezekiel 35

Ezekiel 35:6 Therefore, *as* I live, saith the Lord GOD, I will prepare thee unto blood, and blood shall pursue thee: ~~sith~~ thou hast not hated blood, even blood shall pursue thee.

Therefore, as I live, saith the Lord God, I will prepare thee unto blood, and blood shall pursue thee: **since** thou hast not hated blood, even blood shall pursue thee.

Ezekiel 36

Ezekiel 36:36 Then the heathen that are left round about you shall know that I the LORD build the ruined *places, and* plant that ~~that~~ was desolate: I the LORD have spoken *it,* and I will do *it.*

Then the heathen that are left round about you shall know that I the Lord build the ruined places, and plant that **which** was desolate: I the Lord have spoken it, and I will do it.

Ezekiel 48

Ezekiel 48:35 *It was* round about eighteen thousand *measures:* and the name of the city from *that* day *shall be,* The LORD ~~*is*~~ there.	It was round about eighteen thousand measures: and the name of the city from that day shall be **called holy**, **for** the Lord **shall be** there.

Daniel

Daniel 5	
King James Version	Joseph Smith Translation
Daniel 5:28 ~~PERES~~; Thy kingdom is divided, and given to the Medes and Persians.	**Upharsin**; Thy kingdom is divided, and given to the Medes and Persians.

Hosea

Hosea 11

King James Version	Joseph Smith Translation
Hosea 11:8 How shall I give thee up, Ephraim? *how* shall I deliver thee, Israel? how shall I make thee as Admah? *how* shall I set thee as Zeboim? ~~mine~~ heart is turned ~~within me~~, my ~~repentings~~ are ~~kindled together~~.	How shall I give thee up, Ephraim? how shall I deliver thee, Israel? how shall I make thee as Admah? how shall I set thee as Zeboim? **my** heart is turned **toward thee**, **and** my **mercies** are **extended to gather thee**.
Hosea 11:9 I will not execute the fierceness of mine anger, I will not return to destroy Ephraim: for I *am* God, and not man; the Holy One in the midst of thee: and I will ~~not~~ enter into the city.	I will not execute the fierceness of mine anger, I will not return to destroy Ephraim: for I am God, and not man; the Holy One in the midst of thee: and I will enter into the city.

Joel

Joel 1	
King James Version	Joseph Smith Translation
Joel 1:6 For a nation is come up upon my land, strong, and without number, whose teeth *are* the teeth of a lion, and he hath the cheek teeth of a great lion.	For a nation is come up upon my land, strong, and without number, whose teeth are **as** the teeth of a lion, and he hath the cheek teeth of a great lion.
Joel 2	
Joel 2:13 And rend your heart, and not your garments, and turn unto the LORD your God: for he *is* gracious and merciful, slow to anger, and of great kindness, and ~~repenteth him of~~ the evil.	And rend your heart, and not your garments, **and repent,** and turn unto the Lord your God: for he is gracious and merciful, slow to anger, and of great kindness, and **he will turn away** the evil **from you**.
Joel 2:14 Who knoweth ~~*if*~~ he will return ~~and repent~~, and leave a blessing behind him; ~~*even*~~ a meat offering and a drink offering unto the LORD your God?	**Therefore, repent, and** who knoweth **but** he will return, and leave a blessing behind him; **that you may offer** a meat offering and a drink offering unto the Lord your God?

AMOS

Amos 3

KING JAMES VERSION	JOSEPH SMITH TRANSLATION
Amos 3:6 Shall a trumpet be blown in the city, and the people not be afraid? shall there be evil in a city, and the LORD hath not ~~done~~ *it?*	Shall a trumpet be blown in the city, and the people not be afraid? shall there be evil in a city, and the Lord hath not **known** it?
Amos 3:7 Surely the Lord GOD will do nothing, ~~but~~ he revealeth ~~his~~ secret unto his servants the prophets.	Surely the Lord God will do nothing, **until** he revealeth **the** secret unto his servants the prophets.

Amos 4

KING JAMES VERSION	JOSEPH SMITH TRANSLATION
Amos 4:3 And ye shall go out at the breaches, every ~~*cow at that which is*~~ before ~~her~~; and ye shall cast ~~*them* into the palace~~, saith the LORD.	And ye shall go out at the breaches, every **one** before **his enemy**; and ye shall **be** cast **out of your palaces**, saith the Lord.
Amos 4:5 And offer a sacrifice of thanksgiving with leaven, and proclaim *and* publish the free offerings: for ~~this liketh you~~, O ye children of Israel, saith the Lord GOD.	And offer a sacrifice of thanksgiving with leaven, and proclaim and publish the free offerings: for **thus do ye**, O ye children of Israel, saith the Lord God.
Amos 4:6 ~~And~~ I also have given you cleanness of teeth in all your cities, and want of bread in all your places: yet have ye not returned unto me, saith the LORD.	**Therefore** I also have given you cleanness of teeth in all your cities, and want of bread in all your places: yet have ye not returned unto me, saith the Lord.

Amos 7	
Amos 7:3 The LORD ~~repented~~ for this: ~~It shall~~ not ~~be~~, saith the LORD.	**And** the Lord **said, concerning Jacob, Jacob shall repent** for this: **Therefore I will** not **utterly destroy him**, saith the Lord.
Amos 7:6 The LORD ~~repented for this: This also~~ shall not ~~be~~, saith the Lord GOD.	**And** the Lord **said, concerning Jacob, Jacob** shall **repent of his wickedness; therefore; I will** not **utterly destroy**, saith the Lord God.

Jonah

Jonah 3

King James Version	Joseph Smith Translation
Jonah 3:9 Who can tell *if* ~~God~~ will ~~turn and~~ repent, and turn away from his fierce anger, that we perish not?	Who can tell if **we** will repent, and **turn unto God, but he will** turn away from **us** his fierce anger, that we perish not?
Jonah 3:10 And God saw their works, that they turned from their evil way; and ~~God~~ repented ~~of~~ the evil, that he had said ~~that~~ he would ~~do unto~~ them; ~~and he did *it* not~~.	And God saw their works, that they turned from their evil way; and repented**; and God turned away** the evil, that he had said he would **bring upon** them.

Zechariah

Zechariah 4

King James Version	Joseph Smith Translation
Zechariah 4:10 For who hath despised the day of small things? for they shall rejoice, and shall see the plummet in the hand of Zerubbabel *with* those seven; they *are* the ~~eyes~~ of the Lord, which run to and fro through the whole earth.	For who hath despised the day of small things? for they shall rejoice, and shall see the plummet in the hand of Zerubbabel with those seven; they are the **servants** of the Lord, which run to and fro through the whole earth.
Zechariah 4:14 Then said he, These *are* the two anointed ones, that stand ~~by~~ the Lord of the whole earth.	Then said he, These are the two anointed ones, that stand **before** the Lord of the whole earth.

Zechariah 6

King James Version	Joseph Smith Translation
Zechariah 6:5 And the angel answered and said unto me, These *are* the four ~~spirits~~ of the heavens, which go forth from standing before the Lord of all the earth.	And the angel answered and said unto me, These are the four **servants** of the heavens, which go forth from standing before the Lord of all the earth.
Zechariah 6:6 The black horses which *are* therein go forth ~~into~~ the north country; and the white go forth after them; and the grisled go forth toward the south country.	The black horses which are therein go forth **unto** the north country; and the white go forth after them; and the grisled go forth toward the south country.

Zechariah 8

Zechariah 8:7 Thus saith the LORD of hosts; Behold, I will ~~save~~ my people from the east country, and from the west country;	Thus saith the Lord of hosts; Behold, I will **gather** my people from the east country, and from the west country;[1]
Zechariah 8:13 And it shall come to pass, *that* as ye were a curse among the heathen, O house of Judah, and house of Israel; so will I ~~save~~ you, and ye shall be a blessing: fear not, *but* let your hands be strong.	And it shall come to pass, that as ye were a curse among the heathen, O house of Judah, and house of Israel; so will I **gather** you, and ye shall be a blessing: fear not, but let your hands be strong.

1. OT2 contains the word "gather" but without any indication of where the change should be placed in verse 13. Following "gather" the manuscript reads, "Malicah Correct. Finished on the 2nd day of July 1833."